The S Corporation Answer Book

1990 Edition

Sydney S. Traum, Esq., CPA
Judith Rood Traum, Esq.

The Panel Answer Book Series
Panel Publishers, Inc.

This publication is designed to provide accurate and authoritative information in regard to the subject matter covered. It is sold with the understanding that the publisher is not engaged in rendering legal, accounting or other professional services. If legal advice or other professional assistance is required, the services of a competent professional person should be sought.

> — *From a Declaration of Principles jointly adopted by a Committee of the American Bar Association and a Committee of Publishers and Associations.*

Copyright 1990 by Panel Publishers, Inc. All rights reserved. No part of this book may be reproduced in any form or by any means without permission in writing from the authors and the publisher.

Printed in the United States of America

For more information on other titles in the

Panel Answer Book Series

Contact: Panel Publishers, Inc.
Customer Service
14 Plaza Road
Greenvale, NY 11548
(516) 484-0006

About Panel Publishers, Inc.

Panel derived its name from the panel of business professionals who organized it in 1964 to publish authoritative, timely books and information services written by specialists to assist the tax and business practitioner.

This is still Panel's mission.

Panel's list of publications that are designed to assist the practitioner in providing tax and related advice include such highly regarded publications as **The S Corporation: Planning and Operation, S Corporation Practice Manual, Partnership Tax Practice Manual, The Pension Answer Book,** and **The Multistate Corporate Tax Almanac.**

Introduction

Subchapter S was added to the Internal Revenue Code in 1958. Its announced purpose was to permit closely held businesses to choose a legal entity without having to consider the tax treatment of the entity. In other words, it would permit a small business to (1) incorporate without being subject to corporate tax and (2) be taxed as a partnership. In its original form, it did not, however, achieve the second goal—and Subchapter S rules were arcane and full of pitfalls and traps. All of that changed with the Subchapter S Revision Act of 1982 (Revision Act), which made the S corporation much more like a partnership and made it a more viable form of business operation.

Then came the Tax Reform Act of 1986 (TRA '86), with its introduction of corporate tax rates that exceed individual rates and its repeal of the tax-free liquidation sections of the Internal Revenue Code. TRA '86 made the S corporation increasingly important in the tax planner's arsenal. In fact, many tax practitioners think of it as *the* vehicle for small and medium-sized businesses, and its popularity can be expected to continue.

But TRA '86 also contained some new pitfalls—restricting the S corporation's ability to use a noncalendar taxable year, imposing a new corporate-level built-in gains tax on some S corporations, and restricting the ability of passive investors to use S corporation deductions and losses (a restriction that also applies to passive investors in partnerships). And even as companies were electing S corporation status in record numbers, Congress—in two short years—changed the ground rules again, not once but twice: The Revenue Act of 1987 (Revenue Act) altered the taxable-year rules once again, by adding the "Section 444 election." And both the Revenue Act and the Technical and Miscellaneous Revenue Act of 1988 (TAMRA) tinkered with the built-in gains tax and added the concept of "LIFO recapture."

How is the practitioner going to keep track—much less advise clients on how to operate their S corporations if they have them (and when it might be better to select another entity instead)?

The S Corporation Answer Book is designed to provide quick, accurate, and up-to-date answers to questions in the complex area of the S corporation. TAMRA and Revenue Act provisions are fully integrated into its question-and-answer format, as are temporary regulations on such topics as Section 444 elections and the passive activity loss rules, and recently proposed regulations on various aspects of S corporation qualification and termination.

The questions are organized in a logical sequence so that the reader can use the book in either of two ways: to find an answer to a specific question or to use his or her question as a stepping stone upon which to build a body of information. For either application, the materials contained in this book serve as an invaluable aid.

The following overview explains how this easy-to-use volume provides information about S corporations.

Organization of the Book: The book has been divided into 14 chapters. The questions in each chapter are numbered independently from those in all other chapters—for example, 1:2 or 13:1. In some cases, a question will discuss certain points raised in other questions; in those cases, cross-references are made to the other questions. Question number guides are provided at the upper outer margins of each page, so that a quick glance tells you which questions are covered within the span of two facing pages.

Detailed Listing of Questions: The detailed listing of questions in the front of the book assists the reader in locating the subject matter being researched. The chapter headings are followed by a list of all the questions that are answered in that chapter, with each question identified by a question number and showing the page number on which it appears. This makes it easy to locate the area of interest and the specific questions to which answers are desired.

Glossary: A glossary of basic S corporation terms is included to enable readers who wish to do so to familiarize themselves with basic S corporation concepts and vocabulary. The definitions in the glossary are cross referenced to more detailed discussions in the main body of the text.

Reference Guides: Reference guides, or finding lists, keyed to question numbers, are provided for Internal Revenue Code and regulation sections, revenue rulings, revenue procedures private letter rulings, and court cases.

Index: At the back of the book is a traditional topical index as a further aid to locating specific information. The references in the index are to question numbers, not page numbers.

Sydney S. Traum
Judith Rood Traum
December 15, 1989

About the Authors

SYDNEY S. TRAUM, a tax attorney and CPA, is sole shareholder and employee of Sydney S. Traum, P.A., which is of counsel to the law firm of Semet, Lickstein, Morgenstern & Berger, P.A., in Coral Gables, Florida. He has a B.B.A. from the City College of New York, a J.D. from Harvard Law School, and an LL.M. in Taxation from New York University. He has been an adjunct professor at the University of Miami Law School and at Florida International University. Mr. Traum has also been a frequent lecturer before numerous professional groups, including the New York State Society of CPAs, the Greater Miami Tax Institute, the Georgia Tax Conference, the Florida Institute of CPAs, the Florida Bar, the Philip E. Heckerling-University of Miami Institute on Estate Planning, Accounting Firms Associated, Inc., and the Miami Chapter of the American Society of CLUs. Mr. Traum recently completed his term as President of the American Association of Attorney-CPAs. He is also a past President of the Florida Association of Attorney-CPAs, the Greater Miami Tax Institute, and the Dade County Chapter of the Florida Institute of CPAs. He is recognized by the Florida Bar as both a Board Certified Tax Lawyer and a Board Certified Estate Planning and Probate Lawyer. Mr. Traum is the author of Panel's bestselling looseleaf reference, *THE S CORPORATION: Planning & Operation*.

JUDITH ROOD TRAUM is an attorney at law in solo practice in Coral Gables, Florida. She has a J.D. cum laude from the University of Miami School of Law, as well as an A.B. magna cum laude from Radcliffe College (Harvard). Ms. Traum was formerly a Law Associate with the firm of Wellisch, Metzger & Leone, P.A., in Coral Gables, and previous to that, with Robert Bakerman, Attorney at Law, in Miami, Florida. She has also been on the Adjunct Faculty of the Miami-Dade Community College Legal Assistant Program.

Acknowledgments

There are always many people behind the scenes who contribute to the content and quality of a book.

The authors and the publisher first wish to acknowledge the efforts of Sara Piovia, Esq., now Managing Editor of Panel Publishers' Tax Information Center, and Mark D. Persons, Esq., LL.M. (Taxation), Manager, New Product Development and former Managing Editor. Through their incisive technical editing and broad overview, Ms. Piovia and Mr. Persons have contributed significantly to the quality and the concept of *The S Corporation Answer Book—1990 Edition,* as well as to earlier editions.

Thanks are also due to the staff of Panel Publishers' publishing services department who contributed to the timely production of this latest edition of the book.

Table of Contents

Listing of Questions xv

Chapter 1: Qualifying as an S Corporation 1

Chapter 2: Elections and Consents 23

Chapter 3: Taxable-Year Rules 37

Chapter 4: Terminations and Revocations 55

Chapter 5: Reorganizations of S Corporations 69

Chapter 6: Protecting the S Corporation Election; Invalid Elections 81

Chapter 7: Passive Investment Income 93

Chapter 8: S Corporations' Taxable Income and Losses; Taxation of the S Corporation 111

Chapter 9: Taxation of S Corporation Shareholders—Basic Pass-Through and Allocation Principles 137

Table of Contents

Chapter 10: Taxation of S Corporation Shareholders—Limitations on Losses 147

Chapter 11: Shareholders' Basis in S Corporation Stock and Loans 195

Chapter 12: S Corporation Distributions to Shareholders 209

Chapter 13: Compensation; Fringe and Retirement Benefits 223

Chapter 14: Tax Administration of S Corporations 231

Glossary 249

Reference Guides

    Code Sections 259

    Regulation Sections 267

    Revenue Rulings 271

    Revenue Procedures 273

    Letter Rulings 275

    Cases 277

Index 281

Listing of Questions

Chapter 1 Qualifying as an S Corporation

Basic Considerations

Q. 1:1	What is an S corporation?	1
Q. 1:2	What are the general requirements for S corporation status?	1
Q. 1:3	What is a domestic corporation?	2
Q. 1:4	Must the S corporation be operated for profit?	2
Q. 1:5	Do the "hobby-loss" rules apply to S corporations?	3
Q. 1:6	What other loss limitation rules apply to S corporations?	4
Q. 1:7	Is an S corporation an appropriate vehicle for a tax shelter?	4
Q. 1:8	What types of corporations are ineligible?	4

Ownership and Business Considerations

Q. 1:9	Can an S corporation have a subsidiary?	5
Q. 1:10	Can an S corporation be a subsidiary of another corporation?	5
Q. 1:11	Are there any types of business that an S corporation is prohibited from performing?	5
Q. 1:12	Can an insurance company elect S corporation status?	6
Q. 1:13	What casualty insurance companies can continue to rely on old S corporation elections?	6
Q. 1:14	What special rules apply to a "qualified oil corporation"?	7
Q. 1:15	If spouses own shares in an S corporation separately, how are they counted for purposes of the 35-or-fewer-shareholders test?	7
Q. 1:16	Can the number-of-shareholders test be circumvented by using nominees or agents?	7

Q. 1:17	May a partnership hold stock of an S corporation as nominee for its individual partners?	8
Q. 1:18	Can an S corporation be a partner?	8
Q. 1:19	What types of trusts may own S corporation stock without destroying the election?	9
Q. 1:20	What is a "qualified Subchapter S trust"?	10
Q. 1:21	What type of trust is eligible to be a qualified Subchapter S trust?	10
Q. 1:22	How strictly does IRS construe qualified Subchapter S trust eligibility requirements?	11
Q. 1:23	Are all trusts with more than one beneficiary ineligible for qualified Subchapter S trust status?	12
Q. 1:24	Must the beneficiary of a qualified Subchapter S trust consent to the S corporation election?	12
Q. 1:25	How does the beneficiary of a qualified Subchapter S trust make the special trust election?	13
Q. 1:26	Can the beneficiary of a qualified Subchapter S trust revoke the election?	14
Q. 1:27	What happens when the beneficiary of a qualified Subchapter S trust dies?	14
Q. 1:28	What problems may arise when an S corporation shareholder (other than the beneficiary of a qualified Subchapter S trust) dies?	15
Q. 1:29	May a corporation qualify for S corporation status if it has a shareholder whose interest in the stock is that of a legal life estate or the equivalent?	16

Capital Structure

Q. 1:30	Must S corporation shares be equal in all respects?	16
Q. 1:31	How can the permissible differences in stock be used as a planning tool?	17
Q. 1:32	May a shareholders' agreement vary the rights of the shareholders without creating a second class of stock that would destroy the S corporation election?	18
Q. 1:33	Can warrants, options, convertible debentures, or proxies be treated as a second class of stock?	19
Q. 1:34	Can loans to the corporation be treated as a second class of stock?	19
Q. 1:35	What are the "straight-debt" safe-harbor rules?	20

Listing of Questions

Chapter 2 Elections and Consents

Manner and Time of Election

Q. 2:1	How does a corporation elect to become an S corporation?	23
Q. 2:2	When must an existing corporation make the election to become an S corporation?	23
Q. 2:3	When must a newly formed corporation make the election to become an S corporation?	24
Q. 2:4	Can an extension of time be obtained for filing the S corporation election?	25
Q. 2:5	What should be done to protect against an IRS claim that it never received the S corporation election?	26
Q. 2:6	What happens when the due date for filing the election is a nonbusiness day or a legal holiday?	26
Q. 2:7	When does an S corporation election become effective?	27

Consents

Q. 2:8	Who must consent to the election to become an S corporation?	27
Q. 2:9	How do the shareholders make their consents to the S corporation election?	29
Q. 2:10	When must the shareholders make their consents to the election?	29
Q. 2:11	What happens if a shareholder fails to consent?	29
Q. 2:12	Can an extension of time be obtained for filing the consents?	30
Q. 2:13	How is an extension of time for filing consents obtained?	30
Q. 2:14	When a new shareholder acquires S corporation stock, must the shareholder file anything?	31

Withdrawal and Amendment

Q. 2:15	Can an S corporation election be amended?	31
Q. 2:16	If the shareholders change their minds about the advisability of S corporation status, can the election be withdrawn before it becomes effective?	31

Reelection

Q. 2:17	If an S corporation election has been terminated, when can the corporation reapply for S corporation status?	32
Q. 2:18	When will IRS consent to an early reelection of S corporation status?	33

Chapter 3 Taxable-Year Rules

Taxable-Year Options

Q. 3:1	What is the difference between a fiscal year and a calendar year?	37
Q. 3:2	Are there any restrictions on an S corporation's choice of taxable year?	37
Q. 3:3	What is a "permitted year" for an S corporation?	38
Q. 3:4	What is a "natural business year"?	39
Q. 3:5	What is an "ownership tax year"?	40
Q. 3:6	How might an S corporation establish a "business purpose" justifying a fiscal year?	40
Q. 3:7	If an S corporation does not qualify for any ownership or business-purpose year, must it use a calendar year?	43
Q. 3:8	Can an S corporation that holds a partnership interest make a Section 444 election?	43
Q. 3:9	Can the limitations on electing Section 444 be avoided by transferring assets to other corporations owned by the same shareholders?	44
Q. 3:10	How many Section 444 elections may an S corporation make?	45

Taxable-Year Election Mechanics

Q. 3:11	How does a corporation electing S corporation status request a fiscal year (other than one under Section 444)?	45
Q. 3:12	How can a newly electing S corporation protect S corporation status in case its business-purpose fiscal-year request is denied?	46
Q. 3:13	How does an existing S corporation change its taxable year?	47
Q. 3:14	When will IRS grant expeditious approval of an existing S corporation's use of a business-purpose fiscal year?	47
Q. 3:15	How is a Section 444 election made?	48
Q. 3:16	How is a backup Section 444 election made?	49
Q. 3:17	Will IRS impose a fee for a fiscal-year request?	50

Maintenance and Termination of Section 444 Election

Q. 3:18	How does an S corporation electing Section 444 calculate its required payment?	50
Q. 3:19	When and how are required payments made?	52

Listing of Questions

Q. 3:20	What happens to an S corporation electing under Section 444 that fails to make required payments?	52
Q. 3:21	How is a Section 444 election terminated, and what happens then?	53
Q. 3:22	When should a Section 444 election be terminated?	53
Q. 3:23	How does an S corporation terminating a Section 444 election claim a refund of its required payments?	53
Q. 3:24	Is interest paid on refunds of required payments?	54

Chapter 4 Terminations and Revocations

Basic Considerations

Q. 4:1	When does an S corporation cease to be an S corporation?	55
Q. 4:2	What is the effect of termination or revocation of S corporation status?	55

Terminations

Q. 4:3	How does an S corporation become disqualified, causing a termination?	55
Q. 4:4	Can an S corporation intentionally disqualify itself?	56
Q. 4:5	How many shareholders are needed to intentionally disqualify an S corporation and terminate the election?	56
Q. 4:6	Can S corporation status be preserved if it is accidentally terminated?	57
Q. 4:7	When will IRS consider a termination "inadvertent" or accidental?	57
Q. 4:8	What must an S corporation do to have a termination treated as inadvertent?	58
Q. 4:9	What is the effective date of a termination?	58

Revocations

Q. 4:10	What is a revocation?	59
Q. 4:11	How many shareholders are needed to revoke an S corporation election?	59
Q. 4:12	How is a revocation made?	59
Q. 4:13	What is the effective date of revocation?	60
Q. 4:14	Why would the shareholders want to revoke an election (or permit one to terminate)?	60

Q. 4:15	If the shareholders change their minds about the advisability of a revocation, can they withdraw it before it becomes effective?	61

Accounting for a Termination or Revocation

Q. 4:16	Must IRS be notified of a termination or revocation?	61
Q. 4:17	What happens if S corporation status ends in the middle of a corporation's taxable year?	62
Q. 4:18	Who pays tax on the corporation's income if S corporation status ends in the middle of the taxable year?	62
Q. 4:19	How are income, losses, and deductions allocated between the part of the termination year to which the S corporation election applies and the part to which it does not apply?	63
Q. 4:20	How is a pro rata daily allocation made?	63
Q. 4:21	When is the pro rata daily allocation method unavailable?	64
Q. 4:22	How does the corporation elect to close its books on the day of termination in order to allocate items between the S corporation and C corporation portions of the termination year?	64
Q. 4:23	How is the tax calculated for the C corporation portion of the termination year?	65
Q. 4:24	When are the tax returns due for the termination year of a corporation whose S corporation status has ended in the middle of its taxable year?	66

Post-Termination Estimated Tax

Q. 4:25	If an S corporation loses its election, will it be subject to the estimated tax requirements?	66
Q. 4:26	Will a former S corporation be subject to estimated tax underpayment penalties for its first C corporation year?	66

Chapter 5 Reorganizations of S Corporations

Basic Considerations

Q. 5:1	What is a reorganization?	69
Q. 5:2	Can an S corporation be a party to a tax-free reorganization?	70

Listing of Questions

| Q. 5:3 | Why are reorganizations of special concern to S corporations? | 70 |

Mergers and Consolidations

Q. 5:4	What happens to the S corporation election if an S corporation merges into a C corporation?	71
Q. 5:5	How does a merged S corporation treat the portion of its taxable year that elapsed prior to the merger?	72
Q. 5:6	If an S corporation merges into a C corporation, will the surviving C corporation be able to elect S corporation status?	72
Q. 5:7	Will S corporation status be lost if a C corporation merges into an S corporation?	72
Q. 5:8	Will S corporation status be lost if several S corporations merge into one corporation?	73
Q. 5:9	Will S corporation status be lost if several S corporations are consolidated into a new corporation?	73

Divisions, Acquisitions, and Sales

Q. 5:10	Will S corporation status be lost if an S corporation splits into more than one corporation?	74
Q. 5:11	Will S corporation status be lost if an S corporation purchases, or exchanges stock for, another corporation's assets?	74
Q. 5:12	Will S corporation status be lost if an S corporation acquires another corporation's stock in order to obtain that corporation's assets?	75
Q. 5:13	Can an S corporation acquire stock and then obtain a basis step-up for the acquired corporation's assets?	76
Q. 5:14	What happens to the acquired corporation if the stock of an S corporation is acquired by another corporation?	76

Other Transactions

Q. 5:15	How does a recapitalization affect S corporation status?	77
Q. 5:16	Will changes in identity or place of incorporation change the S corporation status of a single corporation?	77
Q. 5:17	How would a bankruptcy reorganization or similar situation affect S corporation status?	78

Special Considerations

| Q. 5:18 | What special considerations are of continuing concern to an S corporation surviving a reorganization with a C corporation? | 78 |

Chapter 6 Protecting the S Corporation Election; Invalid Elections

Threats to the Election

Q. 6:1	What events might cause a loss of S corporation status?	81
Q. 6:2	How can a shareholder intentionally destroy the election?	81
Q. 6:3	Does the death of a shareholder endanger the S corporation election?	83
Q. 6:4	Does the death of a beneficiary of a qualified Subchapter S trust endanger the election?	83
Q. 6:5	What dangers to the S corporation election may arise if a shareholder holds some shares as a nominee for another?	83
Q. 6:6	Can the existence of corporate indebtedness endanger the S corporation election?	84
Q. 6:7	Can the type of income the corporation receives endanger S corporation status?	84

Protective Measures

Q. 6:8	What can be done to prevent loss of S corporation status?	86
Q. 6:9	How does a shareholders' agreement prevent loss of S corporation status?	86
Q. 6:10	What types of provisions should be included in a shareholders' agreement to prevent loss of S corporation status?	87
Q. 6:11	Is a shareholders' agreement binding on IRS?	88
Q. 6:12	Are there any means, other than shareholders' agreements, of protecting the election against shareholders' disqualifying acts?	89

Failure to Protect the Election

Q. 6:13	What problems will the corporation have if its S corporation status is terminated despite all attempts to protect the election?	90

Invalid Elections

Q. 6:14	What happens if the original election was invalid?	90
Q. 6:15	Can an invalid election be cured?	91
Q. 6:16	How long must a corporation making an invalid election wait before reelecting S corporation status?	92

Listing of Questions

Q. 6:17	If the taxpayer mistakenly believes that an S corporation election is valid, will the filing of an S corporation tax return provide any protection against back taxes?	92

Chapter 7 Passive Investment Income

Basic Considerations

Q. 7:1	What is passive investment income?	93
Q. 7:2	When can passive investment income create problems for an S corporation?	94
Q. 7:3	What problems can passive investment income cause?	94
Q. 7:4	When and how is the S corporation taxed on passive investment income?	94

"Gross Receipts"

Q. 7:5	Are the "gross receipts" used to measure passive investment income synonymous with "gross profits"?	95
Q. 7:6	How is the term "gross receipts" defined?	95
Q. 7:7	How are gross receipts calculated?	96
Q. 7:8	What impact do deductions have on gross receipts?	98
Q. 7:9	When are installment-sale proceeds included in gross receipts?	98
Q. 7:10	How is partnership income treated for gross receipts purposes?	98
Q. 7:11	What special rules apply to calculating gross receipts from the sale of capital assets?	99
Q. 7:12	Are all gross receipts from sales of stock used to calculate passive investment income?	99

Income Characterization

Q. 7:13	Is rental income always passive investment income?	100
Q. 7:14	What level of services is required to make rental income active instead of passive?	101
Q. 7:15	Is income from hotels, motels, and the like passive or active?	102
Q. 7:16	What about income from mobile-home and trailer parks?	102
Q. 7:17	Will income from office building rentals be treated as active or passive?	103

The S Corporation Answer Book

Q. 7:18	Can rental of buildings before an intended demolition create a passive investment income problem?	104
Q. 7:19	Is income from parking facilities and airfields passive investment income?	104
Q. 7:20	Do storage and warehousing activities create passive investment income from rents?	105
Q. 7:21	If the S corporation operates a recreational facility, will it have passive investment income from rents?	105
Q. 7:22	Do farming operations present passive income problems?	105
Q. 7:23	How are receipts from renting or leasing personal property classified as active or passive?	105
Q. 7:24	How is income from charters classified?	107
Q. 7:25	Can a "sale" ever be construed as a rental that creates a passive investment income problem?	108
Q. 7:26	Is interest income ever excluded from the definition of passive investment income?	108

Corporate Planning

Q. 7:27	What can be done to reduce a corporation's passive investment income?	109

Chapter 8 S Corporations' Taxable Income and Losses; Taxation of the S Corporation

Fundamental Principles

Q. 8:1	How is S corporation income generally taxed?	111
Q. 8:2	How, generally speaking, is the S corporation's taxable income computed?	111
Q. 8:3	How does the S corporation treat dispositions of capital assets?	112
Q. 8:4	Is the S corporation's taxable income affected if the corporation distributes appreciated property to its shareholders?	112
Q. 8:5	Are losses from transactions with "related parties" recognized in computing the S corporation's taxable income?	113
Q. 8:6	Can an S corporation deduct accrued expenses that are payable to its shareholders?	114
Q. 8:7	What limitations on deductions apply to the S corporation?	114

Listing of Questions

Q. 8:8	Which elections affecting the computation of an S corporation's income, deductions, and credits are made by the corporation, and which are made by the shareholders?	114
Q. 8:9	Under what circumstances may the S corporation itself be subject to income taxes?	115

Tax on Excess Passive Investment Income

Q. 8:10	When is an S corporation subject to the tax on excess passive investment income?	115
Q. 8:11	How is excess passive investment income taxed?	116
Q. 8:12	Is there any limit on the amount of excess net passive income that can be taxed?	117
Q. 8:13	Can IRS waive the tax on excess passive investment income?	118
Q. 8:14	How does an S corporation request a waiver of the tax on excess passive investment income?	118

Gains and Dispositions—An Overview

Q. 8:15	Can long-term capital gains or other gains and dispositions trigger a corporate-level tax?	119

Long-Term Capital Gains

Q. 8:16	Must all S corporations be concerned with the corporate-level capital gains tax?	119
Q. 8:17	Can an S corporation subject to the capital gains tax avoid the tax by transferring assets to one that is not?	120
Q. 8:18	What level of capital gain, and level of income, trigger the corporate-level capital gains tax?	120
Q. 8:19	How is the corporate-level capital gains tax computed?	121
Q. 8:20	Do gains already taxed as excess passive investment income enter into this corporate-level capital gains tax computation?	122

Built-in Gains

Q. 8:21	What are "built-in gains"?	122
Q. 8:22	Which S corporations are subject to the built-in gains tax?	123
Q. 8:23	Which S corporations are not subject to the built-in gains tax?	124
Q. 8:24	What types of dispositions trigger the built-in gains tax?	124
Q. 8:25	How are built-in gains taxed?	125
Q. 8:26	What is net recognized built-in gain?	125

Q. 8:27	Can losses from S corporation years be used to minimize built-in gains tax?	127
Q. 8:28	Is there any overall limitation on the amount of built-in gains tax?	127
Q. 8:29	Can a corporation's shareholders contribute "loss" property before electing S corporation status and thus lower this "net unrealized built-in gain" limitation amount?	129
Q. 8:30	How does the built-in gains tax apply to property the corporation has received in a tax-free transaction?	129
Q. 8:31	Are gains subject to tax as excess passive investment income also subject to tax as built-in gains?	131
Q. 8:32	What transitional relief is provided from the built-in gains tax?	131
Q. 8:33	Which corporations are eligible for this built-in gains tax transitional relief?	132

Investment Tax Credit Recapture

Q. 8:34	When will the S corporation itself be liable for investment tax credit recapture?	132
Q. 8:35	Will the election (or the termination) of S corporation status cause investment tax credit recapture?	133

LIFO Recapture

Q. 8:36	Will the S corporation election itself ever trigger a corporate-level tax?	133
Q. 8:37	What is the LIFO recapture amount?	134
Q. 8:38	How is the total LIFO recapture tax computed?	134
Q. 8:39	When is the LIFO recapture tax payable? How is it reported?	134

Chapter 9 Taxation of S Corporation Shareholders—Basic Pass-Through and Allocation Principles

Pass-Through of Income, Losses, and Other Items

Q. 9:1	How do income, losses, and other specific items affecting shareholder tax liability pass through to the shareholders of an S corporation?	137

Q. 9:2	When do these items pass through to shareholders?	137
Q. 9:3	Does the characterization of items passing through to shareholders of an S corporation ever change in the process?	138
Q. 9:4	Is passed-through S corporation income simply reported as an aggregate on the shareholder's tax return?	138
Q. 9:5	Are any elections concerning the items that are passed through made by shareholders?	140
Q. 9:6	How is the pass-through affected by dispositions of property on which the S corporation has claimed the investment tax credit?	140

Changes in Ownership

Q. 9:7	Do changes in ownership of S corporation stock cause recapture of the investment tax credit?	141
Q. 9:8	When S corporation stock changes hands, how are these pass-through items generally allocated among the shareholders?	141
Q. 9:9	Must shareholders always use this pro rata method of allocating S corporation items?	142
Q. 9:10	What is the alternative allocation method that may be used if a shareholder terminates his or her interest in the S corporation?	143
Q. 9:11	How much of a difference does the method of allocating income, deductions, and the like make?	143
Q. 9:12	How does the S corporation make the election to use the alternative (actual) method of calculating pass-through allocations?	144
Q. 9:13	Do these allocation rules apply if a shareholder dies during the S corporation's taxable year?	144

Other Concerns

Q. 9:14	Can allocated amounts be affected if members of shareholders' families perform services for, or lend money to, an S corporation?	145
Q. 9:15	Is the shareholder limited in the amounts of allocated deductions he or she can claim?	145

Chapter 10 Taxation of S Corporation Shareholders—Limitations on Losses

Basis Limitations

Q. 10:1	How does basis limit losses and deductions passing through to S corporation shareholders?	147
Q. 10:2	What happens to losses that are disallowed because of the basis limitation?	148

At-Risk Rules

Q. 10:3	What are the "at-risk" rules, and how do they differ from the basis limitation?	148
Q. 10:4	When can S corporation activities be aggregated for purposes of the at-risk rules?	150
Q. 10:5	What activities constitute a trade or business for at-risk rule purposes?	150
Q. 10:6	How and when is the amount at risk calculated?	151
Q. 10:7	What happens to losses disallowed under the at-risk rules?	152
Q. 10:8	Do loss deductions decrease the amount at risk?	152
Q. 10:9	What happens if a shareholder has a negative amount at risk?	153

Passive Activity Loss (PAL) Rules—Overview

Q. 10:10	How do the PAL rules limit a shareholder's deductions?	153
Q. 10:11	To what types of activities do the PAL rules apply?	154

PAL Rules—Definition of Activity

Q. 10:12	Why is it important to define the scope of an activity?	155
Q. 10:13	Is the S corporation itself a discrete activity?	155
Q. 10:14	How does the S corporation shareholder identify an undertaking?	156
Q. 10:15	How does the S corporation shareholder identify an activity?	157
Q. 10:16	When are trade-or-business undertakings aggregated in determining a shareholder's activities?	158
Q. 10:17	When are trade-or-business undertakings controlled by the same interests for purposes of these aggregation rules?	159
Q. 10:18	When are undertakings similar for purposes of the first trade-or-business aggregation rule?	159

Listing of Questions

Q. 10:19	When is there an integrated business for purposes of the second trade-or-business aggregation rule?	160
Q. 10:20	Can, and should, a trade-or-business activity ever be disaggregated or fragmented?	161
Q. 10:21	How does a fragmentation election impact the level of participation in a trade-or-business activity?	162
Q. 10:22	What special aggregation rule applies to a professional service undertaking?	162
Q. 10:23	What special rules apply in determining which rental real estate undertakings constitute an activity?	163

PAL Rules—Material Participation

Q. 10:24	How does a shareholder "participate" in an S corporation activity?	164
Q. 10:25	What makes a shareholder's participation "material"?	165
Q. 10:26	Which taxable year is used to measure material participation, the shareholder's or the S corporation's?	166
Q. 10:27	How should the shareholder substantiate participation?	167

PAL Rules—Disallowed Losses and Credits

Q.10:28	If the shareholder does not materially participate in an S corporation activity, how—and why—is passive activity gross income calculated?	167
Q. 10:29	Is income from S corporation investments passive activity gross income?	168
Q. 10:30	How are S corporation distributions treated?	169
Q. 10:31	How is the shareholder's pro rata share treated?	169
Q. 10:32	Is the trade-or-business income from the S corporation always characterized by the nature of the shareholder's participation?	170
Q. 10:33	What deductions are "passive activity deductions"?	171
Q. 10:34	How does the shareholder treat "self-charged interest" passed through on loans to the S corporation?	173
Q. 10:35	What about interest on debt incurred to purchase or carry S corporation shares?	173
Q. 10:36	How do the basis limitation and at-risk rules affect passive activity deductions?	174
Q. 10:37	How do the PAL rules affect credits passed through by the S corporation?	175
Q. 10:38	What must the shareholder do to account for disallowed losses and credits attributable to S corporation activities?	177

PAL Rules—Rental Activities

Q. 10:39	What special rules apply to items from the S corporation's rental activities?	179
Q. 10:40	What happens if the S corporation rents property from a shareholder?	180
Q. 10:41	Is there an exception for the S corporation's rental real estate activities?	180
Q. 10:42	When and how does the shareholder "actively participate" in the S corporation's rental real estate activities?	181

PAL Rules—Dispositions of Property or Interests in Property

Q. 10:43	When does a shareholder recognize gain (or loss) from a corporate disposition of property? How is the gain (or loss) characterized?	182
Q. 10:44	How must the shareholder account for a disposition of S corporation shares?	184
Q. 10:45	What valuation date is used to account for shareholder dispositions?	185
Q. 10:46	What allocation methods can be used in accounting for shareholder dispositions?	186
Q. 10:47	Can a shareholder change the character of gain from a disposition of property by contributing the property to the S corporation?	188
Q. 10:48	When does a disposition trigger suspended losses?	189
Q. 10:49	What is the PAL impact of a revocation or termination of the S corporation election? Is it equivalent to a disposition?	191

PAL Rules—Effective Dates and Transitional Rules

Q. 10:50	When are the PAL rules effective? What phase-in rules apply?	192
Q. 10:51	What happens under the phase-in rules if the shareholder's proportionate holding in a preenactment interest changes?	193

Listing of Questions

Chapter 11 Shareholders' Basis in S Corporation Stock and Loans

Functions of Basis

Q. 11:1	When and why must a shareholder determine his or her basis in an S corporation?	195
Q. 11:2	How is basis used to determine a shareholder's gain or loss on sale or exchange of stock?	195
Q. 11:3	How is basis used to impose a limitation on losses?	196

Determining Basis

Q. 11:4	How is a shareholder's basis in S corporation stock determined?	196
Q. 11:5	What yearly adjustments must be made to each shareholder's basis in his or her S corporation stock?	197
Q. 11:6	Which items increase a shareholder's basis in his or her S corporation stock?	198
Q. 11:7	Which items decrease a shareholder's basis in his or her S corporation stock?	198
Q. 11:8	What happens if the adjustments would decrease the basis in stock to below zero?	199
Q. 11:9	What is the shareholder's basis in loans made to the S corporation?	199
Q. 11:10	Is basis in loans ever reduced below zero?	200
Q. 11:11	What happens when the S corporation repays loans in which the shareholder's basis has been reduced?	200
Q. 11:12	How are payments on more than one outstanding loan allocated between return of basis and income?	201

Structuring Loans to Increase Basis

Q. 11:13	What type of loan to the corporation gives the shareholder additional basis for losses and deductions?	201
Q. 11:14	Can a shareholder obtain basis for purposes of the limitation on losses and deductions by guaranteeing a loan the corporation obtains from a third party?	202
Q. 11:15	Does the situation change if the shareholder-guarantor actually has to make payments on the loan?	202
Q. 11:16	If a shareholder substitutes his or her own obligation for corporate obligations to a third party, will this create basis for purposes of the limitation on losses and deductions?	203

The S Corporation Answer Book

Q. 11:17	Do loans from a related third party give the shareholder basis for deducting passed-through deductions and losses?	203
Q. 11:18	Will co-making or cosigning a corporate loan give a shareholder basis for purposes of the limitation on deductions and losses?	204

Contributions to Capital—A Planning Tool

Q. 11:19	Is a loan the only way, other than a stock purchase, to increase the shareholder's basis?	204
Q. 11:20	What is a contribution to capital?	205
Q. 11:21	What types of payments can be contributions to capital?	205
Q. 11:22	How do contributions to capital increase basis?	205
Q. 11:23	What are the advantages of a contribution to capital, as compared to a loan?	206
Q. 11:24	How does a contribution to capital solve the problem of repayment of a reduced-basis loan?	206
Q. 11:25	What might make a contribution to capital inadvisable?	207

Chapter 12 S Corporation Distributions to Shareholders

Fundamental Concepts

Q. 12:1	How, generally speaking, are S corporation distributions treated?	209
Q. 12:2	What concepts are important in characterizing distributions from an S corporation?	210
Q. 12:3	What is earnings and profits (E&P)?	210
Q. 12:4	When will an S corporation have E&P?	210
Q. 12:5	How can an S corporation acquire E&P from another corporation?	211
Q. 12:6	When is an S corporation's E&P reduced?	211

Corporations Without E&P

Q. 12:7	How are distributions from an S corporation taxed if the corporation has no E&P?	211
Q. 12:8	Is it important for an S corporation without E&P to make distributions to its shareholders each year?	212

Listing of Questions

Corporations With E&P

Q. 12:9	How are distributions from an S corporation generally taxed if the corporation does have accumulated E&P?	213
Q. 12:10	What is the accumulated adjustments account that an S corporation with E&P generally distributes first?	214
Q. 12:11	How are adjustments to the accumulated adjustments account made?	214
Q. 12:12	How is the accumulated adjustments account reduced, and what is the impact?	215
Q. 12:13	How does a redemption reduce the accumulated adjustments account?	215
Q. 12:14	If distributions in a taxable year exceed the amount in the accumulated adjustments account, how are distributions allocated to that account?	216
Q. 12:15	Can the accumulated adjustments account become negative?	216
Q. 12:16	Can S corporation distributions be timed to prevent problems that arise from a zero or negative accumulated adjustments account?	216
Q. 12:17	Do tax-exempt earnings affect the accumulated adjustments account?	217
Q. 12:18	Can a corporation with accumulated E&P distribute E&P before distributing the accumulated adjustments account?	218
Q. 12:19	Why would a corporation want to distribute E&P before distributing the accumulated adjustments account?	218
Q. 12:20	How does the corporation elect to distribute accumulated E&P first?	219
Q. 12:21	Are these distribution rules modified if an S corporation has undistributed pre-1983 S corporation income that has previously been taxed?	220
Q. 12:22	What is previously taxed income?	220

Post-Termination Distributions

Q. 12:23	Can a corporation make tax-free distributions of S corporation income after the election has been terminated or revoked?	221
Q. 12:24	What is the post-termination transition period?	221
Q. 12:25	Can—and should—the corporation opt out of this post-termination transition-period rule?	222

Chapter 13 Compensation; Fringe and Retirement Benefits

Compensation

Q. 13:1	Can a shareholder who works fulltime for his or her S corporation take zero compensation and have profits distributed as dividends to avoid unemployment tax, Social Security, and withholding requirements?	223

Fringe Benefits

Q. 13:2	Can the S corporation deduct the cost of providing fringe benefits to a shareholder who is also an employee?	224
Q. 13:3	How is ownership calculated for purposes of the rule treating more-than-2% shareholders as partners?	224
Q. 13:4	How might the S corporation handle benefits for more-than-2% shareholders?	225
Q. 13:5	What deductible fringe benefits are available to 2%-or-less shareholders and other employees?	226
Q. 13:6	What tax-favored death benefits may S corporations pay on behalf of employees—including more-than-2% shareholders?	227

Retirement Plans

Q. 13:7	Can all shareholders participate in the S corporation's qualified retirement plan(s)?	227
Q. 13:8	What are the tax advantages of qualified retirement plans?	227
Q. 13:9	Can an S corporation take shareholder-employees' shares of undistributed net profits into account in setting a retirement plan benefit or contribution formula?	228
Q. 13:10	Are there any types of qualified plans that an S corporation may not adopt?	229
Q. 13:11	Can a shareholder borrow from the S corporation's qualified retirement plan?	229

Chapter 14 Tax Administration of S Corporations

Returns

Q. 14:1	Must an S corporation file an income tax return?	231

Listing of Questions

Q. 14:2	When must an S corporation file its income tax return?	231
Q. 14:3	How does an S corporation obtain an extension of time for filing its return?	232
Q. 14:4	Must an S corporation furnish its shareholders with copies of the Form 1120S?	232
Q. 14:5	What happens if an S corporation fails to supply a shareholder with the information necessary to include the pro rata share of each S corporation item on his or her tax return for the taxable year?	233

S Corporation Audits Generally

Q. 14:6	How are audits of the S corporation and its shareholders handled?	233
Q. 14:7	How do the S corporation audit provisions operate?	233
Q. 14:8	Are any S corporations exempt from these audit rules?	234

"Subchapter S" Items

Q. 14:9	What is a "Subchapter S item" for income tax purposes?	235
Q. 14:10	Which factors affecting contributions and distributions are Subchapter S items?	236
Q. 14:11	What does "corporate-level determination" mean?	237
Q. 14:12	Must all shareholders follow the corporation's treatment in reporting Subchapter S items on their tax returns?	238
Q. 14:13	When and how may a shareholder ask that Subchapter S items be treated differently from the way in which the S corporation treated them?	238

"Small Corporation" Audit Exception

Q. 14:14	Are there any exceptions to this general rule that Subchapter S items must be determined at the corporate level?	239
Q. 14:15	What is a "small corporation" to which the Subchapter S item rules do not apply?	240
Q. 14:16	Is every S corporation that meets the small-corporation ownership requirements eligible for this special rule?	240
Q. 14:17	When is eligibility for small-corporation treatment determined?	241
Q. 14:18	When can the tax treatment of a small corporation's Subchapter S items be determined at the corporate level?	241
Q. 14:19	When is an election to determine a small corporation's Subchapter S items at the corporate level effective?	241

Notice; Tax Matters Person

Q. 14:20	Must a shareholder be given notice of an administrative or judicial proceeding involving the S corporation?	241
Q. 14:21	Why and how might an S corporation designate one of its shareholders as a tax matters person (TMP) for a specific corporate year?	242
Q. 14:22	What are the powers and responsibilities of the TMP?	242

Statute of Limitations and Other Matters

Q. 14:23	How long does IRS have to challenge items reported on returns of the S corporation and its shareholders?	243
Q. 14:24	When does IRS have an extended time to challenge items of income and deduction on the returns of the S corporation and its shareholders?	244
Q. 14:25	What is the "innocent spouse" rule?	245
Q. 14:26	How is gross income of an S corporation shareholder calculated for purposes of extending the statute of limitations under the substantial omission rule and for applying the innocent spouse rule?	246
Q. 14:27	Can an S corporation be used to shield a person's business from his or her creditors?	247

Chapter 1

Qualifying as an S Corporation

Basic Considerations

Q. 1:1 What is an S corporation?

An S corporation is one whose shareholders will report the corporation's taxable income or loss on their own tax returns in a manner similar to that of partnerships and partners. The S corporation, unlike a regular or "C" corporation, will generally not be subject to tax at the federal level. Thus, S corporations escape the so-called double taxation of corporate profits—that is, once at the corporate level and again at the shareholder level when corporate earnings and profits, in the form of a dividend, are paid. At the same time, the S corporation retains the nontax legal and practical advantages of corporate status.

To achieve this beneficial tax treatment, a corporation must meet the general requirements for S corporation status (see Question 1:2) and make an election to be governed by the provisions of Subchapter S of the Internal Revenue Code. (see Chapter 2.)

Q. 1:2 What are the general requirements for S corporation status?

In order for a corporation to be eligible to elect S corporation status, it must meet all of the following requirements (Section 1361(b)):

1. It must be a domestic corporation (see Question 1:3);
2. It must not be an ineligible corporation (see Question 1:8);
3. It must not have more than 35 shareholders (see Questions 1:15–1:16 for the method of counting shareholders);

4. It must have only individuals, estates (including estates in bankruptcy), or certain trusts as shareholders (see Question 1:19 for an explanation of what types of trusts qualify);
5. It must not have nonresident aliens as shareholders;
6. It must have only one class of stock (see Questions 1:30–1:35); and
7. It must make an election to which all shareholders consent. (See Chapter 2.)

Q. 1:3 What is a domestic corporation?

A domestic corporation is, first and foremost, a real corporation organized in the United States. In no sense is it a "pseudo" corporation. In most respects, therefore, an S corporation is just like any other corporation, having all the legal attributes and subject to all the rules, regulations, benefits, and burdens of the corporate form, except that—because of the election—it is not ordinarily subject to *federal* corporate income tax. (Note, however, that many states imposing franchise or excise taxes on corporate businesses impose the same tax on S corporations.)

An election to be taxed as an S corporation is not valid if the corporation has not, on the date of the election, acquired a legal existence—that is, it must be incorporated and holding a charter. (See, for example, *Frentz,* 44 TC 485 (1965), *aff'd,* 375 F.2d 662 (6th Cir. 1967); *Ratcliff,* TC Memo 1980-12.)

S Corporation Is Not a Partnership or Proprietorship: Although the income and loss of an S corporation are treated in much the same way as partnership income and loss, the S corporation is nevertheless a corporation and not a partnership. A number of decisions under the law prior to the Subchapter S Revision Act of 1982 (Revision Act) make that clear (and there are no provisions in the Revision Act that would contradict those cases).

Q. 1:4 Must the S corporation be operated for profit?

Although it may be self-evident, the courts and IRS have long taken the position that losses from S corporations are available only to a corporation that is operated for profit (or with the intention of making a profit). Losses are not available to a corporation maintained as a hobby or for the recreation or other personal gratification of its shareholders.

(*DuPont*, 234 F. Supp. 681 (D. Del. 1964); *Demler*, TC Memo 1966-117) Hence, the fact that one clothes personal, recreational, and non-profit-making activities in the cloak of an S corporation will not serve to raise such activities to deductible status for purposes of federal income tax. The profit motive remains a necessary requirement in establishing the validity of deductions from an S corporation. (*Curran*, TC Memo 1970-160)

Q. 1:5 Do the "hobby-loss" rules apply to S corporations?

Although S corporation deductions generally pass through to the shareholders, an S corporation is subject to the same limitations on the deductibility of so-called hobby losses as is an individual.

The deductibility of all expenses (with certain exceptions noted later) incurred in connection with any *activity not engaged in for profit* is limited to the income derived from such activity. A deduction is allowed, however, for those expenses ("specially treated deductions") that would otherwise be deductible, regardless of the fact that they are incurred in connection with an activity not engaged in for profit—for example, interest that would be deductible in any event and state and local taxes. (Section 183)

The rule of Section 183 also provides a presumption for the taxpayer that if profits are derived from an activity in three years out of any consecutive five-year period (the period is seven years for the racehorse industry), then the activity will be deemed "engaged in for profit" and not a "hobby." This presumption is rebuttable by IRS. Section 183(e) lets the taxpayer elect to postpone such a determination, provided he or she consents to an extension of the statute of limitations for the years involved. In the case of an S corporation, each shareholder must consent to the corporation's election to postpone the determination. (See also TIR-1278 (3/21/74).) Making the election will extend the statute of limitations only with respect to the activity involved pursuant to Section 183(e)(4).

Treatment of "Special Deductions": Note that the so-called specially treated deductions (that is, interest and taxes) referred to previously must be used to reduce the gross income from a not-for-profit activity to arrive at the amount of such gross income against which all other expenses may be deducted. Presumably, the same rule applies in determining whether profits were derived in three out of five consecutive taxable years for purposes of invoking the presumption of profitability referred to above.

Q. 1:6 What other loss limitation rules apply to S corporations?

Even if a hobby-loss operation meets all of the tests of Section 183 (see Question 1:5), IRS still has another weapon in its arsenal. Loss pass-throughs can be disallowed if the expenses of the corporation are not paid or incurred in carrying on a trade or business within the meaning of Section 162(a). (See *Eppler,* 58 TC 691 (1972), *aff'd in an unpublished opinion* (7th Cir. 1973); *Brown,* TC Memo 1977-15; *Lemler,* TC Memo 1979-308; *Lemler,* TC Memo 1980-507; *Appley,* TC Memo 1979-433; *Blake,* TC Memo 1981-579.)

Other limitations are basis (see Questions 10:1–10:2), the at-risk rules (see Questions 10:3–10:9), and the passive activity loss rules (see Questions 10:10–10:50).

Q. 1:7 Is an S corporation an appropriate vehicle for a tax shelter?

Because the Revision Act liberalized S corporation rules, more interest has been generated in S corporations as tax-shelter planning vehicles. Even though the 1984 and 1986 Tax Reform Acts severely curtailed tax shelters generally, interest in S corporations has continued insofar as tax-shelter activities remain possible. However, IRS may claim that such corporations are not operated with the expectation of earning profits (*Pike,* 78 TC 58 (1982); see Question 1:4), or it may attempt to ignore the S corporation as a separate tax entity. (See *Packard,* 85 TC 397 (1985).)

Q. 1:8 What types of corporations are ineligible?

An ineligible corporation is one that fits into any of the following categories (Section 1361(b)(2)):

1. A member of an affiliated group (that is, a member of a parent-subsidiary controlled group) determined under Section 1504 without the exceptions of Section 1504(b) (see Question 1.9);
2. A financial institution that is eligible for the special bad-debt deductions of Section 585 or 593;
3. An insurance company subject to tax under Subchapter L of the Code (see Questions 1:12–1:13);
4. A Puerto Rican or possessions corporation for which a tax credit has been elected under Section 936; or
5. A domestic international sales corporation (DISC) or a former DISC.

Ownership and Business Considerations

Q. 1:9 Can an S corporation have a subsidiary?

Generally, if an S corporation owned 80% or more of another corporation, it would, as a member of a parent-subsidiary controlled group, be an ineligible corporation. Section 1504 defines parent-subsidiary controlled groups. In applying this definition for S corporation purposes, the Section 1504(b) exclusions (tax-exempt corporations, insurance companies, foreign corporations, corporations for which a Section 936 election has been made, investment companies, real estate investment trusts, DISCs, and former DISCs) are not taken into account. Thus, a corporation that has any 80%-or-more-owned subsidiary will generally not be permitted Subchapter S treatment.

However, an S corporation may own stock of another corporation—even a majority or controlling interest—so long as the total owned is less than 80%. There is no attribution rule; so, for example, the corporation can own 79% of another corporation and its shareholders 21%.

Brother-Sister Corporations: S corporations may be commonly owned by the same shareholders as brother-sister corporations—that is, the same individuals (or eligible estates and trusts) may own 80%, or even 100%, of two or more corporations, and any or all of these corporations will be eligible to elect S corporation status.

Inactive Subsidiary Exception: In addition, there is one special exception to the 80% rule. An S corporation may have an inactive subsidiary that has not begun business and does not have gross income. (Section 1361(c)(6)) Such a subsidiary is sometimes used, for example, to prevent other corporations from using a particular name in states where the S corporation is not doing business.

Q. 1:10 Can an S corporation be a subsidiary of another corporation?

No, an S corporation may not have a corporation as a shareholder.

Q. 1:11 Are there any types of business that an S corporation is prohibited from performing?

Certain corporations are ineligible for S corporation status. (See Question 1:8.) These include financial institutions, insurance companies, possessions corporations, and domestic international sales corporations (DISCs).

Q. 1:12 Can an insurance company elect S corporation status?

No, an insurance company subject to tax under Subchapter L of the Internal Revenue Code is an ineligible corporation and can no longer elect S corporation status. In certain cases, a casualty insurance corporation that had an election in effect for its 1985 tax year may continue to use the provisions of Subchapter S as in effect on July 1, 1982—prior to the Revision Act. (See Question 1:13.)

Q. 1:13 What casualty insurance companies can continue to rely on old S corporation elections?

Despite the rule that insurance companies are ineligible for S corporation status, there are special exceptions for casualty insurance companies that satisfy any one of the following three criteria (Section 6(c)(2)(B) of the Revision Act):

1. The corporation was an S corporation casualty insurance company on July 12, 1982;
2. The corporation was formed before April 1, 1982, and had proposed in a written private offering circulated to investors prior to that date that it would elect to be taxed as an S corporation and be operated on an established insurance exchange; or
3. The corporation was approved for membership on an established insurance exchange pursuant to a written agreement entered into before December 31, 1982, and the corporation was engaged in the casualty insurance business before the end of 1984.

If one of these requirements was met, and the corporation had an S corporation election in effect for its first taxable year beginning after 1984, the status continues until there is a termination of the election or more than a 50% change in stock ownership after 1984. (Section 6(c)(4) of the Revision Act) Such corporations, however, will continue to function under the old Subchapter S rules as in effect on July 1, 1982. (Sections 6(c)(2)(A) and 6(c)(4) of the Revision Act) (Those rules, which are far more restrictive than those now in effect, generally are not discussed in this book.)

Q. 1:14 What special rules apply to a "qualified oil corporation"?

The Revision Act provides that the old Subchapter S law (as in effect on July 1, 1982) may apply to a "qualified oil corporation." In order to be qualified, *all* three of the following requirements must have been satisfied (Section 6(c)(3)(B) of the Revision Act):

1. The corporation either (a) was an S corporation on September 28, 1982, or (b) made an S corporation election after December 31, 1981, but before September 28, 1982 (the election could be effective after that date);
2. The combined average daily production of domestic crude oil or natural gas of the corporation plus that of its substantial shareholders (those who owned more than 40% in value of the stock of the corporation on July 1, 1982) exceeded 1,000 barrels for calendar year 1982; and
3. The corporation had made an election to be treated as an S corporation under the old Subchapter S law (prior to the Revision Act).

The election to continue under the old Subchapter S law continues until either the election to have the old law apply is terminated or more than 50% of the stock becomes owned by persons who were not shareholders on July 1, 1982. (Sections 6(c)(3)(A) and 6(c)(4) of the Revision Act)

Q. 1:15 If spouses own shares in an S corporation separately, how are they counted for purposes of the 35-or-fewer-shareholders test?

Regardless of how they own their shares, spouses are treated as one shareholder for purposes of the number-of-shareholders test. (Section 1361(c)(1)) Thus, they are one shareholder if they own shares jointly, or even if they own shares separately in their own individual names.

Q. 1:16 Can the number-of-shareholders test be circumvented by using nominees or agents?

No, it cannot be. When stock is held by a nominee, agent, guardian, or custodian for an individual, the individual for whom the stock is being held is the shareholder. The beneficial or equitable owner, not the owner of record, is counted in the number-of-shareholders test—and must consent to the initial S corporation election. (See Question 2:8.) The equitable owner is treated as the shareholder for these purposes. (*Kean*, 51 TC 337 (1968), *aff'd on this point,* 469 F.2d 1183 (9th Cir. 1972))

Q. 1:17 May a partnership hold stock of an S corporation as nominee for its individual partners?

No, a partnership may not be a shareholder of an S corporation. However, a partnership can become an S corporation. (See below.) An S corporation can also be a partner. (See Question 1:18.)

Tax-Free Transfer of Partnership Assets to an S Corporation: There are two ways in which a partnership can transfer its assets to an S corporation in a tax-free (Section 351) transaction. The partnership may first liquidate by distributing its assets, subject to liabilities, to its partners. If this course is chosen, the partners should simultaneously transfer these assets and liabilities to their corporation, either as a contribution to capital or for additional stock.

Alternatively, the partners may transfer their interests in the partnership directly to the corporation, thus automatically terminating the partnership. The partnership's assets and liabilities become those of the corporate transferee.

The partnership should not, however, transfer all of its assets (subject to liabilities) to the corporation in exchange for its stock. If this happens, the corporation will have a disqualified shareholder—the partnership—and it will not qualify under Subchapter S. Even if the partnership liquidates and dissolves by distributing the corporate stock to its partners in proportion to their respective partnership interests, there is a danger that IRS will disqualify the corporation because the partnership is a shareholder.

Q. 1:18 Can an S corporation be a partner?

An S corporation can be a partner. Thus, it can participate in a joint business venture or make investments via a partnership vehicle.

An S corporation-partnership combination can also enable the owners to enjoy the advantages of both forms of ownership while avoiding the disadvantages of both. Stated simply, greater flexibility can be achieved in structuring a business or investment venture as a partnership. However, the general partners' exposure to liability generally discourages the use of partnerships. Using an S corporation as general partner may provide the insulation from liability, the flexibility afforded a C corporation, and the elimination of double taxation. Assuming all partners other than the S corporation were limited partners, any claims arising from the venture would have to be satisfied from the assets of either the partnership or the S corporation. Of course, the venture would have to adhere to the strict rules IRS sets for corporate general partners to ensure that the corporate general partners are adequately capitalized. (See *Rev. Proc. 89-12,* 1989-7 IRB 22, and *Ann. 88-118.*)

Q. 1:19 What types of trusts may own S corporation stock without destroying the election?

The types of trusts that qualify as S corporation shareholders are explained below. Under no circumstances, however, may a foreign trust be an S corporation shareholder—even if one of the provisions discussed below would otherwise apply. (Section 1361(c)(2))

Grantor Trust: A trust that is treated for income tax purposes as owned by one individual who is a citizen and resident of the United States under Sections 671–678 (sometimes called a "grantor" trust) may be a shareholder of an S corporation. (Section 1361(c)(2)(A)(i)) A trust that was a grantor trust before the death of the deemed owner and that continues in existence after the deemed owner's death will still qualify as an S corporation shareholder for the 60-day period beginning on the deemed owner's death If such a trust is completely includible in the gross estate of the deemed owner, the 60-day period is lengthened to two years. (Section 1361(c)(2)(A)(ii))

Trust Created by Will: A "testamentary" trust that receives S corporation stock pursuant to the terms of a will may qualify for a limited period of 60 days beginning on the day on which the stock is transferred to the trust. (Section 1361(c)(2)(A)(iii)) This provision gives the trust time to sell the stock or distribute the stock to beneficiaries in order to enable the corporation to avoid the loss of S corporation status.

Voting Trusts: A voting trust—that is, one to which stock is transferred so the trust can exercise voting rights—is permitted to be a shareholder of an S corporation. (Section 1361(c)(2)(A)(iv); Prop. Reg. §1.1361-1A(h)(3)(ii)) Under the proposed regulations, a written agreement or document (for example, a will) would have to delegate the right to vote to a trustee or trustees. To qualify as a voting trust, the document would also have to require corporate distributions to be paid to, or on behalf of, the beneficial owners of the stock—that is, to the people who have transferred their stock to the voting trust. Additionally, title and possession of the stock would have to be delivered to the beneficial owners upon termination of the trust, which would have to be on or before a specific date or event that is set under the terms of the trust or by state law.

Qualified Subchapter S Trust: A qualified Subchapter S trust may also be an S corporation shareholder. (See Questions 1:20–1:27.)

Q. 1:20 What is a "qualified Subchapter S trust"?

A qualified Subchapter S trust is one that meets certain requirements set forth in Section 1361(d)(3) (see Questions 1:21–1:23) and whose beneficiary has made a special election with respect to an S corporation (see Questions 1:24 and 1:25). When this election is made, the trust is permitted to be a shareholder of the S corporation with respect to which the beneficiary's election is made. (Section 1361(d)(1)(A)) The trust is treated as though it were a grantor trust, with the beneficiary as the owner of the trust. (Section 1361(d)(1)(B))

Q. 1:21 What type of trust is eligible to be a qualified Subchapter S trust?

There are two basic requirements for a qualified Subchapter S trust. One relates to income distributions, and the other relates to the terms of the trust.

Income Distributions: All of the trust income must be actually distributed or required to be distributed under the terms of the trust on a current basis to one individual who is a U.S. citizen or resident. (Section 1361(d)(3)(B))

Trust Terms: The terms of the trust must require the following:
1. That there be only one income beneficiary of the trust (Section 1361(d)(3)(A)(i));
2. That any corpus (or principal amount) of the trust that is distributed during the life of the current income beneficiary be distributed only to that beneficiary and not to some other person (Section 1361(d)(3)(A)(ii));

3. That the current income beneficiary's income interest in the trust terminate at the earlier of his or her death or the termination of the trust (Section 1361(d)(3)(A)(iii)); and
4. That, if the trust terminates during the life of the current income beneficiary, all trust assets be distributed to such beneficiary (Section 1361(d)(3)(A)(iv)).

In proposed regulations, which will not be effective unless they are adopted in final form, IRS says that a trust must meet these criteria under both the trust instrument (that is, the document creating the trust) and state law governing the trust. For example, if a trust instrument said that A was the sole income beneficiary, but application of state law said that B was also an income beneficiary, A and B would both be income beneficiaries. If the terms of the trust left open the possibility that any of the requirements would not be met, the trust would not qualify. For example, if the trust instrument was silent about distributions of principal, and state law allowed such distributions to someone other than the current income beneficiary, the trust would not qualify. However, the fact that the current beneficiary could, under the terms of the trust, transfer his or her interest would not prevent the trust from qualifying. (Prop. Reg. §1.1361-1A(i)(2))

Q. 1:22 How strictly does IRS construe qualified Subchapter S trust eligibility requirements?

IRS construes these requirements very strictly, as illustrated in two Revenue Rulings issued during 1989.

The fact pattern for the first ruling was as follows. A donor established a qualified Subchapter S trust for each of his grandchildren. Each trust held the same number of shares in an S corporation. Additionally, in order to provide for future grandchildren, each trust contained a provision providing for the creation of a new trust for any new grandchildren born after the trust was created. The new trust was to be funded by transferring shares of the S corporation from each existing trust to the new trust, so that all of the grandchildren's trusts would hold the same number of shares. IRS held that these trusts could not qualify because it was possible for trust corpus to be distributed to someone other than the current income beneficiary during a current income beneficiary's lifetime. (*Rev. Rul. 89-45*, 1989-14 IRB 15)

Q. 1:22 The S Corporation Answer Book

A second ruling emphasizes that a trust will not be a qualified Subchapter S trust if the assets of the trust could *ever* be distributed to someone other than the current income beneficiary during the current income beneficiary's lifetime. The trust instrument involved in this ruling contained all four of the required trust terms. (See Question 1:21.) The trust instrument also contained a provision to the effect that if the trust did not own any stock of an S corporation, on termination of the trust, distributions could be made to the current income beneficiary and/or to other relatives of the grantor. Even though the distribution provision relating to other beneficiaries could be effective only if the corporation did not own S corporation stock, IRS held that it violated the requirement that no one but the current income beneficiary could receive trust assets during the current income beneficiary's lifetime. (*Rev. Rul. 89-55*, 1989-15 IRB 14)

Q. 1:23 Are all trusts with more than one beneficiary ineligible for qualified Subchapter S trust status?

According to the original definition of a qualified Subchapter S trust, a qualified Subchapter S trust was strictly limited to the terms described at Question 1:21. However, the Tax Reform Act of 1986 (TRA '86) amended Section 1361(d)(3) to permit separate shares of a single trust to be treated as separate trusts for purposes of qualification as a qualified Subchapter S trust if such treatment is permitted for distribution purposes under Section 663(c). Section 663(c) permits a trust with more than one beneficiary to be treated as separate trusts for distribution purposes when the beneficiaries have substantially separate and independent shares.

The amendment, which is termed a technical correction to the Revision Act, is retroactive to taxable years beginning after December 31, 1982 (the effective date of the Revision Act).

Q. 1:24 Must the beneficiary of a qualified Subchapter S trust consent to the S corporation election?

If a new election is being made, the beneficiary of the qualified Subchapter S trust must consent to the Form 2553 (S corporation election form) being filed, just as all of the other shareholders must consent. (See Chapter 2.) In addition, the current income beneficiary of a qualified Subchapter S trust must make a separate election under Section 1361(d)(2) with respect to each S corporation for which the trust seeks to be a qualified Subchapter S trust. The election is irrevocable and may be retroactive for up to 2 months and 15 days. (See Question 1:25.)

There have been some private letter rulings issued that permitted the beneficiary to make the election at a later time because he or she was unaware of the requirement at the time the S corporation election was originally made. Other private letter rulings have taken the position that substantial compliance with this requirement occurs when the beneficiary consents to the S corporation election on the Form 2553.

Q. 1:25 How does the beneficiary of a qualified Subchapter S trust make the special trust election?

The current income beneficiary of the trust, or his or her legal representative, makes the election. If the beneficiary is a minor, the election is made by his or her appointed legal representative, and if no legal representative has been appointed, by the natural or adoptive parent. (Section 1361(d)(2)(A); Temp. Reg. §1.1361-1T(a)) (See Question 2:8.)

Where and What to File: The election is in the form of a signed statement filed with the IRS Service Center with which the *corporation* files its tax return. (Temp. Reg. §1.1361-1T(a)) It should contain the following information:

1. Name, address, and taxpayer identification number of (a) the current income beneficiary, (b) the trust, and (c) the S corporation;
2. A statement that this is an election under Internal Revenue Code Section 1361(d)(2);
3. The date on which the election is to become effective (not earlier than 2 months and 15 days before the date of the election); and
4. All information necessary to show that the current income beneficiary is entitled to make the election.

Election on Form 2553: Part III of Form 2553, the IRS form used to make the S corporation election, can be used to make the qualified Subchapter S trust election if (1) stock of the corporation has been transferred to the trust on or before the date the S corporation election is made, and (2) the corporation's and the trust's elections have the same effective date.

When to File: The trust beneficiary's election must be filed within the 2-month-and-15-day period beginning on the later of the date the stock is transferred to the trust or the first day of the taxable year for which

Q. 1:25   **The S Corporation Answer Book**

the corporation's Subchapter S election is effective. (Temp. Reg. §1.1361-1T(a)) (Prop. Reg. §1.1361-1A(i)(3) would permit the beneficiary's election to be made within 2 months and 16 days of the later of the two dates. However, this change will become effective only if the proposal is adopted as a final regulation.)

Q. 1:26 Can the beneficiary of a qualified Subchapter S trust revoke the election?

A trust beneficiary's election under Section 1361(d)(2) may be revoked only with IRS consent. (Section 1361(d)(2)(C)) An application for IRS consent must be signed by the current income beneficiary and filed with the IRS Service Center where the corporation files its tax returns. (Temp. Reg. §1.1361-1T(c)) The application for IRS consent must contain the following information:

1. Name, address, and current taxpayer identification number of (a) the current income beneficiary, (b) the trust, and (c) the corporation;
2. Identification of the election that the current beneficiary is seeking to revoke as an election under Section 1361(d)(2); and
3. The reason the current beneficiary seeks to revoke the election.

Q. 1:27 What happens when the beneficiary of a qualified Subchapter S trust dies?

So long as the trust still qualifies—that is, still has only one beneficiary and meets the other requirements explained at Questions 1:20–1:22—the trust will continue to qualify. Each successive beneficiary is considered to have made the special trust election unless that beneficiary affirmatively refuses to consent to the election. (Section 1361(d)(2)(B)(ii))

Ending "Qualified Subchapter S Trust" Status: The affirmative refusal must be filed within 60 days after the date on which the successor beneficiary became the income beneficiary. It is filed with the IRS Service Center where the corporation files its tax return. The refusal becomes effective as of the date the successor income beneficiary became the income beneficiary. (Temp. Reg. §1.1361-1T(b)) The affirmative refusal to consent must contain the following information:

1. Name, address, and taxpayer identification number of (a) the successor beneficiary, (b) the trust, and (c) the S corporation;

2. A statement that this is an affirmative refusal to consent under Section 1361(d)(2);
3. The date on which the successor beneficiary became the income beneficiary; and
4. Information necessary to show that the successor beneficiary is entitled to make the refusal.

Q. 1:28 What problems may arise when an S corporation shareholder (other than the beneficiary of a qualified Subchapter S trust) dies?

Upon the death of an S corporation shareholder, his or her shares will pass to the shareholder's estate unless they are jointly held with another. The estate is a qualified shareholder (see Question 1:2), and this should present no problem. However, if the actual heir who will receive the S corporation stock from the estate is a disqualified shareholder (for example, a nonresident alien or a testamentary trust that does not qualify; see Question 1:19), S corporation status is in jeopardy.

There have been instances in which a decedent's estate was transmuted into a testamentary trust because the period of estate administration was prolonged beyond a reasonable length of time. (See *Old Virginia Brick Co., Inc.*, 367 F.2d 276 (4th Cir. 1966), *aff'g* 44 TC 69 (1965); and *Fulk & Needham, Inc.*, 228 F. Supp. 39 (D. N.C. 1968), *aff'd*, 411 F.2d 1403 (4th Cir. 1969).)

> **Planning Pointer.** If the administration of the estate is to be prolonged, there should be a good nontax reason for doing so. For example, the estate will continue to be an eligible shareholder of an S corporation when the sole purpose of holding the stock in the estate, instead of distributing it, is to comply with the provisions of Section 6166. (*Rev. Rul. 76-23*, 1976-1 CB 264) Section 6166 permits a long-term payout of estate taxes for up to 15 years.

In appropriate cases, this installment-payment provision might be used to prolong the period during which a corporation will be able to maintain S corporation status when the proceeds of the estate are payable to a trust that does not qualify as an S corporation shareholder.

The problem of an heir who is an ineligible shareholder might be avoided by a shareholders', or "buy-sell," agreement. (See Questions 6:9–6:11.)

Q. 1:29 May a corporation qualify for S corporation status if it has a shareholder whose interest in the stock is that of a legal life estate or the equivalent?

Under pre-Revision Act law, IRS looked at this question in the context of a Louisiana usufruct, which is roughly comparable to a legal life estate in property in a common-law jurisdiction, and ruled that an individual usufructuary under the Louisiana law could hold shares in an S corporation. (*Rev. Rul. 64-249,* 1964-2 CB 332)

Prop. Reg. §1.1361-1A(f) would continue this approach for usufruct interests and life estates created under a will executed before January 1, 1983, by a decedent who died before January 1, 1986, without republishing the will. Otherwise, the proposed regulation would permit such a shareholder to qualify only if all of the following criteria were met:

1. The interest is owned by only one individual who is a citizen or resident of the United States;
2. The individual for whom that interest was created has not transferred that interest to any other person; and
3. That interest will terminate upon the death of the individual for whom it was created.

These three requirements somewhat resemble those for a qualified Subchapter S trust. (See Question 1:21.) If any one of them is not met, the proposed regulations say that the S corporation election will terminate as of the first date on which the requirement ceases to be met. However, unless the regulations (proposed on October 7, 1986) are adopted, they will not be binding on IRS.

Capital Structure

Q. 1:30 Must S corporation shares be equal in all respects?

With the exception of voting rights, all rights must be identical with respect to each outstanding share of the S corporation. (Sections 1361(b)(1)(D) and 1361(c)(4))

The rule allowing variations in voting rights provides flexibility in tax planning. Stock without voting rights or with lesser voting rights can be given to inactive shareholders, thus concentrating the control of the corporation in the active shareholders. Similarly, nonvoting shares may be given to children and other family members in connection with estate planning.

Meaning of "Outstanding" Stock: Outstanding stock is stock that the corporation has actually issued to a shareholder. It does not include stock that the corporation's charter (or certificate or articles of incorporation, as the charter is called in some states) permits it to issue but that the corporation has never issued. Nor does it include treasury stock—that is, stock that it had issued but redeemed.

Thus, a corporation may have, or be authorized to have, both common stock and preferred stock. It may even have had both common shareholders and preferred shareholders at some time. But it cannot have both for any period for which the S corporation election is in effect. (For a fuller explanation of how the period is calculated in the year the election is made, see Question 2:2.)

Meaning of "Identity of Rights": Each share of stock must be identical to every other share of stock with respect to the profits and assets of the corporation—such as dividend rights and liquidation preferences.

Q. 1:31 How can the permissible differences in stock be used as a planning tool?

The prohibition against two or more classes of stock has long precluded the use of the technique of "freezing" the value of the estate of the principal shareholders of a small corporation by issuing preferred stock to the older generation (thereby "freezing" the value as of the date of the issuance) and issuing common stock to the younger generation (which shares in the increase in value of the corporation after the date of the recapitalization). The two classes of stock—preferred for the older generation and common for the younger generation—will result in a disqualification of S corporation status. However, it may be possible to pass some portion of the worth of the corporation to the next generation using the one exception permitted to the one-class-of-stock rule. The S corporation is permitted to issue voting and nonvoting common stock, as long as the two kinds are identical in all other ways except the voting rights. (see Question 1:30.) The older generation can retain the voting stock, issuing nonvoting stock to its offspring, and thereby pass some of the value of the corporation to the younger generation while retaining control for itself.

However, Section 2036(c)—added by the Revenue Act of 1987 (Revenue Act) and amended by the Technical and Miscellaneous Revenue Act of 1988 (TAMRA)—throws serious doubt on the use of the transfer of nonvoting S corporation stock to younger generations as an estate planning tool. Section 2036(c) clearly prevents the traditional C corporation "preferred stock freeze." As amended by TAMRA, Section 2036(c) appears to apply to the situation in which one individual retains all of the S corporation voting stock and transfers the nonvoting stock to his or her children. Regulations yet to be issued may also shed light on the operation of this provision.

Planning Pointer. Despite the foregoing, the use of voting and nonvoting stock is still a valuable income-tax planning tool. It enables the older generation to retain control while shifting tax on most of the income to the younger generation. For example, a mother may own 1% of the outstanding stock of an S corporation, which is the only voting stock. Her adult children may own 99% of the stock of the corporation, which is all nonvoting stock. Although mother retains control of the corporation, the adult children are taxed on 99% of the corporation's income. (Of course, the "kiddie tax" applies if children under 14 are involved.)

In addition, TAMRA, although extending the scope of Section 2036(c), mitigates some of its impact by allowing for recognition of bona fide family sales and providing for estate tax contribution by the transferee stock owner when Section 2036(c) does apply.

Q. 1:32   May a shareholders' agreement vary the rights of the shareholders without creating a second class of stock that would destroy the S corporation election?

Yes, it may. *Rev. Rul. 85-161,* 1985-2 CB 191 permitted a shareholders' agreement to include restrictions that prohibited one of the shareholders from transferring his stock without the consent of the other three shareholders. Stating that the agreement restricting the transfer of the shareholder's stock did not affect his interest in corporate profits or in corporate assets while he was a shareholder, IRS ruled that there was only one class of stock.

Planning Pointer. Care must be taken to avoid agreements in which rights to corporate profits, dividends, or liquidating distributions are different for different shareholders. In such cases, IRS may well take the position that there are two classes of stock, even though the shares are identical except as modified by the shareholders' agreement. The law in this area is not as clear as it might be, so caution is advised. (For a further discussion of shareholders' agreements, see Questions 6:9–6:11.)

Q. 1:33 Can warrants, options, convertible debentures, or proxies be treated as a second class of stock?

IRS and the courts have ruled that unexercised options, warrants, and convertible debentures do not constitute a second class of stock. (*Rev. Rul. 67-269,* 1967-2 CB 298; *Helvering v. Southwest Consolidated Corp.,* 315 U.S. 194 (1942); *LeVant,* 45 TC 185 (1965), *rev'd on other issue,* 376 F.2d 434 (7th Cir. 1967)) Care should be taken, however, to ensure that these rights are issued only with regard to the corporation's only class of stock (see Question 1:30) and that the corporation does not run afoul of the other eligibility requirements discussed in this chapter.

Inasmuch as voting trusts may be used to hold S corporation stock (see Question 1:19), and disproportionate voting rights are permitted, there appears to be little or no need for irrevocable proxies. But S corporation status will not be jeopardized if they are used.

Q. 1:34 Can loans to the corporation be treated as a second class of stock?

Loans may be treated as a second class of stock when the corporation is thinly capitalized—that is, when there is a relatively small investment in corporate stock or equity—and the loans made by the shareholders are disproportionate to their ownership of stock. Thus, loans from shareholders, as well as from others, can pose a threat to S corporation status if the rules are not followed.

However, as explained below, debt obligations held solely by shareholders and held in proportion to their interests in the nominal stock of the corporation (that is, stock that is called stock) should not constitute a second class of stock that will jeopardize the S corporation election. In addition, a safe-harbor exception for "straight debt," enacted as part of the Revision Act, ensures that certain debt obligations will not be recharacterized as a second class of stock regardless of whether they are held in proportion to nominal shareholdings; straight debt may even be held by nonshareholders. (See Question 1:35.)

"Debt-Equity" Debate: To understand the law here, it is necessary to understand a little history. At one time, IRS took the position that if it or the courts decided for other reasons that debt was really stock, there was a second class of stock that voided the S corporation election. (These disputes usually arise because IRS wants to characterize payments to the holders of debts as dividends and stock redemption payments rather than interest and repayments of loan principal.) After a series of court defeats, IRS issued regulations under the Subchapter S law in effect prior to the Revision Act. Those regulations provided that debt obligations would not be considered a second class of stock if they were owned solely by the owners of the nominal stock of the corporation and if the shareholders held the obligations in substantially the same proportions as they owned the nominal stock. (Former Reg. §1.1371-1(g)) In such a case, even though the corporation was thinly capitalized, the purported debt obligations would be treated as contributions to capital rather than as a second class of stock. Under this regulation, however, there can still be problems if the debt obligations vary the rights, preferences, or privileges of the shareholders.

In 1969, Congress enacted Section 385. This provision, which was designed to deal with the overall debt-versus-equity problem as it applied to all closely held corporations (not just the special one-class-of-stock issue), instructed IRS to issue regulations that provided criteria for distinguishing between debt and equity. Proposed regulations were issued in 1980, revised in 1981, and then withdrawn. So there is still no overall definition of what is debt and what is equity.

In summary, the Revision Act did not change the one-class-of-stock requirement, other than to add the "straight-debt" exception. The old rule continues to apply at least until new regulations are issued.

> **Planning Pointer.** Reliance on the straight-debt exception is preferable, because unless that rule applies, the result is not certain. IRS can look at all elements of the debt instrument and might decide that they vary the rights, preferences, or privileges of the shareholders. In short, there might still be a second class of stock.

Q. 1:35 What are the "straight-debt" safe-harbor rules?

Section 1361(c)(5) provides that straight debt will not be treated as a second class of stock. "Straight debt" is defined as any written unconditional promise to pay on demand or on a specified date a sum certain in money if the following three conditions are met:

1. The interest rate and interest payment dates are not contingent on profits, the borrower's discretion, or similar factors;
2. The debt is not convertible into stock, either directly or indirectly; and
3. The creditor is an individual, estate, or trust that would qualify as an S corporation shareholder (see Question 1:19).

If these conditions are met, the straight debt will not be treated as a second class of stock that would disqualify the corporation from electing S corporation status.

Chapter 2

Elections and Consents

Manner and Time of Election

Q. 2:1 How does a corporation elect to become an S corporation?

A corporation, if it meets the requirements of Subchapter S (see Question 1:2), makes its election on a timely filed Form 2553, "Election by a Small Business Corporation." The form must be signed by a corporate officer authorized to sign the corporation's tax return, Form 1120S.

Q. 2:2 When must an existing corporation make the election to become an S corporation?

An eligible corporation that has operated as a C corporation may make an election that will be effective for the following year at any time during the year. (Section 1362(b)) In order for the election to be effective for the year in which it is made, however, all three of the following conditions must be met (Section 1362(b)(2)):

1. The election must be made on or before the fifteenth day of the third month of the taxable year;
2. The corporation must have been eligible to make the election for all days during the taxable year that preceded the date of the election; and
3. All persons who held stock of the corporation during the part of the year prior to the date of the election must consent to the election, regardless of whether they are still shareholders on the date of the election.

Q. 2:2   The S Corporation Answer Book

Rules two and three above are best explained by example.

■ **Example.** An existing calendar-year corporation, A, makes an election to be treated as an S corporation on March 2, 1990. The corporation must have met all of the eligibility requirements discussed in Chapter 1 for the period from January 1 through March 2, in order for the election to be effective in 1990. Similarly, all persons who were shareholders from January 1 through March 2 must consent, even if they are no longer shareholders on the date of the election, in order for the election to be valid for 1990.

If the corporation fails any one of these three requirements, its election will be treated as having been made for the following year.

Q. 2:3   When must a newly formed corporation make the election to become an S corporation?

The rules that apply for newly formed corporations are the same as those that apply to preexisting corporations. (See Question 2:2.) However, when a newly formed corporation wants to start out as an S corporation, it is necessary to determine (1) when the taxable year begins and (2) which day is the fifteenth day of the third month in order to determine the deadline for the election.

Determination of Beginning of First Taxable Year: The regulations under Subchapter S as it existed prior to the Subchapter S Revision Act of 1982 (Revision Act) and the proposed regulations under the current version of Subchapter S both say that the corporation's first taxable year begins when the *first* of the following three events has occurred (Former Reg. §1.1372-2(b)(1); Prop. Reg. §1.1362-1):

1. The corporation first had shareholders;
2. The corporation first acquired assets; or
3. The corporation began doing business.

Planning Pointer. As a precautionary measure, it is often advisable to use the date of incorporation, because there is usually no question about the date on which the corporation was incorporated.

Determination of Fifteenth Day of Third Month: Once the beginning date has been determined, it is necessary to calculate when the fifteenth day of the third month occurs. In Temp. Reg. §18.1362-1T(b), IRS gives the example of a corporation that began its first taxable year on January 5. The temporary regulation says that for the election to be effective for the corporation's first taxable year, it must be made within the period beginning on January 5 and ending on March 19. Similar examples are set forth in Prop. Reg. §1.1362-1(e).

A method that can be used in making this calculation, which is based on regulations under pre-Revision Act law, is as follows:
1. The first month ends on the day before the beginning date of the following month. Thus, in the example in the temporary regulation, the first month began on January 5 and ended on February 4.
2. The second month ends on the same-numbered day in the following month. In the example, the second month ended on March 4.
3. After the end of the second month, 15 days are added. In the example, that would be 15 days from March 4—or March 19.

Q. 2:4 Can an extension of time be obtained for filing the S corporation election?

IRS and the courts have strictly enforced the filing deadline for the S corporation election. Since the election is optional and the law does not require it, and since it does not constitute a "return, declaration, statement or document required" to be filed under the Code, IRS takes the position that it has no authority to grant an extension of time to file the election.

Numerous hard-luck stories have been heard in the courts during the years since Subchapter S was first enacted—without changing the results of this rigid rule. When, for example, an accountant given the duty of filing an S corporation election suffered a heart attack, the Tax Court held that the late-filed election was invalid, even though the court had sympathy with the taxpayer's predicament. (*Pestcoe*, 40 TC 195 (1963))

An attempt to alter the impact of a late filing by hand delivering the election on the date that IRS would normally have received it by mail was held untimely. (*Simons*, 208 F. Supp. 744 (D. Conn. 1962))

An election that was mailed on the last day for filing, but postmarked on the next day, was invalid. (*Feldman*, 47 TC 329 (1966)) An election was deemed untimely when it was filed in the name of a corporation prior to the time the corporation had acquired legal existence. (*Frentz*, 44 TC 485 (1965), *aff'd*, 375 F.2d 662 (6th Cir. 1967)) (For further discussion on this point, see Question 1:3.)

Attorney or Accountant Mistake: A timely instruction to an attorney or accountant to file an election will not salvage the election if the practitioner fails to make a timely filing. (*Thaddeus J. Zalewski,* TC Memo 1988-340; *George R. Taylor,* TC Memo 1987-399)

Q. 2:5 What should be done to protect against an IRS claim that it never received the S corporation election?

If IRS loses the election, or says it was not received, the taxpayer must be able to show that it was filed—and timely filed. The safest course of action is to have the election filed by hand at an IRS office and to insist on receiving a copy of the election stamped with the IRS "RECEIVED" stamp, should indicate the date on which the election was filed. Then, even if IRS loses the election, the taxpayer can prove that it was timely filed.

The second best course of action is to send the election by certified mail, getting a stamped receipt from the post office for the certified mailing. In addition, if the taxpayer takes this second course of action, the people who placed the signed and completed election in the envelope, affixed proper postage to the envelope, and/or hand delivered it to the post office should immediately sign affidavits stating these facts. The affidavits, should be promptly and properly notarized and kept in the taxpayer's files.

Failure to follow either of these procedures has, in several cases, resulted in determinations that the election was never filed because, without evidence, the taxpayer could not meet its burden of proving that the election was timely filed. (See *Mora,* TC Memo 1972-123; *Jones,* TC Memo 1973-238; *Gripentrog,* TC Memo 1975-334; *Ober,* TC Memo 1980-513; *Parkin,* TC Memo 1986-59.)

In contrast, if appropriate steps are taken, it is possible to prove by testimony that the S corporation elections were prepared and filed on time. (See, for example, *Zaretsky,* TC Memo 1967-247; *Mitchell Offset Plate Service, Inc.,* 53 TC 235 (1969), *acq.,* 1970-1 CB xvi; *Thompson,* 66 TC 737 (1976), *acq. in result,* 1977-1 CB 1; *Leve,* TC Memo 1985-255.)

Q. 2:6 What happens when the due date for filing the election is a nonbusiness day or a legal holiday?

Generally, the Internal Revenue Code provides that when the due date for filing a form or document falls on a Saturday, Sunday, or day that is a legal holiday in the District of Columbia, the filing is timely if made on the next succeeding business day—that is, a day that is not a Saturday, Sunday, or legal holiday. (Section 7503)

Although the S corporation election must be filed within a prescribed time period, rather than on a prescribed date, the rules of Section 7503 nevertheless apply. (See Reg. §301.7503-1(a).) Thus, for example, if the last day for filing an S corporation election is March 15 (when the 2½-month rule applies; see Question 2:2), and March 15 is a Saturday, the election may be timely filed by March 17 (the following Monday).

IRS has in the past indicated that it may challenge the applicability of Section 7503 when it deals with time limitations in other than general procedural rules. (See *Rev. Rul. 83-116.*)

Prop. Reg. §1.1362-1(c)(4) would apply Section 7503 and the regulations thereunder to the making of an S corporation election. However, until the proposed regulation is adopted, the best practice is to follow the suggestion set forth below.

Planning Pointer. When the filing deadline falls on a Saturday, Sunday, or legal holiday, it is best to file the election on the day before the deadline. For example, if March 15 is the deadline and March 15 is a Saturday, file on Friday, March 14, if possible.

Q. 2:7 When does an S corporation election become effective?

The S corporation election becomes effective on the date set forth on the election, Form 2553. (See Questions 2:2 and 2:3 for information about the due dates of the election.)

Consents

Q. 2:8 Who must consent to the election to become an S corporation?

Each individual, estate, or trust that is a shareholder on the date the election is made must consent to such election. (Section 1362(a)(2)) In addition, when the election is made within the 2½-month period and is to be retroactive to the first day of the taxable year, any persons that are no longer shareholders on the date of the election but that were shareholders at any time during the taxable year must also consent. If their consents are not obtained, the election will be effective for the following year. (See Question 2:2.)

Special Situations: In general, the individual shareholder or the person who is treated as a shareholder for purposes of determining whether a trust is a shareholder must make the consent. (Temp. Reg. §18.1362-2T(b)(1)) Special rules clarify some situations (Temp. Reg. §18.1362-2T(b)(2)):

- If stock is held as community property, both spouses must file consents;
- If stock is held by tenants in common, joint tenants, or tenants by the entirety, all such parties must sign the consent;
- If stock is held by a minor, the consent may be made by the minor, by the minor's legal representative, or, if the minor has no legal representative, by the minor's natural or adoptive parent (when stock is held by a custodian under the Uniform Gifts to Minors Act, it is the minor who is considered the owner of the shares, and the consent is to be signed by the legal guardian or natural guardian of the minor, not by the custodian; see *Rev. Rul. 66-116*, 1966-1 CB 198, and *Rev. Rul. 68-227*, 1968-1 CB 381);
- If stock is held by an estate, the consent is made by the personal representative (executor or administrator) of the estate;
- If stock is held by a grantor trust or other trust of which a third party is deemed the owner (such as a qualified Subchapter S trust; see Question 1:20), the deemed owner of the trust is treated as the shareholder who must file the consent;
- If a trust holds stock transferred to it by a will, the estate of the decedent, which is considered to be the shareholder (see 1:19) is treated as the owner of the stock, and the personal representative of the estate must file the consent; and
- If a voting trust holds the stock, each beneficiary is deemed to be a shareholder, and therefore each beneficiary must file a consent.

Beneficial Owners: Sometimes the person who owns stock according to a corporation's records is not the actual or "beneficial" owner of the stock. Under the law prior to the Revision Act, IRS ruled that each beneficial owner of the stock must consent. When the record owner of stock in an S corporation has no beneficial interest in the shares of stock, he or she is not required to consent. (*Rev. Rul. 70-615*, 1970-2 CB 169, clarified by *Rev. Rul. 75-261*, 1975-2 CB 350) Although this ruling was issued under prior law, it would still seem to be effective, since the Revision Act did not change the law in this respect.

Q. 2:9 How do the shareholders make their consents to the S corporation election?

The shareholders may consent directly on Form 2553 or on a separate statement attached to Form 2553. (Temp. Reg. §18.1362-2T(a)) If a separate statement is used, it must include the following information:

1. The name, address, and taxpayer identification numbers of the shareholder and of the corporation;
2. The number of shares the shareholder owns;
3. The date or dates on which the shares were acquired; and
4. The month with which the shareholder's taxable year ends.

Q. 2:10 When must the shareholders make their consents to the election?

The shareholder consents are due at the same time as the S corporation election. (See Questions 2:2 and 2:3 for the due date of the election; see Question 2:12 for information relating to extensions of time for filing the consents.)

Q. 2:11 What happens if a shareholder fails to consent?

Failure of a shareholder to consent will invalidate the S corporation election. Many cases involving this point arose under the law in effect prior to the Revision Act. However, since the Revision Act did not change the requirement dealing with the consent of shareholders, these cases should be equally valid under current law.

Failure by one spouse to sign a consent when corporate stock was held as community property has caused failure of the S corporation election in several cases. (*Forrester*, 49 TC 499 (1968); *Clemens*, TC Memo 1969-235, *aff'd*, 453 F.2d 869 (9th Cir. 1971); *Seely*, TC Memo 1986-216)

When a stockholder held stock in his own name, but half of his stock was held as a nominee for his brother, both brothers were required to consent. (*Kean*, 51 TC 337 (1968), *aff'd on this point*, 469 F.2d 1183 (9th Cir. 1972)) (For more on beneficial ownership, see Question 2:8.)

Q. 2:12 Can an extension of time be obtained for filing the consents?

In contrast to the S corporation election itself (see Question 2:4), the consent is a requirement of law that the corporation must meet to make the election valid. Thus, IRS will grant extensions of time to file consents. Temp. Reg. §18.1362-2T(c) sets forth the conditions under which IRS will not invalidate an S corporation election even though consents are late. They are:

1. It must be shown to the satisfaction of the District Director or the Director of the Service Center with which the corporation files its income tax return that (a) there was reasonable cause for the failure to file the consent on time and (b) the interest of the government will not be jeopardized by allowing the S corporation election to stand;
2. The shareholder who failed to file the consent on time must file the consent within the extension period granted by IRS; and
3. New consents must be filed by (a) all persons who were shareholders at any time during the taxable year in which the shareholder applying for the extension failed to file his or her consent and (b) all persons who became new shareholders after the end of that taxable year but before the end of the period of extension that IRS granted to the shareholder who failed to file the consent on time.

According to the Ninth Circuit, an extension of time for filing consents must be granted when there is reasonable cause for the failure to file a timely consent and the government's interest will not be jeopardized. (*Kean*, 469 F.2d 1183 (9th Cir. 1972)) The Tax Court has refused to permit IRS to revoke an extension of time for filing a consent when the only reason for the revocation was the disputed validity of the election. (*Hicks Nurseries, Inc.*, 62 TC 138 (1974), *rev'd on other grounds*, 517 F.2d 437 (2d Cir. 1975))

Q. 2:13 How is an extension of time for filing consents obtained?

A request for an extension of time to file a consent is made to the

District Director or the Director of the Service Center with which the corporation files its income tax return. The request must show that there was reasonable cause for the failure to file such consent on time and that the interest of the government will not be jeopardized by treating the election as valid. (See also Question 2:12.)

Q. 2:14 When a new shareholder acquires S corporation stock, must the shareholder file anything?

No, the shareholder need not file anything—unless the new shareholder is a qualified Subchapter S trust. If the new shareholder is a qualified Subchapter S trust, the beneficiary must file a special election with respect to the S corporation whose stock the trust has just acquired. (See Question 1:25.)

Withdrawal and Amendment

Q. 2:15 Can an S corporation election be amended?

Someone might make a mistake on an S corporation election. For example, the information on Form 2553 might be complete, but contain an error. Or the information might be incomplete. Or the shareholders might change their minds about requesting a fiscal year as the corporation's taxable year. However, there seems to be no law regarding the right to amend an S corporation election. In some cases in which information on the election is incomplete, IRS will send a request for additional information, and the information supplied will relate back to the date of the original filing of Form 2553.

IRS has permitted an election to be effective January 1, 1987, when the taxpayer had erroneously inserted the date "January 1, 1988" as the effective date of the S corporation election. (*Letter Ruling 8836031;* see also *Thompson v. Commissioner,* 66 TC 737 (1976), *acq.,* 1977-1 CB 1.)

Q. 2:16 If the shareholders change their minds about the advisability of S corporation status, can the election be withdrawn before it becomes effective?

Nothing in the law mentions the right to withdraw an S corporation election before it becomes effective. Regulations under the law in effect prior to the Revision Act took the position that once an election was made it was binding and could not be withdrawn, even if the withdrawal was attempted prior to the last day on which the election could have been filed. (Former Reg. §1.1372-2(b)(3))

Planning Pointer. The shareholders could still cause the corporation to file a revocation prior to the effective date of the election (see Question 4:10), or could cause the corporation to commit a disqualifying act so that the corporation no longer qualifies for S corporation status (see Question 4:3). (See Question 4:12 for a discussion of when the shareholders might wish to terminate S corporation status.)

Also, revoking the election before it becomes effective may enable the corporation to avoid the five-year waiting period for reelection. (See Question 2:18.)

Reelection

Q. 2:17 If an S corporation election has been terminated, when can the corporation reapply for S corporation status?

If an S corporation election has been terminated, neither the corporation nor any successor corporation will be eligible for a new election until its fifth taxable year that begins after the first taxable year for which the termination was effective, unless IRS consents to an early reelection. (Section 1362(g)) Thus, if an S corporation terminates its election during calendar year 1990, it will not be able to reelect until its 1995 calendar year—the fifth taxable year following 1990—unless it receives IRS permission. (See Question 2:18.)

Successor Corporation: Although Section 1362(g) does not define a successor corporation, regulations under pre-Revision Act law did contain a definition. Under Former Reg. §1.1372-5(b), a successor corporation was defined as any corporation:

(1) *50%* or more of the stock of which is owned, directly or indirectly, by the same persons who, at any time during the first taxable year for which such termination was effective, owned 50% or more of the stock of the small business corporation with respect to which the election was terminated, *and*
(2)(i) which acquires a *substantial portion* of the assets of such small business corporation, *or*

(ii) A *substantial portion* of the assets of which were assets of such small business corporation. [Emphasis added.]

Regulations proposed under the current law, issued on December 27, 1988, would use the same definition, except that the reference to the persons owing 50% or more of the stock would be to those persons holding such interests *on the date of termination.* (Prop. Reg. §1.1362-6(b))

The provision dealing with a successor corporation is important because a former S corporation might otherwise be able to circumvent the five-year waiting period by liquidating and then reincorporating under a new name, perhaps even in a different state, but with substantially the same shareholders and assets that it had prior to liquidation.

Q. 2:18 When will IRS consent to an early reelection of S corporation status?

Regulations governing IRS consents to early reelections were issued under the law as it existed prior to the Revision Act. Since this part of the law has not been changed, it is believed that these regulations will still be valid. Former Reg. §1.1372-5(a) set forth the circumstances under which IRS might consent to an early reelection. This regulation states:

> The fact that more than 50% of the stock in the corporation is owned by persons who did not own any stock in the corporation during the first taxable year for which the termination is applicable will tend to establish that consent should be granted. In the absence of such fact, consent will ordinarily be denied unless it can be shown that the event causing the termination was not reasonably within the control of the corporation or shareholders having a substantial interest in the corporation, and was not part of a plan to terminate the election in which plan such shareholders participated.

Regulations proposed on December 27, 1988 under the current law would adopt a similar test and contain similar, but not identical, language. (Prop. Reg. §1.1362-6(a)) The proposed regulations state:

> The fact that more than fifty percent of the stock in the corporation is owned by persons who did not own any stock in the corporation on the date of the termination will tend to establish that consent should be granted. In absence of such fact, consent will ordinarily be denied unless it can be shown that the event causing termination was not reasonably within the control of the corporation or shareholders having a substantial

interest in the corporation, and was not part of a plan on the part of the corporation or of such shareholders to terminate the election.

Many private letter rulings have been issued that indicate that IRS is following these general principles. (For examples in which consent to early reelection was granted, see *Letter Rulings 7809078, 7743011,* and *7741019.* For examples in which consent was denied, see *Letter Rulings 7805036* and *7730071.*) Several revenue rulings also set forth situations in which permission to reelect will be granted before the end of the five-year waiting period. These revenue rulings involved situations prior to the time IRS could ignore an inadvertent termination (that is, pre-Revision Act terminations) and illustrate circumstances under which the shareholders inadvertently terminated the election. Among these are *Rev. Rul. 78-274,* 1978-2 CB 220; *Rev. Rul. 78-332,* 1978-2 CB 223; *Rev. Rul. 78-333,* 1978-2 CB 224; and *Rev. Rul. 78-364,* 1978-2 CB 225. For rules regarding inadvertent termination, see Question 4:6.

In *Rev. Rul. 78-332,* the sole owner of an S corporation sold all his stock to an unrelated third party in an arm's-length transaction. The new owner caused the S corporation election to be revoked. About a year later, the new owner decided that the investment was not profitable, and he sold the stock back to the old owner. The old owner requested permission for an early reelection. In granting permission, IRS noted that the shareholder owned no stock during the first taxable year of the corporation for which the termination of S corporation status was applicable.

In *Rev. Rul. 78-364,* the shareholders of an S corporation entered into a plan for a type "B" reorganization with a public corporation in which they exchanged their stock in the S corporation for stock in the public corporation. Since the public corporation became a shareholder, the S corporation election was automatically terminated. Two years later, because of conflicts concerning management and policy, the parties agreed to reverse the transaction. The corporation, which had formerly been an S corporation, became owned again by the same individuals who previously owned it. Permission for an early reelection was requested and denied. The event that caused the termination—the "B" reorganization—was within the control of the shareholders and was part of a plan to terminate the election in which all the shareholders participated. Therefore, the loss of S corporation status was within the control of the corporation and its shareholders. (See also *Versitron* (Ct. Cl. 1976).)

Prior Election Revoked Before Effective Date: IRS has also waived the five-year waiting period (see Question 2:17) when the prior election had been revoked before it would have become effective, reasoning that the corporation had never received any of the tax benefits of S corporation status. (*Letter Ruling 8842007*)

Proposed regulation would waive the five-year waiting period and IRS consent to re-election automatically in situations where the corporation either (1) revoked its election effective on the first day of the first taxable year for which the election was to be effective or (2) failed to meet the definition of an S corporation on the first day of the first taxable year for which the election was to be effective. (Prop. Reg. §1.1362-6(c))

Chapter 3

Taxable-Year Rules

Taxable-Year Options

Q. 3:1 What is the difference between a fiscal year and a calendar year?

A calendar year ends on December 31. (Section 441(d)) A fiscal year is one that ends at any other time. All tax years must end on the last day of a calendar month, except for so-called 52–53-week years. (Section 441(e)) A year consisting of 52–53 weeks is one that always ends on the same day of the week, on whatever date that day of the week either (1) last occurs in a calendar month, or (2) falls closest to the last day of a calendar month (even if the day on which the year closes actually falls in the first few days of the following month). (Section 441(f))

Q. 3:2 Are there any restrictions on an S corporation's choice of taxable year?

Section 1378(a) provides the general rule that the taxable year of an S corporation must be a "permitted year." Generally, a permitted year is a calendar year, although fiscal years are still permitted years in some instances. (See Question 3:3.)

Additionally, some S corporations may adopt fiscal years pursuant to the provisions of Sections 444 and 7519. (See Questions 3:7–3:10.)

Shareholder Relief Provision: Many of the S corporations that were not using calendar years on the effective date of the Tax Reform Act of 1986 (TRA '86) were required to change their tax years. If an S corporation was required to make a change in its taxable year, it would have had two tax years ending during 1987. The first year was the full 12-month year of its former fiscal year. The second year was the one starting on the date its former fiscal year began and ending on December 31, 1987.

Normally the shareholders would have had to report, and pay tax on, more than 12 months' income on their 1987 returns. However, if the corporation was an S corporation for a taxable year that began in 1986, a relief provision allowed the shareholders to report the S corporation income from the short-period year ending December 31, 1987, in four separate taxable years: 1987, 1988, 1989, and 1990. (Section 806(e)(2)(C) of the 1986 Act) Under the temporary regulations, the four-year spread applies only when the income for the short period required by the change in fiscal year exceeded the expenses for that period. If the result of all income and expense items was a net loss, the four-year spread does not apply. (Temp. Reg. §18.1366-5)

Transfers of Stock: Under TRA '86, as amended by the Technical and Miscellaneous Revenue Act of 1988 (TAMRA), and the temporary regulations, if the stock is transferred by sale, exchange, gift, or death, the unamortized items remaining to be spread will be realized in the year of the transfer. The temporary regulations say that partial transfers may result in partial realization of the unamortized income. (Temp. Reg. §18.1366-5(f))

Impact on Basis: TRA '86, as amended by TAMRA, and the temporary regulations also provide that the basis of the shareholder's interest (in stock and loans) in the S corporation is determined as if all of the income had been included in 1987, even though the four-year-spread provision applies for income recognition. (Temp. Reg. §18.1366-5(d)) (The importance of basis is discussed in Chapter 11.)

Q. 3:3 What is a "permitted year" for an S corporation?

A permitted year for an S corporation is (1) a taxable year ending December 31 (that is, a calendar year) or (2) any other accounting period for which the corporation establishes a business purpose satisfactory to IRS. Objective business purposes that will be acceptable to IRS are (1) a natural business year and (2) an ownership tax year. (*Rev. Proc.* 87-32, 1987-2 CB 396) Deferral of income to shareholders is not a business purpose. (Section 1378(b)) (See Question 3:4 for a discussion of how a corporation establishes its natural business year, Question 3:5 for the definition of ownership tax year, and Question 3:6 for examples.)

(Some S corporations may also elect fiscal years pursuant to the provisions of Sections 444 and 7519. (See Questions 3:7–3:10.))

Q. 3:4 What is a "natural business year"?

The natural business year of an S corporation is determined by using the following 25% test as quoted from Section 4.01(1) of *Rev. Proc. 87-32,* 1987-2 CB 396:

> (a) Gross receipts from sales and services for the most recent 12-month period that ends before the filing of the request and that ends with the last month of the requested fiscal year are computed. This amount is divided into the amount of gross receipts from sales and services for the last two months of this 12-month period.
> (b) The same computation as in (a) above is made for the two 12-month periods immediately preceding the 12-month period described in (a).
> (c) If each of the three results described in (a) and (b) equals or exceeds 25 percent, then the requested fiscal year is the taxpayer's natural business year.
> (d) Notwithstanding (c), if the taxpayer qualifies under (c) for more than one natural business year, the fiscal year producing the highest average of the three percentages (rounded to 1/100 of a percent) described in (a) and (b) is the taxpayer's natural business year.
> To apply the 25-percent test described above for any particular year, the taxpayer must compute its gross receipts under the method of accounting used to prepare the tax returns for such tax year.
> If a taxpayer has a predecessor organization and is continuing the same business as its predecessor, the taxpayer must use the gross receipts of its predecessor for purposes of satisfying the 25-percent test. If the taxpayer (including any predecessor organization) does not have a 47-month period of gross receipts (36-month period for requested tax year plus additional 11-month period for comparing requested tax year with other potential tax years), then it cannot establish a natural business year under section 4.01(1) of this revenue procedure.
> If the requested tax year is a 52–53-week tax year, the calendar month ending nearest to the last day of the 52–53-week tax year [is used] for purposes of computing the 25-percent test described above.

Q. 3:4 The S Corporation Answer Book

If the corporation does not meet this test, it may still, based on its individual facts and circumstances, try to convince IRS that a fiscal year is its natural business year. (See Question 3:6.)

Q. 3:5 What is an "ownership tax year"?

According to *Rev. Proc. 87-32*, 1987-2 CB 396:

> An S corporation or a corporation electing to be an S corporation meets the "ownership tax year test" if the corporation is adopting, retaining, or changing to a tax year and shareholders holding more than one-half of its issued and outstanding shares of stock (as of the first day of the tax year to which the request relates) have, or are concurrently changing to, the same tax year. A shareholder in an S corporation that desires to change its tax year concurrently should see the instructions generally applicable to taxpayers changing their tax years. These instructions are contained in section 1.442-1(b)(1) of the regulations.
>
> If, as of the first day of any tax year, the S corporation no longer meets the ownership tax year test, it must change its tax year to a permitted year by following the instructions for a change in tax year contained in this revenue procedure.

Planning Pointer. Since most S corporation shareholders will be using calendar years, the ownership tax year test will generally not be met for a noncalendar year.

Q. 3:6 How might an S corporation establish a "business purpose" justifying a fiscal year?

Simultaneously with its release of *Rev. Proc. 87-32*, 1987-2 CB 396, IRS issued *Rev. Rul. 87-57*, 1987-2 CB 117. The ruling examined whether each of eight factual situations established a business purpose for adopting, retaining, or changing an S corporation's taxable year. In each instance, the shareholders of the S corporation have different tax years from that requested by the corporation. Also, the requested tax year is not a "grandfathered fiscal year" within the meaning of Section 5.01(2) of *Rev. Proc. 87-32*—that is, a fiscal year for which permission was granted on or after July 1, 1974, that did not result in a three-month or less deferral of income. The following is a discussion of the factual patterns set forth in *Rev. Rul. 87-57*.

Situation 1: The S corporation wants to use a January 31 tax year end because it corresponds to the natural business year for its type of business, as suggested by the Natural Business Year Committee of the American Institute of CPAs (AICPA) in an official release published in the Journal of Accountancy in 1955. The taxpayer corporation also uses a January 31 fiscal year end for financial reporting purposes. As stated in the Conference Committee Report to TRA '86, the use of a particular year for financial accounting purposes is not considered sufficient to meet the business-purpose requirement. In addition, the natural business year suggested by the AICPA is not based on this taxpayer's own facts and circumstances.

Situation 2: The taxpayer corporation wants to use a September 30 tax year end because the taxpayer's accountant is extremely busy during the first six months of the year. The accountant has told the taxpayer corporation that if it uses a September 30 year end, it will receive a reduced charge for the accountant's services. The reason here is one of convenience to the taxpayer. Convenience to the taxpayer will not be considered a sufficient business reason for the use of a requested tax year.

Situation 3: The taxpayer corporation desires to retain its November 30 tax year end. The reasons it gives for this are that it has used a November 30 year end since the inception of its business 15 years ago and that if it were required to change its tax year, it would lose its recordkeeping consistency and would suffer financial hardship in changing its records to another year. This is also not considered a sufficient business reason, because it is merely for the convenience of the taxpayer.

Situation 4: The taxpayer corporation desires to use a September 30 tax year end. Its reason for this request is that it desires to issue timely tax information (Schedules K-1) to its shareholders to facilitate the timely filing of shareholders' returns. This is also not a valid business purpose, because it is merely for the convenience of the taxpayers.

Situation 5: The taxpayer wishes to use a November 30 tax year end. The corporation can establish a natural business year ending on January 31 under the 25% test of Section 4.01(1) of *Rev. Proc. 87-32.* (See Question 3:4.) If the taxpayer had not satisfied the natural business year test for January 31, it would have met the natural business year test for November 30. Use of a November 30 tax year end would be permitted by IRS because the November 30 fiscal year also satisfies the 25% test and results in less deferral to the shareholders than the January 31 tax year.

Situation 6: The taxpayer desires to use a June 30 tax year end, claiming that it coincides with the taxpayer's natural business year. For this taxpayer, June 30 is not a natural business year end within the meaning of the 25% test of *Rev. Proc. 87-32.* (See Question 3:4.) The corporation has failed to meet the 25% test because of unusual gross receipts figures for several months during the 47-month test period. The figures for these months were unusual because a labor strike closed the taxpayer's business during a period that included its normal peak season. The taxpayer has data for the most recent five years demonstrating that the requested tax year would have satisfied the 25% test if the strike had not occurred. Since the taxpayer's failure to establish a natural business year under the 25% test is due to unusual circumstances during the test period that were beyond the taxpayer's control, and the historical data support the taxpayer's contention that in the absence of these unusual circumstances the requested year would have qualified, IRS is satisfied that a sufficient business purpose has been established for the requested tax year.

Situation 7: The taxpayer wishes to use a May 31 tax year end. Its reason for the requested tax year is that because of weather conditions, its business is operational only during the period from September 1 through May 31. For the 10 years it has been in business, the corporation has had insignificant gross receipts for the period June 1 through August 31. The facility used by the taxpayer is not used for any other purpose during the three months of insignificant gross receipts. The taxpayer does not meet the 25% test of *Rev. Proc. 87-32.* (See Question 3:4.) IRS rules that a valid business purpose for using the May 31 tax year end exists because the year coincides with the time that the taxpayer has closed down operations for the past 10 years, and closing because of weather conditions is not within the taxpayer's control.

Situation 8: The taxpayer wishes to continue to use a March 31 tax year end. The taxpayer changed its method of accounting to the accrual method for the March 31 tax year end just completed. The taxpayer's reason for the requested tax year is that it coincides with the taxpayer's natural business year. The taxpayer failed the 25% test for March 31 because the 25% test in Section 4.01(1) of *Rev. Proc. 87-32* requires the taxpayer to compute the gross receipts on the method of accounting used to file its income tax returns for each year of the test period. (See Question 3:4.) This requires the taxpayer to compute gross receipts on a cash method of accounting for tax years prior to the March 31 tax year end just completed. The taxpayer has audited financial statements prepared on the accrual basis that would be acceptable for tax purposes. Using the gross receipts based on the accrual method, the corporation would satisfy the 25% test for the tax year ending March 31. Under these circumstances, it is reasonable for IRS to allow the taxpayer to use a March 31 tax year end if the accrual method, which will be used for all future tax years, would pass the 25% test and establish a natural business year ending on March 31.

Q. 3:7 If an S corporation does not qualify for any ownership or business-purpose year, must it use a calendar year?

Section 444 permits an S corporation to elect a taxable year other than the required taxable year. The general rule provides that the election may be made only if the deferral period of the elected taxable year does not exceed three months. If the corporation has a fiscal year with a deferral period of less than three months, the deferral period may not be increased. For example, a corporation that as a C corporation had an October 31 year end may make a Section 444 election to use that year end, or a November 30 year end, when it elects Subchapter S. It may not elect a September 30 year end.

Calendar-year corporations may not use the election.

However, as a trade-off for this election, the corporation must make a "required payment" that is in the nature of a deposit on shareholder tax deferral. (See Questions 3:18-3:19.)

(Special rules also applied to S corporations making the election in 1987, to S corporations forced to change their taxable years because of the 1986 Act, and to certain reactivated S corporation elections. The deadlines for these special rules have expired.)

Q. 3:8 Can an S corporation that holds a partnership interest make a Section 444 election?

This is sometimes, but not always, possible. An S corporation that owns a partnership interest is generally considered a member of a "tiered structure" of "deferral entities," subject to taxable-year restrictions. If this is true, the S corporation can make a Section 444 election only if the structure is composed of one or more partnerships or S corporations that all have the same taxable year. (Section 444(d)(3))

However, not all S corporations that own partnership interests are deemed to belong to tiered structures. An S corporation that is not deemed to be a member of a tiered structure may make a Section 444 election.

Q. 3:8   **The S Corporation Answer Book**

Generally, an S corporation is a member of a tiered structure if it *directly* owns any portion of a deferral entity (a deferral entity is an S corporation, a partnership, a personal service corporation, or certain type of trust). (Temp. Reg. §1.444-2T) However, a "downstream" *de minimis* rule disregards ownership if, in the aggregate, all deferral entities accounted for not more than either:

1. 5% of the S corporation's adjusted taxable income, or
2. 2% of its gross income for the taxable year that ends immediately prior to the taxable year for which the corporation is making its Section 444 election.

Thus, for example, the S corporation might be able to make a Section 444 election even though its working capital reserve is invested in a limited partnership.

For a newly formed S corporation, this two-part test is replaced by a 5%-of-assets test. Thus, if the newly formed S corporation attributes 5% or less of its tax basis in its assets to its ownership in deferral entities, the deferral entities will be considered *de minimis* and will be disregarded. Mid-year acquisitions are tested pro rata, and newly formed deferral entities in which the S corporation owns an interest are tested by comparing adjusted taxable income or gross income including the new entities and adjusted taxable income or gross income without them.

The measurement is made as of the last due date of the required taxable year (without taking any business-purpose year into account). The testing period used for purposes of the *de minimis* rule is the taxable year ending immediately before the taxable year for which the S corporation wants to make or continue a Section 444 election. Additional rules are provided when the deferral entity was not in existence during the entire testing period. Adjusted taxable income is the aggregate amount of S corporation items described in Section 1366(a) (See Questions 9:1–9:2), other than credits and tax-exempt income, plus "applicable payments" as defined in Section 7519(d)(3) (see Question 3:18). Losses and deductions are treated as negative income.

An antiabuse rule may also apply in some cases. (See Question 3:9.)

Q. 3:9   **Can the limitations on electing Section 444 be avoided by transferring assets to other corporations owned by the same shareholders?**

Under an antiabuse rule in the temporary regulations, a transfer by an existing S corporation to a related party will be disregarded for purposes of Section 444 if the principal purpose of the transfer is to either (Temp. Reg. §1.444-1T(b)(5)(iii)):

1. Create a deferral period greater than the deferral period of the predecessor corporation's taxable year; or
2. Make a Section 444 election following the termination of the predecessor corporation's Section 444 election.

This rule applies even if the tax deferral created by the change is effectively eliminated by a required payment made under Section 444.

Additionally, an S corporation is deemed to be a member of a tiered structure, and thus eligible for the election only under limited circumstances (See Question 3:8), if the corporation or related taxpayers have organized or reorganized their ownership structure or operations for the principal purpose of obtaining a significant unintended tax benefit from making or continuing a Section 444 election. The regulations specify that a significant unintended tax benefit results when an S corporation makes a Section 444 election and someone (not necessarily the S corporation making the election) obtains a significant deferral of income, substantially all of which is not eliminated by a required payment under Section 7519. (Temp. Reg. §1.444-2T(b)(3))

Q. 3:10 How many Section 444 elections may an S corporation make?

An S corporation may make only one Section 444 election. That election remains in effect until the S corporation changes its taxable year, which might occur in a number of ways.

Taxable-Year Election Mechanics

Q. 3:11 How does a corporation electing S corporation status request a fiscal year (other than one under Section 444)?

Any corporation electing S corporation status—either a newly formed corporation that elects S corporation status for its first fiscal year or an existing regular (C) corporation that elects S corporation status—selects a fiscal year (other than one elected under Section 444, for which procedures are discussed at Questions 3:15–3:16) by indicating its choice of tax year at Item I, Part I, of Form 2553, the form on which the S corporation election is made. Any request for a permitted year other than one ending on December 31 must be made as part of the election, on page 2 (the back page) of Form 2553.

As a preliminary question, Item O, at the beginning of Part II of Form 2553, asks whether the corporation is adopting the fiscal year entered on page 1, retaining the fiscal year entered on page 1, or changing to the fiscal year entered on page 1. The corporation then checks applicable boxes.

Ownership Year: In the unlikely event that the corporation is relying on the ownership-year provision of *Rev. Proc. 87-32*, 1987-2 CB 396 (see Question 3:5), the first box in Item P, Part II, is checked to indicate that the shareholders holding more than half of the outstanding stock on the first day of the S corporation year either (1) have the same tax year or (2) are currently changing to the same fiscal year that the corporation shows on page 1. This representation is made under penalties of perjury.

Natural Business Year: The second box in Item P, Part II, is checked if the corporation is adopting, retaining, or changing to a tax year that coincides with its natural business year as verified by satisfaction of the requirements set forth in *Rev. Proc. 87-32*. (See Question 3:4.) This representation is also made under penalties of perjury.

Other Business-Purpose Years: The first box in Item Q, Part II, is checked if the corporation is selecting a fiscal year under the provisions of *Rev. Proc. 87-32* that require IRS approval because the automatic provisions are not met. (See Questions 3:3–3:6.)

Checking this box enables the corporation to ask IRS to determine whether the corporation qualifies for the requested fiscal year based on the information submitted.

Q. 3:12 How can a newly electing S corporation protect S corporation status in case its business-purpose fiscal-year request is denied?

Items on page 2 of Form 2553, the form on which the election is made, permit a corporation that is initially selecting a fiscal year to make a backup request.

Item Q also permits the corporation to signify whether it is making a backup Section 444 election (see Question 3:16) and whether the corporation agrees to use a calendar year ending December 31, if necessary, for IRS to accept the election for S corporation status in the event that the corporation does not qualify for a fiscal year.

Item R permits the corporation to signify whether the corporation is making a Section 444 election (see Question 3:15) and whether the corporation agrees to use a December 31 year end in the event that it does not qualify for a Section 444 election.

These are optional boxes to be checked if the corporation agrees to adopt a calendar tax year if IRS requires this year as a condition of the S corporation election. Checking this box means that the corporation agrees to forgo the use of the fiscal year requested in order to be sure of qualifying for S corporation status if IRS refuses to grant the requested year (or backup Section 444 year). If the fiscal year is granted, checking the box will make no difference. If the fiscal year requested is denied, then the box will preserve the S corporation election, and the corporation will automatically be on a calendar year for federal income tax purposes.

Q. 3:13 How does an existing S corporation change its taxable year?

In order to change its taxable year, an S corporation must file a Form 1128, "Application for Change in Accounting Period," with the Director of the IRS Service Center where the taxpayer files its income tax returns. The taxpayer must generally request permission to change to the desired tax year in accordance with Reg. §1.442-1(b)(1), which requires the corporation to establish to IRS's satisfaction that the year is a permitted year. In some cases, however, the corporation may request expeditious approval. (See Question 3:14.)

The corporation may also, if eligible, elect a fiscal year under the special procedures for Section 444. (Eligibility is discussed at Questions 3:7–3:10 and the procedures are discussed at Questions 3:15–3:16.)

Q. 3:14 When will IRS grant expeditious approval of an existing S corporation's use of a business-purpose fiscal year?

IRS has announced that it will grant expeditious approval to those

Q. 3:14   The S Corporation Answer Book

existing S corporations requesting that they be permitted to use the natural business year (see Question 3:4) or the ownership tax year (see question 3:5). (*Rev. Proc. 87-32*, 1987-2 CB 396)

Procedure and Time to File: The procedure for effecting the change requires filing a current Form 1128, "Application for Change in Accounting Period," with the Director of the IRS Service Center where the taxpayer files its income tax returns, directed to "Attention: ENTITY CONTROL." The Form 1128 must be filed on or before the fifteenth day of the second calendar month following the close of the short period for which a return is required in order to effect the change in accounting period (see (2) in the list below). If no short period is created because the taxpayer is retaining its fiscal year, Form 1128 must be filed on or before the seventy-fifth day of the tax year. In order to assist processing of the retention or change in tax year, taxpayers should type or print "Filed Under Rev. Proc. 87-32" at the top of page 1 of Form 1128.

Contents: In order for an S corporation to obtain expeditious approval to adopt, retain, or change its tax year, it must comply with each of the following conditions:

1. The corporation must file a federal income tax return (Form 1120S) for any short period required to effect the change, adoption, or retention of the desired tax year by the due date of the return;
2. If a short period is required to effect the change, it begins with the day following the close of the old tax year and ends with the day preceding the first day of the new tax year;
3. The books of the corporation must be closed as of the last day of the short period in the case of a change or adoption that establishes a new tax year (returns for subsequent years must generally be made on the basis of a full tax year); and
4. The taxpayer's books and records, including financial reports and statements for credit purposes, must be kept on the basis of the selected tax year.

Q. 3:15   How is a Section 444 election made?

The election is made by filing a properly prepared Form 8716, "Election To Have a Tax Year Other Than a Required Tax Year," with the Internal Revenue Service Center shown on the instructions to the form. In addition, a copy of the Form 8716 must be attached to the

Form 1120S for the first taxable year for which the Section 444 election is made. Form 8716 must be signed by a person authorized to sign the Form 1120S. (Temp. Reg. §1.444-3T)

The due date for filing the Form 8716 is generally the earlier of:

1. The fifteenth day of the fifth month following the month that includes the first day of the taxable year for which the election will first be effective; or
2. The due date (without regard to extensions) of the Form 1120S resulting from the Section 444 election.

Newly Electing S Corporations: In addition to satisfying the requirements set forth above, a corporation electing to be an S corporation after September 26, 1988, is required to state on its Form 2553 its intention to (Temp. Reg. §1.444-3T(b)(3)):

1. Make a Section 444 election if qualified; or
2. Make a backup Section 444 election (see Question 3:16).

If a corporation fails to state either of the above intentions on its Form 2553, the District Director has discretion to disregard the Section 444 election.

Q. 3:16 How is a backup Section 444 election made?

The S corporation must file and, if necessary, activate a backup Section 444 election.

A corporation making a backup Section 444 election should type or print the words "BACKUP ELECTION" at the top of Form 8716. If the corporation is requesting a change in its accounting period (see Question 3:13), and the Form 8716 is filed on or after the date a Form 1128 is filed with respect to a period that begins on the same date, the words, "FORM 1128 BACKUP ELECTION" should be typed or printed at the top of Form 8716. (Temp. Reg. §1.444-3T(b)(4)(ii)) A newly electing corporation must also indicate the backup election in Items Q and R on page 2 of Form 2553. (See Question 3:12.)

The election is activated by filing the appropriate return and making any required payment. The due date for the payment is the later of (1) the due date for the required payment under the general rules, or (2) 60 days after IRS denies the business-purpose request. (The general procedures for the required payment are discussed at Questions 3:18–3:19.)

The return form must bear these words at the top: "ACTIVATING BACKUP ELECTION." (Temp. Reg. §1.444-3T(b)(4)(iii))

Interest will be assessed on any payment made after the general due date, calculated from the due date to the date the amount is actually paid. It is separate from the required payment and is not refunded if the corporation cancels the Section 444 election.

Q. 3:17 Will IRS impose a fee for a fiscal-year request?

A $150 user fee is charged on all applications for a change of accounting period filed by existing S corporations on Form 1128. This fee should accompany the application.

A user fee of $150 will also be imposed on Forms 2553 that request a determination under *Rev. Proc. 87-32*, 1987-2 CB 396, regarding a fiscal year. In this case the corporation will be billed by the IRS National Office after its application is forwarded by the Service Center where the Form 2553 was filed.

These fees remain in effect through September 30, 1990. (See *Rev. Proc. 88-13*, 1988-1 CB 639.)

Maintenance and Termination of Section 444 Election

Q. 3:18 How does an S corporation electing Section 444 calculate its required payment?

If an election under Section 444 is in effect for a taxable year, the S corporation is required to make a payment computed under the provisions of Section 7519, unless the total amount due is $500 or less. The amount due for the current year is called the "required payment." (Section 7519(b)) It is defined as an amount equal to the excess of the current year's payment over the required payment for the preceding applicable year.

The current amount is the product of the applicable percentage of the adjusted highest Section 1 rate times the net base year income of the S corporation. For this purpose, the term "adjusted highest Section 1 rate" means one percentage point over the highest rate of tax in effect under Section 1 as of the end of the base year. However, in the case of applicable election years beginning in 1987, the adjusted highest Section 1 rate was specified as 36%. If the payment for the current year exceeds the amount of required payment for the preceding applicable election year, the S corporation will receive a refund of such excess. No interest will be paid on that refund.

Applicable Percentage: The applicable percentage is determined in accordance with the following table:

If the Applicable Election Year of the S Corporation Begins During	The Applicable Percentage Is
1987	25
1988	50
1989	75
1990 or later	100

However, TAMRA provided that the applicable percentage does *not follow the table for taxable years beginning after 1987* if more than 50% of the S corporation's net income for the short taxable year that would have resulted without the Section 444 election would have been allocated to shareholders who were not entitled to four-year spread relief for the change of a taxable year. (See Question 3:2.) In this case, the applicable percentage is 100%.

Net Base Year Income: For purposes of these calculations, net base year income is equal to the sum of two components:

1. The deferral ratio multiplied by the corporation's net base year income for the base year; and
2. The excess (if any) of the deferral ratio, multiplied by the aggregate amount of "applicable payments" made by the corporation to a shareholder during the base year, over the aggregate amount of such "applicable payments" made during the deferral period of the base year.

Deferral Ratio: Deferral ratio means the ratio that the number of months in the deferral period of the base year bears to the number of months in the S corporation's taxable year.

Net Income: Net income for the S corporation is the amount (but not less than zero) determined by taking into account the aggregate of the corporation's Section 1366(a) items, other than credits. If the S corporation was a C corporation for the base year, its taxable income for that year is treated as its net income. Limitations (that is, basis limitations) are disregarded in computing the taxable income of an S corporation for this purpose.

Applicable Payment: Applicable payment means amounts paid or incurred by the S corporation that are includible in the gross income of a shareholder, other than dividends paid by the corporation and gains from the sale or exchange of property between the corporation and a shareholder.

Applicable Election Year: The applicable election year is the taxable year of the S corporation for which a Section 444 election is in effect.

Base Year: The base year is the taxable year of the S corporation immediately preceding the applicable election year.

Q. 3:19 When and how are required payments made?

For applicable election years beginning after 1987, the required payment is due and payable without assessment or notice on or before May 15 of the calendar year following the calendar year in which the applicable election year begins.

Payments due under Section 7519 are made with Form 720, Quarterly Federal Excise Tax Return, unless IRS prescribes another form. (Temp. Reg. §1.7519-2T(a)(2)) If the amount due for an applicable election year and all preceding years does not exceed $500, the S corporation is not required to make a payment under Section 7519 and should type or print "zero" on the appropriate line of the Form 720.

The required payment must be made by a check or money order that indicates the S corporation's taxpayer identification number and also includes the statement: "IRS NO. 11 PAYMENT." The check or money order must be sent together with the Form 720 to the Service Center indicated by the instructions for the Form 720.

Q. 3:20 What happens to an S corporation electing under Section 444 that fails to make required payments?

The basic penalty for failure to pay is 10% of the underpayment. In addition, the negligence and fraud penalties of Section 6653 may be applied. If the S corporation willfully fails to make a required payment, the Section 444 election will cease to apply. (Section 7519(f)(4))

Q. 3:21 How is a Section 444 election terminated, and what happens then?

Generally, the election is terminated by a change to another taxable year (either a calendar year or, with IRS permission, a business-purpose year). In that event, the corporation is entitled to apply for a refund of required payments. (Temp. Reg. §1.444-1T(c)(2)) (See Question 3:23.) (As there is no longer a deferral, there is no further need for the deposit that the required payment represents.)

Q. 3:22 When should a Section 444 election be terminated?

There is no easy answer to this question. It is important to monitor cash flow and related benefits. In other words, if retention of the election produces more upfront expense than a calendar year, and the situation does not appear temporary, termination of the election is usually desirable.

Practical considerations, such as financial accounting, shareholder year-end planning, and possible reductions in professional fees, should also be taken into account.

Q. 3:23 How does an S corporation terminating a Section 444 election claim a refund of its required payments?

Regulations have yet to be promulgated. Temp. Reg. §1.7519-2T(a)(6)(ii) is reserved for this purpose. However, IRS has provided temporary guidance that technically applies only in 1989. (*Notice 89-41,* 1989-15 IRB 16) The Notice provided that a refund should be requested using Form 720, "Quarterly Federal Excise Tax Return" (revised January, 1989). In addition, the taxpayer must type or print at the top of Form 720 whichever one of the following statements applies:

A. "TERMINATION OF §444 ELECTION BY CHANGE TO REQUIRED YEAR."

B. "TERMINATION OF §444 ELECTION OTHER THAN BY CHANGE TO REQUIRED YEAR."

C. "CONTINUING SECTION 444 ELECTION."

In the case of any termination of a Section 444 election, the taxpayer should indicate its eligibility for a complete refund of any required payment which is on deposit by inserting the word "zero" on the line for "IRS No. 11" and including the amount paid with respect to the applicable election year on line 4(d), Part II of Form 720.

IRS has indicated that it may change these procedures for 1990 and subsequent years. In no event will a refund be made prior to April 15 of the second calendar year that follows the calendar year in which an applicable election year (as defined at 3:18) begins. Thus, for example, if an S corporation elected to retain its taxable year beginning October 1, 1987, made a required payment for that year, and terminated its election for its taxable year beginning October 1, 1988, it would not be entitled to a refund before April 15, 1989.

Q. 3:24 Is interest paid on refunds of required payments?

No, interest is not paid on refunds of required payments. (Section 7519(f)(3))

Chapter 4

Terminations and Revocations

Basic Considerations

Q. 4:1   When does an S corporation cease to be an S corporation?

S corporation status ceases when:

1. The election is terminated because the corporation becomes disqualified (see Question 4:3); or
2. The election is revoked (see Question 4:1).

Q. 4:2   What is the effect of termination or revocation of S corporation status?

The termination or revocation of S corporation status means that the S corporation will no longer be shielded from the double tax provisions of Subchapter C of the Code. The corporation will become a regular C corporation and will be subject to all corporate taxes. The corporation will no longer file Form 1120S, but will instead file Form 1120. In the event that the loss of S corporation status occurs in the middle of the corporation's taxable year, the corporation will have to file two tax returns for the year (see Question 4:17), allocating income and deductions (see Question 4:19).

Terminations

Q. 4:3   How does an S corporation become disqualified, causing a termination?

An S corporation is disqualified when it fails to meet any of the general requirements for S corporation status. (See Question 1:2.) Thus, for example, an S corporation will become disqualified if it has more than 35 shareholders; has more than one class of stock; acquires an active subsidiary; or has a disqualified shareholder, such as a nonresident alien, a corporation, or a partnership. (See Prop. Reg. §1.1362-3(c).)

In addition, the corporation will lose S corporation status if (1) it has earnings and profits from years when it was a C corporation (not an S corporation) and (2) it has passive investment income exceeding 25% of its gross receipts for three consecutive years. (Section 1362(d)(3)) (See Question 7:3.) (Prop. Reg. §1.1362-3(d))

(A special aspect of terminations—corporate reorganizations—is discussed separately in Chapter 5.)

Q. 4:4 Can an S corporation intentionally disqualify itself?

Yes, an S corporation can intentionally disqualify itself by intentionally failing to meet the general requirements for S corporation status. (See Question 1:2.) Thus, for example, issuance of a *single* share of stock to a nonresident alien individual, a corporation, or a trust that does not qualify as a shareholder will terminate the S corporation status. So, too, will the issuance of a second class of stock (see Question 1:2) or the acquisition of 80% or more of the stock of an active subsidiary (see Question 1:9).

Q. 4:5 How many shareholders are needed to intentionally disqualify an S corporation and terminate the election?

There is no minimum. Any shareholder can cause the election to be terminated by transferring *one* of his or her shares to a disqualified shareholder. (See Question 1:2.) This can happen if the transfer occurs by way of a trust instrument or a will (See Questions 1:28-1:29), as well as in a direct sale, exchange, or gift.

Planning Pointer. It may be possible to prevent a shareholder from intentionally disqualifying the corporation by prohibiting the transfer of shares to disqualified shareholders in the charter, bylaws, or a shareholders' agreement, depending on the state law governing the corporation. There do not seem to be any cases covering this point at the present time. (Shareholders' agreements, sometimes called buy-sell agreements, are discussed at Questions 6:9-6:11.)

Q. 4:6 Can S corporation status be preserved if it is accidentally terminated?

Yes, if the termination was brought about because of a disqualifying act (see Questions 4:3–4:5) or because the passive income restrictions were violated (see Question 7:3), the corporation may nevertheless still be treated as an S corporation during a period specified by IRS, if all the following conditions are met (Section 1362(f)):

1. IRS determines that the termination was inadvertent;
2. Within a reasonable period after discovering the terminating event, steps are taken to correct the situation so that the corporation once more qualifies as an S corporation; and
3. The corporation and each person who was a shareholder at any time during the period between the terminating event and the corrective action agree to make the adjustments required by IRS (such adjustments, of course, must be consistent with the treatment of the corporation as an S corporation).

Q. 4:7 When will IRS consider a termination "inadvertent" or accidental?

Proposed regulations published on December 27, 1988, provide guidelines indicating when the IRS will agree that a termination was inadvertent (Prop. Reg. §1.1362-5(b)):

> The fact that the terminating event was not reasonably within the control of the corporation and was not part of a plan to terminate the election, or the fact that the event took place without the knowledge of the corporation notwithstanding its due diligence in the course of its business to safeguard itself against such an event, tends to establish that the termination was inadvertent. For example, if a corporation, in good faith and using due diligence, determined that it had no subchapter C earnings and profits, but it was later determined on audit that its election terminated by reason of violating the passive investment income test for three consecutive years because the corporation in fact had accumulated earnings and profits, it may be appropriate for the Commissioner to find that the terminating event was inadvertent.

Of course, these regulations for the moment are only proposed.

At least one earlier IRS ruling also provides guidance. *Rev. Rul.* 86-

110, 1986-2 CB 150, illustrates a situation in which the majority shareholder of an S corporation, upon advice of his attorney, transferred shares of stock to two irrevocable trusts for the benefit of his minor children. Neither trust was an eligible shareholder. Within a reasonable time after discovering that neither trust was eligible and that the S corporation election had terminated, the shareholder took steps to correct the problem so that the corporation once more qualified as an S corporation. The ruling does not specify what actions he took. In addition, the shareholder and all other shareholders of the corporation agreed to make any adjustments required by IRS with respect to the period during which S corporation status was terminated. Under these facts, IRS held that the termination was inadvertent because the shareholder acted on the advice of his attorney and would not have made the transfers but for this advice. Further, since he took the necessary steps to correct the problem within a reasonable time after discovery of the termination, and the shareholders agreed to make whatever adjustments were required by IRS, the corporation was allowed to continue its election during the period when it had ineligible shareholders.

Q. 4:8 What must an S corporation do to have a termination treated as inadvertent?

The proposed regulations state that a corporation requesting inadvertent termination status must request a private letter ruling. The request must contain information required by regulations and revenue procedures pertaining to a ruling request. The request must set forth all relevant facts pertaining to the terminating event, such as the date of the corporation's S corporation election, a detailed explanation of the event causing termination, when and how the event was discovered and the steps taken to return the corporation to S corporation status. Requests for a determination of inadvertent termination should be sent to: Internal Revenue Service, Associate Chief Counsel (Technical), Att: CC:PS, 1111 Constitution Avenue, N.W., Washington, DC 20224. (Prop. Reg. §1362-5(c).)

Q. 4:9 What is the effective date of a termination?

The effective date of a termination is the date on which the corporation first fails to meet the requirements for qualification as an S corporation. (See Question 1:2.)

There was a time under prior law when the termination of an S corporation related back to the first day of the taxable year. That law was repealed by the Subchapter S Revision Act of 1982 (Revision Act), so the termination is now effective on the date on which the corporation fails to meet one of the requirements. When this causes a termination during the taxable year, the rules discussed at Questions 4:17–4:26 will be applicable.

Revocations

Q. 4:10 What is a revocation?

An S corporation may voluntarily give up its status by revoking its election. Shareholders holding more than 50% of the shares of stock outstanding on the date on which the revocation is made must consent to the revocation. (Section 1362(d)(1)) (For the effective date of the revocation, see Question 4:13.)

Q. 4:11 How many shareholders are needed to revoke an S corporation election?

Shareholders holding more than one-half the shares of the corporation's stock on the day on which the revocation is made must consent to the revocation. (Section 1362(d)(1)(B)) (For techniques for dealing with this rule in a shareholders' agreement and providing more flexibility, see Question 6:10.)

Q. 4:12 How is a revocation made?

The corporation must file a written statement with the IRS Service Center with which the S corporation election was filed. The statement should be signed by a person authorized to sign the corporation's tax returns and should include the following information (Temp. Reg. §18.1362-3T; Prop. Reg. §1.1362-3(b)(1).):

1. The fact that the corporation is revoking its S corporation election made under Section 1362(a);
2. The number of shares of stock (including nonvoting stock) issued and outstanding at the time the revocation is made; and

Q. 4:12   The S Corporation Answer Book

3. The date on which the revocation is to be effective.

Attached to the corporation's statement of revocation should be a statement of consent signed by each shareholder who consents to the revocation. The shareholders' statements of consent should include the following information (Temp. Reg. §18.1362-3T):

1. The fact that the shareholder consents to the corporation's revocation of its S corporation election under Section 1362(a); and
2. The number of issued and outstanding shares (including nonvoting stock) held by the shareholder at the time of the revocation.

Q. 4:13   What is the effective date of revocation?

The rules are as follows (Section 1362(d)(1)(C)):

1. If the revocation is made on or before the fifteenth day of the third month of the taxable year, the revocation is retroactive to the first day of the taxable year in which it is filed, unless the corporation chooses otherwise;
2. If the revocation is made after the fifteenth day of the third month of the taxable year, it will become effective on the first day of the following year, unless the corporation chooses otherwise; or
3. The corporation can specify the date on which the revocation will take effect, provided that the effective date can be no earlier than the date on which the revocation is filed.

(See also Prop. Reg. §1.1362-3(b)(2) and (3).)

If the revocation is effective on a date other than the first day of a taxable year, the rules described at Questions 4:17–4:26 will be applicable.

Q. 4:14   Why would the shareholders want to revoke an election (or permit one to terminate)?

The shareholders may want to end S corporation status for a number of reasons. For example, the corporation's income level may be such that the corporation's income tax bracket would be lower than the shareholders' income tax brackets. In such a case, it may be desirable for the corporation, rather than the shareholders, to pay the tax. This would be especially true if the corporation needs to reinvest income in its business and does not have cash to distribute to the shareholders.

Another example is a conflict among the shareholders that results in a failure to distribute the S corporation's income, or at least enough of it to enable the shareholders to pay the tax on the S corporation income passed through to them. In such a case, shareholders who lack independent sources of funds might want the election terminated so that the corporation itself will pay tax on its income, and they will not have to use their own money to pay tax on the corporation's income.

Q. 4:15 If the shareholders change their minds about the advisability of a revocation, can they withdraw it before it becomes effective?

The law is silent about the right to withdraw an S corporation revocation before it becomes effective. Proposed regulations issued in December 1988 would permit the rescission of a revocation at any time before the revocation becomes effective, but only with the consent (1) of each person who consented to the revocation *and* (2) of each person who became a shareholder of the corporation during the period from the date of the revocation to the date of the rescission. To rescind the revocation, the corporation would file a statement with the IRS Service Center where the revocation was properly filed. The rescission statement would contain the corporation's name, address, and taxpayer I.D. number, be signed by an authorized person, and state that the corporation rescinds the revocation made under Section 1362(d)(1). In addition, the shareholders' statement of consent, signed by each consenting shareholder, must show the name, address, and taxpayer identification number of each consenting shareholder. (Prop. Reg. §1.1362-3(b)(5))

Accounting for a Termination or Revocation

Q. 4:16 Must IRS be notified of a termination or revocation?

When the shareholders revoke the S corporation election, IRS will be notified, because a revocation statement together with the consents of the shareholders holding more than 50% of the shares must be filed. (See Question 4:12.) When S corporation status is terminated by a disqualifying event, there is no definite requirement that IRS be notified.

Q. 4:16   **The S Corporation Answer Book**

The regulations for the law in existence prior to the Revision Act (Former Reg. §1.1372-4(b)(3)) did require a corporation to notify the District Director with whom the original election was filed of any disqualifying event. Those regulations required filing of certain information regarding the cause and the date of the termination, and information about transfers of shares or issuance of a second class of stock if one of these events caused termination. Similar requirements are contained in Prop. Reg. §1.1362-3(c)(1). In any event, it is advisable to notify IRS of a terminating event, so that IRS will adjust its records and send Form 1120 instead of Form 1120S.

In case of either termination or revocation, IRS will be notified by virtue of the fact that a regular C corporation return (Form 1120) will be filed instead of an S corporation return (Form 1120S) after the S corporation status has ended.

Q. 4:17   What happens if S corporation status ends in the middle of a corporation's taxable year?

When this happens, the corporation will be required to file two tax returns for *one* taxable year, which is called the "S corporation termination year." An S corporation tax return on Form 1120S will be required for the period beginning on the first day of the taxable year and ending on the day *before* the date the termination or revocation became effective. A C corporation tax return on Form 1120 will be filed for the balance of the taxable year. (Section 1362(e)(1)) Both returns will be due at the same time. Income, losses, and deductions will be allocated between the two portions of the year in the manner set forth at Questions 4:18–4:21.

Q. 4:18   Who pays tax on the corporation's income if S corporation status ends in the middle of the taxable year?

The shareholders will pay tax on the corporation's income attributable to the portion of the S corporation termination year during which the S election was effective. (See Chapter 9.) The corporation itself will pay tax on the portion of the income attributable to the part of the year after which S corporation status is no longer available (when the corporation is a regular or C corporation). (See Question 4:23.)

Q. 4:19 How are income, losses, and deductions allocated between the part of the termination year to which the S corporation election applies and the part to which it does not apply?

There are two methods for allocating these items between the S corporation portion of the S corporation termination year and the C corporation portion of that year:

1. The pro rata daily allocation method (Section 1362(e)(2)); and
2. The closing of the books method (Section 1362(e)(3)).

The pro rata daily allocation method will apply:

1. Unless more than 50% of the corporation's stock has been sold or exchanged in the termination year (see Question 4:21);
2. Unless and except to the extent that income items are attributable to acquisition of an active subsidiary and a Section 338 basis step-up has been elected (see Question 4:21); or
3. Unless a closing of the books has been elected (see Question 4:22).

Q. 4:20 How is a pro rata daily allocation made?

The general rule when the election is terminated or revoked during a taxable year is that all items of income, deduction, loss, or credit, and all nonseparately computed income or loss, are to be divided between the two portions of the S corporation termination year on a daily basis. (Section 1362(e)(2))

The total dollar amount of each of these items is first divided by the actual number of days in the year, usually 365.

Next, the daily amount for each item is multiplied by the number of days in the S corporation part of the termination year to determine how much of each item is allocated to the S corporation portion of the termination year.

The procedure is repeated by multiplying the daily amount of each item by the number of days in the C corporation part of the termination year to determine how much of each item is allocated to the C corporation portion of the termination year. (See also Prop. Reg. §1.1362-4(b).)

The amounts assigned to the S corporation portion of the termination year will be reported on Form 1120S and passed through to the shareholders, who will pay tax on these items. The allocations for the C corporation portion of the termination year will be reported by the corporation on a regular Form 1120, and any tax will be paid by the corporation. (See Question 4:23.)

Q. 4:21 When is the pro rata daily allocation method unavailable?

If there is a sale or exchange of 50% or more of the stock of the corporation during the year in which the S corporation election terminates, the automatic pro rata daily allocation method does not apply. (Section 1362(e)(6)(D)) Instead, the corporation is required to use its books and records to determine the actual amounts of income, expenses, and the like that are allocable to the various segments of the year.

In addition, the pro rata daily allocation method cannot be used for items resulting from a Section 338 election (when the S corporation has purchased the stock of another corporation, thus causing termination of the S corporation election, and the corporation has made an election under Section 338 to treat the subsidiary as having been liquidated for the purpose of obtaining an increase in its basis in the subsidiary's assets). In this case, any income *caused* by the Section 338 election (such as depreciation recapture) will be reported in the C corporation portion of the year on the regular Form 1120. (Section 1362(e)(6)(C))

(See also Prop. Reg. §§1.1362-4(a), 1.1362-4(c)(3), and 1.1362-4(c)(4).)

Q. 4:22 How does the corporation elect to close its books on the day of termination in order to allocate items between the S corporation and C corporation portions of the termination year?

In cases in which the automatic pro rata daily allocation rules would otherwise apply (see Question 4:19), the shareholders may elect to have an actual allocation of all items of income, expenses, and the like based on the corporation's books and records. (Section 1362(e)(3)) All persons who were shareholders at any time during the S corporation short year, and all persons who were shareholders on the first day of the C corporation short year, must consent to this election. The following procedure must be used for the election (Temp. Reg. §18.1362-4T):

1. A statement signed by the person authorized to sign the corpora-

tion's tax return must be attached to the corporation's Form 1120 for the C corporation portion of the termination year;
2. The statement must indicate that the corporation elects under Section 1362(e)(3) not to have the automatic pro rata daily allocation rules of Section 1362(e)(2) apply;
3. The statement must give the cause of the termination, or say that a revocation has been made, and give the effective date of the termination or revocation; and
4. The shareholders' consent, signed by all those who were shareholders at any time during the S corporation short year and all those who were shareholders on the first day of the C corporation short year, must be attached to the statement.

Substantially the same procedure is contained in Prop. Reg. §1.1362-(c)(2).

Q. 4:23 How is the tax calculated for the C corporation portion of the termination year?

The taxable income for the C corporation short year has to be annualized. This is done by multiplying the taxable income for the short year—determined by either the daily pro rata allocation method (see Question 4:20) or the closing of the books method (see Question 4:22)—by the total number of days in the S corporation termination year (usually 365) and dividing the result by the number of days in the C corporation portion of that year. Once the annualized income is determined, the corporate income tax is calculated on that amount. The result is then multiplied by a fraction (Section 1362(e)(5)(A)):

1. The numerator is the number of days in the C corporation portion of the termination year; and
2. The denominator is the total number of days in the S corporation termination year.

■ **Example.** Assume a calendar-year corporation's S corporation election terminated on October 20, 1990. The S corporation short year would run from January 1, 1990, through October 19, 1990. The C corporation short year would run from October 20, 1990, through December 31, 1990. Assuming that the actual taxable income of the corporation was $30,000 for the C corporation short-year period, the annualization computation would be as follows:

The $30,000 for the C corporation short year would be multiplied by 365, resulting in $10.95 million. This amount would be divided by 73 (the number of days during the period beginning on October 20 and ending on December 31), giving an annualized income of $150,000. The corporate income tax would be calculated on the $150,000. The result of the computation would be multiplied by 73/365 (1/5) to calculate the actual tax due for the short period.

(See also Prop. Reg. §1.1362-4(d).)

Q. 4:24 When are the tax returns due for the termination year of a corporation whose S corporation status has ended in the middle of its taxable year?

When a corporation terminates its S corporation status in the middle of its taxable year, it is required to file two tax returns, one for the portion of the termination year in which it was an S corporation, and the other for the balance of the termination year. Both tax returns are due on the normal due date for the corporation's tax return—that is, on the fifteenth day of the third month following the close of the corporation's taxable year. For a calendar-year corporation, both tax returns would be due on March 15.

(For a further discussion of return due dates and filing extensions, see Questions 14:2 and 14:3.)

Post-termination Estimated Tax

Q. 4:25 If an S corporation loses its election, will it be subject to the estimated tax requirements?

Yes, it will. Since the corporation is a C corporation, it becomes subject to all of the requirements to which C corporations are subject. This rule includes the requirement to pay estimated taxes.

Q. 4:26 Will a former S corporation be subject to estimated tax underpayment penalties for its first C corporation year?

Since the corporation is a C corporation after it loses its S corporation status, it is subject to the estimated tax rules and the penalty provisions for underpayment of estimated taxes. Even when the election is terminated in the middle of the year—so that there are two tax returns required, a Form 1120S for the S corporation period of the year and a regular Form 1120 for the C corporation period of the year (see Question 4:17)—the corporation may be subject to the estimated tax penalties. The Code makes it clear that estimated tax rules do apply to short years. (Section 6144(e))

Chapter 5

Reorganizations of S Corporations

Basic Considerations

Q. 5:1 What is a reorganization?

A reorganization, as the term implies, is basically a change in the ownership structure of the corporation. The Internal Revenue Code defines seven types of tax-free reorganizations (Section 368(a)(1)):

1. A statutory merger or consolidation—that is, a combining of two or more corporations pursuant to state law (an "A" reorganization; Section 368(a)(1)(A)).

2. An acquisition by one corporation, solely for voting stock, of stock of another corporation, immediately after which the acquiring corporation has control of the acquired corporation (a "B" reorganization; Section 368(a)(1)(B)).

3. An exchange of substantially all of the property of the acquired corporation for voting stock of the acquiring corporation (a "C" reorganization; Section 368(a)(1)(C)).

4. A transfer of all or part of a corporation's assets to another corporation that the transferor corporation, its shareholders, or both will control immediately after the transfer (if the requirements of Section 354, 355, or 356 are met) (a "D" reorganization; Section 368(a)(1)(D)). (Sections 354 and 355 deal with taxation of shareholders upon exchanges of stock and securities of a corporation that is a party to a reorganization, and upon distributions of stock and securities of a controlled corporation, respectively; Section 356

Q. 5:1 The S Corporation Answer Book

deals with taxation of "boot" or consideration other than stock or securities received in these transactions.)

5. A recapitalization—that is, a change in the corporation's capital structure (an "E" reorganization; Section 368(a)(1)(E)).
6. A mere change in identity, form, or place of organization of one corporation, however that occurs (an "F" reorganization; Section 368(a)(1)(F)).
7. A transfer by a corporation of all or part of its assets to another corporation in a Title 11 bankruptcy reorganization or similar situation (for example, receivership), if stock or assets distributed meet the requirements of Section 354, 355, or 356 (a "G" reorganization; Section 368(a)(1)(G))

Q. 5:2 Can an S corporation be a party to a tax-free reorganization?

Yes, it can be. A General Counsel's Memorandum issued in December 1988 reaches this conclusion, even though Section 1371(a)(2) treats an S corporation as an individual in its capacity as a shareholder of another corporation. (*GCM 39768*) This ruling apparently lays to rest speculation that IRS and the Treasury Department would not continue to follow rulings in this area under the law as in effect prior to the Subchapter S Revision Act of 1982 (Revision Act).

Q. 5:3 Why are reorganizations of special concern to S corporations?

In the context of a C corporation, the major consequence of having a transaction characterized as falling within one of the seven categories of reorganization defined in Section 368(a)(1) (see Question 5:1) is that the transaction will be characterized as tax-free under Section 361 (which, except in the case of a "D" reorganization, is generally the desired result) if the acquiror has 80% control of the corporation (as defined in Section 368(c)) immediately after the transaction. Otherwise, the transaction is treated as a taxable sale or exchange, unless it falls within some other nonrecognition provision of the Code.

The tax characterization of a transaction as a reorganization is also of concern to S corporations, but S corporation consequences generally follow the same rules, and except as otherwise noted later in this chapter, the intricacies of characterization are beyond the scope of this book.

There is, however, another important concern when an S corporation is involved in a reorganization: *Will the reorganization—regardless of whether it is tax-free or some tax is incurred—cause a termination of the S corporation election?* The results will vary. Some types of reorganizations will cause a loss of S corporation status; some will not; and, in some cases, the results will depend on the particular facts and circumstances.

The problem of a loss of S corporation status is not as troublesome today as it was before the Revision Act. Under the old law, a disqualifying act—such as acquiring a corporate shareholder as a result of a type "B" reorganization (defined at Question 5:1)—would terminate S status retroactively to the beginning of the corporation's fiscal year. Today, a disqualifying act will terminate S corporation status as of the day the disqualifying act or event occurs. Thus, S corporation status will continue through the day *before* the day that the act or event occurs. (See Questions 4:9 and 4:17–4:24 for a more detailed discussion.) However, the impact of a possible termination—even if it is not retroactive—should be considered whenever a reorganization is contemplated.

Reorganizations involving a C corporation can also create problems for an S corporation that survives the transaction. (See Question 5:18.)

Mergers and Consolidations

Q. 5:4 What happens to the S corporation election if an S corporation merges into a C corporation?

If an S corporation "merges into" a C corporation (in an "A" reorganization, defined at Question 5:1), the C corporation is the "surviving" corporation. The S corporation ceases to exist, although, if it is eligible, the surviving C corporation may make its own S corporation election. (See Question 5:6.)

Q. 5:5 How does a merged S corporation treat the portion of its taxable year that elapsed prior to the merger?

Under current law, a termination is never retroactive to the beginning of the year. Thus, it would seem that the S corporation status of the corporation would be preserved up to the date of the "A" reorganization in any event. The corporation's taxable year would, of course, terminate upon merger.

Q. 5:6 If an S corporation merges into a C corporation, will the surviving C corporation be able to elect S corporation status?

Assuming that the C corporation is an eligible corporation (see Chapter 1), it may be able to elect S corporation status. IRS has taken the position that a C corporation into which an S corporation has merged may make its own S corporation election for the first taxable year after the merger (provided it is otherwise qualified) *without* any prior IRS approval. (*Letter Ruling 8007089*)

However, a corporation that has formerly been an S corporation, or the successor to such a corporation, must generally wait five years before it can reelect S corporation status. (See Question 2:17.) Thus, the answer to the question of *when* the surviving C corporation can make this election will depend on its status. If it has never been an S corporation, it will be able to elect S corporation status on the same basis as any other C corporation—that is, without waiting for five years—if it otherwise qualifies as an S corporation. If, however, it has terminated or revoked an S corporation election within the last five years, it will have to wait the full period or get permission from IRS for an early reelection. (See Question 2:18.)

Q. 5:7 Will S corporation status be lost if a C corporation merges into an S corporation?

If a C corporation merges with an S corporation in an "A" reorganization (defined at Question 5:1), and the S corporation is the survivor corporation, the S corporation election is not affected. IRS has viewed this type of statutory merger—in which, of course, the S corporation shareholders become the shareholders of the merged corporation—essentially as an acquisition of assets by the S corporation. (*Rev. Rul. 69-566,* 1969-2 CB 165)

Q. 5:8 Will S corporation status be lost if several S corporations merge into one corporation?

S corporation status can be lost as a result of a merger if the corporation no longer qualifies as an S corporation. (See Chapter 1 for a discussion of qualification requirements.) However, the election can be maintained if the merger is carefully structured so that the surviving corporation continues in existence without running afoul of the qualification rules—for example, if it is structured so that the total number of shareholders is not increased beyond the permissible number. (See Question 1:2.) Another important concern with regard to qualification is the existence, or nonexistence, of a subsidiary as a result of the merger.

Apparently, IRS once took the position that the surviving corporation's election was terminated because a statutory merger technically created a momentary parent-subsidiary relationship, thus resulting in the disqualification of the surviving corporation because it was a member of an affiliated group. (See Question 1:9.) Subsequently, however, IRS has indicated that it would not take this position.

IRS will permit two (or more) S corporations to merge and retain S corporation status for the surviving corporation—provided, of course, that all the other requirements for retaining S corporation status are satisfied. However, if the parent-subsidiary relationship is more than "momentary," both the subsidiary's and the parent's S corporation status will terminate. (*Rev. Rul. 79-52,* 1979-1 CB 283)

Q. 5:9 Will S corporation status be lost if several S corporations are consolidated into a new corporation?

The difference between a merger and a consolidation is that in the former, one of the preexisting corporations survives, while in the latter, a new corporation is formed. As a corollary to the merger rules (see Question 5:8), IRS has ruled that the consolidation of two S corporations into a single new corporation does not result in the termination of S corporation status for the final taxable year of each of the separate corporations. Hence the new corporation resulting from the consolidation may, if it wise qualifies (see Chapter 1), make a valid S corporation election without waiting for five years. (*Rev. Rul. 70-232*, 1970-1 CB 177) (The five-year waiting period is discussed further at Questions 2:17–2:18.)

Divisions, Acquisitions, and Sales

Q. 5:10 Will S corporation status be lost if an S corporation splits into more than one corporation?

S corporation status probably will not be lost as a result of a divisive reorganization. For example, in the case of one "D" divisive reorganization (see Question 5:1 for definition), IRS ignored the transitory parent-subsidiary relationship and held that the S corporation election was not terminated. (*Rev. Rul. 72-320*, 1972-1 CB 270)

> ■ **Example.** In the fact pattern presented in the ruling, one of two divisions of an S corporation was transferred to a newly created corporation in exchange for all its stock. Immediately thereafter, half of the old corporation's shareholders exchanged all of their stock in the old corporation for all of the stock in the new corporation in a transaction qualifying as a distribution of stock and securities of a controlled corporation under Section 355. The ownership by the S corporation of all of the stock of the new corporation made the S corporation a member of an affiliated group, which generally would have been a disqualifying act. (See Question 1:9.) However, IRS held that since the S corporation "never contemplated more than momentary control of" the new corporation, "the affiliation will not be considered as terminating" the S corporation's election.

Note that as with a merger (see Question 5:8), any parent-subsidiary relationship created as a result of a divisive reorganization must be a momentary situation, or the election will be terminated.

Q. 5:11 Will S corporation status be lost if an S corporation purchases, or exchanges stock for, another corporation's assets?

If one corporation wants to acquire another's assets, it may be able to obtain them in exchange for stock and/or money—that is, in a "C" tax-free reorganization (see Question 5:1) or outright purchase.

An outright purchase is just that—a purchase of assets—and would not be a disqualifying event. However, if the S corporation acquires assets in exchange for its own stock, the results will depend on who the new shareholders are and how many of them there are. If the total number of old and new shareholders exceeds the number permitted by the Code, which is currently 35, or if there are disqualified shareholders (see Question 1:2), the S corporation election will terminate. IRS has never indicated that it would overlook a "momentary" disqualification, as it does in some parent-subsidiary situations (see Questions 5:8 and 5:10). It may be possible, though, to ask IRS to permit retention of S corporation status under the rules for an inadvertent termination. (See Question 4:6.)

Planning Pointer. The better practice is to structure the asset acquisition to avoid a situation in which disqualified parties become shareholders, or in which shareholders are too numerous. There is no guarantee that IRS will agree to continue S corporation status under the inadvertent termination rules in this type of reorganization.

Acquisitions of Assets of S Corporation: When the assets of an S corporation are acquired in exchange for stock of a C corporation, the election is not terminated, because a C reorganization is not one of the specified events that terminates an S election. (*Rev. Rul. 71-266,* 1971-1 CB 262) A problem might exist if the S corporation receives 80% or more of the stock of the C corporation (see Question 1:9), but this does not usually happen. If it did, the momentary affiliation would be ignored if it lasted for less than 30 days. In a typical "C" reorganization, the corporation that gives up its assets is subsequently liquidated, distributing the stock it has received for its assets to its shareholders. Upon liquidation, the S corporation will go out of existence.

Q. 5:12 Will S corporation status be lost if an S corporation acquires another corporation's stock in order to obtain that corporation's assets?

Sometimes it is not possible for a corporation that wants the assets of another corporation to acquire them directly, either by purchase or in a "C" reorganization. The acquiring corporation must purchase the stock of the corporation that owns the assets, or exchange stock for them in a "B" reorganization. (See Question 5:1.)

By acquiring stock in a "B" reorganization, the S corporation acquires a subsidiary, an event that would ordinarily cause it to lose its S corporation status. (See Question 1:9.) However, if ownership of the subsidiary is transitory—that is, if the liquidation of the acquired subsidiary takes place within 30 days of the acquisition of the stock of the subsidiary—S corporation status will not be lost. (*Rev. Rul. 73-496*, 1973-2 CB 312; *Letter Ruling 7745041*)

Q. 5:13 Can an S corporation acquire stock and then obtain a basis step-up for the acquired corporation's assets?

If an S corporation acquires the stock of another corporation in order to acquire its assets, the basis of the assets will generally carry over—that is, remain the same as before the acquisition—as long as the acquired corporation remains in existence. If the S corporation is able to make an election to step up the basis of these assets, the newly acquired subsidiary corporation will be treated as though it had been liquidated, and the basis of the assets will be their fair market value. (Section 338)

It is not clear, however, that this election is available to an S corporation, because an S corporation, in its capacity as the shareholder of another corporation, is to be treated as an individual, and the Section 338 election is not available to individuals. (Section 1371(a)(2); see also *Letter Ruling 8818049*.) For individuals, a complete liquidation (under Section 331) would produce the same results as a Section 338 election. However, for individuals, a Section 331 liquidation followed by a transfer of the assets to a new corporation may result in a liquidation-reincorporation. If a liquidation-reincorporation results, then no step-up in basis is permitted for the acquired assets.

> **Planning Pointer.** In view of the unsettled law in this area, it might be wise to request a private letter ruling prior to entering into a transaction if a step-up in basis is desired.

Q. 5:14 What happens to the acquired corporation if the stock of an S corporation is acquired by another corporation?

In a "B" reorganization, one corporation acquires control of another corporation solely in exchange for voting stock of the acquiring corporation. (See Question 5:1.) If the acquired corporation is an S corporation, its S corporation status will terminate because it now has a corporate shareholder. (See Questions 1:2 and 1.10.) Since the termination is effective on the date of acquisition of the stock by the other corporation (see Question 4:9), the period ending on the day before the date of acquisition of the stock would be a short year for the S corporation. (The result would be the same, of course, if the corporate shareholders acquired the stock in a taxable transaction.)

(For a discussion of accounting for the short year, see Questions 4:17–4:24.)

Other Transactions

Q. 5:15 How does a recapitalization affect S corporation status?

An "E" reorganization or mere recapitalization (see Question 5:1) involves a restructuring of the corporation's capital stock—for example, the corporation might convert from stock with a par value to no-par stock. By itself, a recapitalization should have no effect on S corporation status *unless* it results in:

1. Issuance of more than one class of stock (see Questions 1:30–1:35)—for example, common stock and preferred stock; or
2. Some other event that would disqualify the corporation—for example, a disqualified shareholder.

(See Chapter 1, generally, for a discussion of qualification requirements.)

Q. 5:16 Will changes in identity or place of incorporation change the S corporation status of a single corporation?

A corporation might, for various reasons, want to change its name or the state in which it is incorporated. (This is an "F" reorganization, as defined at Question 5:1.) If all other factors remain the same, this should not affect an S corporation election.

■ **Example.** An S corporation was reincorporated in a state other than that of its original incorporation. The reincorporation was effected by forming, in the new state, a second corporation that was intended to qualify in all respects as an S corporation. Then the first corporation was merged into the second and went out of existence. IRS ruled

Q. 5:16   The S Corporation Answer Book

that this was a reorganization under Section 368(a)(1)(F) and that it did *not* terminate the S corporation election with respect to the surviving corporation. (*Rev. Rul. 64-250*, 1964-2 CB 333)

Q. 5:17 How would a bankruptcy reorganization or similar situation affect S corporation status?

Usually the bankrupt corporation would go out of existence, terminating S corporation status. Its assets would be turned over to a new organization, which might or might not qualify for an S corporation election. (See Chapter 1.)

Special Considerations

Q. 5:18 What special considerations are of continuing concern to an S corporation surviving a reorganization with a C corporation?

The Code specifies what items or attributes may be carried over to a surviving corporation. (Section 381) These carryover rules are the same for an S corporation as for a C corporation. Although the application of these rules is, for the most part, beyond the scope of this book, three items merit special attention when an S corporation and a C corporation are involved in a reorganization and the S corporation is the survivor:

1. Loss carryovers from the C corporation;
2. Earnings and profits (E&P); and
3. Capital gain or built-in gain tax under Section 1374.

Loss Carryovers: C corporation loss carryovers can be ignored for Subchapter S purposes, since they remain in a state of limbo and cannot be used by the S corporation unless it terminates its S corporation status and becomes a C corporation.

Earnings and Profits: The C corporation carryover of the greatest concern to the S corporation is earnings and profits. The carryover rules are mandatory, not elective. If the acquired corporation (regardless of whether it is an S corporation or a C corporation immediately prior to acquisition) has C corporation earnings and profits that must be carried over, the surviving S corporation will be affected in two ways:

1. Carryover earnings and profits will affect the distribution rules (see Question 12:9); and
2. Passive investment income limitation rules apply (see Question 7:3).

An S corporation with accumulated earnings and profits from C corporation years is subject to a limitation on passive investment income, which cannot exceed 25% of its gross receipts. If an S corporation exceeds this limitation, it is subject to a tax on excess passive income at the highest corporate rates. (See Question 8:11.) If the S corporation exceeds the limitation for more than three consecutive years, it will lose its S corporation status.

Planning Pointer. When planning a reorganization in which the surviving corporation will be an S corporation, the planner should be aware of any accumulated earnings and profits in the corporation to be acquired. It may be desirable to have that earnings and profits distributed before or during the reorganization so that the accumulated earnings and profits does not cause problems for the surviving corporation.

Section 1374 Tax: Disposition of carryover-basis assets that the S corporation receives from the C corporation may be subject to a tax under either:

1. The capital gain tax if the disposition is within three years (see Questions 8:16–8:20); or
2. The built-in gain tax if the disposition is within ten years (see Questions 8:24–8:33).

Chapter 6

Protecting the S Corporation Election; Invalid Elections

Threats to the Election

Q. 6:1 What events might cause a loss of S corporation status?

There are several different types of events that might cause the loss of S corporation status. A majority of the shareholders may have revoked the S corporation election. (See Questions 4:10 and 4:11.)

Termination of existing S corporation status may occur because a corporation no longer meets the general requirements for S corporation status. (See Question 1:2.) Thus, the corporation may have exceeded the permissible number of shareholders, or it may have acquired an ineligible shareholder (corporation, partnership, nonresident alien, or disqualified trust). (See Questions 1:2 and 1:15–1:19.) The corporation may have issued a second class of stock. (See Questions 1:30–1:35.) Loans made to the corporation may be deemed to be a second class of stock. (See Question 1:34.) The corporation may have acquired 80% or more of the stock of an active subsidiary corporation. (See Question 1:9.)

The corporation may have earnings and profits from years prior to the S corporation election and more than 25% of its gross receipts as passive investment income for three consecutive years. If this situation occurs, the S corporation election will automatically terminate, effective on the first day of the fourth taxable year. (Section 1362(d)(3)) (See Question 6:7 and Chapter 7.)

In addition, the original election may have been invalid. (See Chapter 2 and Questions 6:14–6:17.)

Q. 6:2 How can a shareholder intentionally destroy the election?

A termination may be deliberately caused by a shareholder seeking to end the S corporation election at a time when the other shareholders wish to keep the election in effect. It takes only one shareholder to transfer one of his or her shares to an ineligible shareholder—that is, to a thirty-sixth shareholder, a corporation, a partnership, a nonresident alien, or a trust that is not qualified to hold stock in an S corporation. (See Question 4:5 for a further discussion of this problem, and Chapter 1 for a discussion of the eligibility rules.) That shareholder might have a number of reasons for intentionally destroying the election. (See Question 4:14.)

In addition, a disqualifying event may occur via a transfer in a will (see Question 6:3) or a change in the beneficiary of a qualified Subchapter S trust (see Question 6:4).

Q. 6:3 Does the death of a shareholder endanger the S corporation election?

Sometimes the death of a shareholder can endanger the election. If a shareholder dies and his or her shares are held by the shareholder's estate, no problem is presented by the shareholder's death. However, if the shares are distributable under the shareholder's will to a disqualified shareholder (for example, a nonresident alien or a disqualified trust), then the election is in jeopardy. (See Question 1:19 for a discussion of qualified trusts, and Question 1:28 for a discussion of the special problem of unintended testamentary trusts.)

If the shareholder who dies was considered the owner of a grantor trust that no longer qualifies as an S corporation shareholder after his or her death, then the election continues in effect for a 60-day period beginning on the deemed owner's death. If the trust is completely includible in the deemed owner's gross estate for federal estate tax purposes, the 60-day period is lengthened to two years. (See the discussion of trusts at Question 1:19.)

The S corporation election also may be endangered by the death of a shareholder if the beneficiary who inherits the stock of the deceased shareholder:

1. Owns more than 50% of the stock and revokes the election (see Questions 4:10–4:11); or

2. Causes a terminating event by transferring all or some of his or her shares to a disqualified shareholder (see Question 4:5).

Q. 6:4 Does the death of a beneficiary of a qualified Subchapter S trust endanger the election?

When the shareholder is a qualified Subchapter S trust and the income beneficiary has filed the special consent to have the trust treated as a qualified Subchapter S trust (see Question 1:25), the death of the income beneficiary may cause a termination of the trust's status as a qualified Subchapter S trust because either:

1. The trust itself no longer qualifies; or
2. The successor beneficiary does not want the trust to be a qualified Subchapter S trust.

Trust Disqualification: If, upon the death of a beneficiary, there are two or more successor beneficiaries, the presence of more than one income beneficiary may cause disqualification of the trust as a qualified Subchapter S trust and therefore the loss of S corporation status to the corporation. (See Question 1:21, generally, and Question 1:23 for the rule that may continue to qualify the trust despite the existence of more than one beneficiary.)

Beneficiary Action: Alternatively, even though there may be only one successor beneficiary, the successor beneficiary has the right to file an affirmative refusal to consent. (See Question 1:27.) If the beneficiary does file the affirmative refusal to consent, the trust will no longer be a qualified Subchapter S trust, and the corporation's S corporation status will be terminated.

Q. 6:5 What dangers to the S corporation election may arise if a shareholder holds some shares as a nominee for another?

The election may be lost for one of the following reasons if the "record" shareholder is an agent or nominee:

1. Lack of proper shareholder consent to the election; or
2. Presence of an ineligible shareholder.

Planning Pointer. One method of attempting to prevent such a problem is to have each shareholder enter into a shareholders' agreement that states that he or she is the sole beneficial owner and is not the nominee of another with respect to the S corporation stock. It would probably also be advisable to have the agreement spell out that S corporation status is endangered if this representation is not true. (See Questions 6:9–6:10 for a discussion of shareholders' agreements.)

Consent to the Election: If a shareholder holds shares as nominee for another, or even partially as nominee for another, the equitable owner of the shares is required to have consented to the S corporation election. (See Question 2:9.) If the consent has not been filed, then the election may be invalid.

Planning Pointer. To remedy this situation, an immediate request for extension of time to file consents should be requested. (See Question 2:12.)

Ineligible Shareholder: It is also possible that the equitable owner of the shares held by the nominee is a person or entity that cannot own S corporation stock (for example, a nonresident alien or a corporation). (See Questions 1:2 and 1:10.) In such case, the election would not be valid.

Ineligible Trust: The nominee arrangement may be construed as a trust that is ineligible to be an S corporation shareholder. (See Question 1:19.)

Q. 6:6 Can the existence of corporate indebtedness endanger the S corporation election?

When the indebtedness is deemed to be a second class of stock, it will jeopardize the election. (See Question 1:34.) However, there is a "safe harbor" for what the Code defines as "straight debt." (Section 1361(c)(5)) (See Question 1:35.)

Q. 6:7 Can the type of income the corporation receives endanger S corporation status?

S corporation status will be in danger when the corporation has previously been a C corporation and has accumulated earnings and profits (E&P) from years prior to its S election. If the S corporation has C corporation E&P, and if more than 25% of its gross receipts for three consecutive years is passive investment income, the election will be terminated beginning on the first day of the fourth year. (Section 1362(d)(3))

Planning Pointer. Since the election will not be terminated until the first day of the fourth year, the corporation should have sufficient time to take steps in order to eliminate the problem. There are several possible solutions, including:

1. Dividend payments; and
2. Acquiring or divesting assets to change the ratio of active and passive income.

Dividend Payments: Although it is true that dividends are ordinary income to the shareholders, the distribution of all E&P will "cleanse" the corporation so that it is not limited in the type of income it may receive without penalty. Furthermore, ordinary income is not as onerous as it used to be, given the current rate structure, and the impact of the additional dividend income taxed to the shareholders may be partially offset by the elimination of the corporate tax on excess net passive income. (See Questions 8:10–8:12 and 12:18–12:19.)

Changing the Active-to-Passive Ratio: Another possible solution to the problem is to decrease the amount of passive investment income and/or increase the gross receipts of the corporation so that net passive investment income will not exceed 25% of the gross receipts. Sometimes this reduction may be accomplished by selling or distributing the assets that produce the passive investment income. At other times, it may mean that the S corporation should acquire an active trade or business in order to increase active gross receipts and thus reduce the passive investment income to less than 25% of the gross receipts.

Transfer of Right to Receive Passive Income: Mere assignment of passive income—for example, passive rents—is probably insufficient. An attempt to assign passive rental income from an S corporation to another entity was unsuccessful in a case in which an S corporation assigned to a charitable foundation "the right to receive the first ninety thousand dollars ($90,000) of rents paid by the tenants." Under the terms of the agreement, the charity was to repay the rents to the corporation in the following year, retaining for itself the interest earned on the rentals received. But the corporation retained ownership, domination, and control over the rental property. This was an imaginative approach, but was not successful.

Under these facts, the Tax Court held that the corporation had merely made an anticipatory assignment of those rents; they were still taxable to the assignor corporation when they were collected by the charity. The opinion relied on a body of cases about the anticipatory assignment of income and also on the fact that the substance of the transaction was a loan of the rental proceeds to the charity. (*Johnston,* TC Memo 1976-142)

Protective Measures

Q. 6:8 What can be done to prevent loss of S corporation status?

If any of the above actions were inadvertent and were rectified within a reasonable time, IRS might ignore the temporary disqualification under the inadvertent-termination provisions. (See Question 4:6.) However, this does not resolve the problem of *deliberate* shareholder action (see Question 6:2), and it leaves much to chance.

A shareholders' agreement is strongly recommended for the purpose of limiting shareholders' ability to revoke the election or to commit a disqualifying act. (See Questions 6:9–6:11.) Additionally, careful monitoring of the corporation and its shareholders is advisable. (For example, this is necessary if there is a potential passive investment income problem; see Question 6:7.)

Q. 6:9 How does a shareholders' agreement prevent loss of S corporation status?

A shareholders' agreement may be effective in preventing the loss of S corporation status. An agreement may have the effect of deterring a shareholder from committing an act that might disqualify the corporation from S corporation status. This deterrent might arise simply because the shareholders' agreement calls these acts to the shareholders' attention. Or the agreement might deter a shareholder from intentionally revoking or causing termination because it contains harsh sanctions against a shareholder who violates its restrictions. Or the agreement might state outright that the transfer is invalid. (See Question 6:10 for types of provisions that might be included in such an agreement.)

Planning Pointer. Quite often, when a shareholders' agreement exists, the stock certificates are "legended" so that a prospective purchaser or transferee will be alerted to this fact—that is, the fact that there is a shareholders' agreement is printed prominently on each stock certificate. Thus, the provisions in the agreement dealing with the preservation of S corporation status will be brought to the attention of the prospective transferee.

Q. 6:10 What types of provisions should be included in a shareholders' agreement to prevent loss of S corporation status?

A shareholders' agreement should include several different types of provisions to prevent loss of S corporation status, including:

- An agreement to continue the S corporation election;
- A mechanism for terminating it; and
- Transfer restrictions.

Additionally, it is desirable for the corporation itself as well as all of the shareholders to be parties to such an agreement. As a party to the agreement, the corporation will also be bound by its provisions. And, as previously discussed, the agreement should contain appropriate protections against nominee shareholders. (See Question 6:5.)

Planning Pointer. It should be kept in mind that the validity of any shareholders' agreement provisions will depend on the law of the state in which the corporation is formed. A discussion of shareholders' agreement restrictions that are permitted or prohibited by state laws is beyond the scope of this book.

The S Corporation Election—Maintenance and Termination: The agreement should recite that the parties agree to continue S corporation status unless there is an agreement to terminate the election. Percentage requirements or unanimity may be required in such an agreement, as negotiated by the parties.

The shareholders' agreement should also provide a mechanism for the shareholders to decide whether they wish to terminate the election. The Code permits a revocation of S corporation status by the corporation if more than one-half of the shareholders consent to the revocation. (Section 1362(d)(1)) (See Questions 4:10 and 4:11.) The shareholders' agreement could provide for a higher or lower requirement for revocation, and if the stated requirement is met, all parties must agree to revoke the election.

Transfer Restriction: The agreement should restrict transfers of S corporation stock to nonqualified shareholders, to too many shareholders, or to any other transferees who might cause termination of S corporation status. (See definitions at Question 1:2 and Chapter 1 generally.) Alternatively, the agreement could require an opinion of counsel that S corporation status will not be jeopardized prior to the effectiveness of any transfer of stock.

Notice and Presale Approval: Provision may be made for prior notification before the transfer of any stock so that a determination may be made as to whether the transfer would jeopardize the election. Consent of a certain percentage of the shareholders might be required prior to the effectiveness of a proposed transfer of stock.

Buy-Sell Provisions: The shareholders might provide a stock repurchase provision, a buyout provision, or a right of first refusal provision with respect to a shareholder who attempts to transfer shares in contravention of the shareholders' agreement. In such case, it might be wise to provide a formula in the shareholders' agreement to fix the price for the shares. The buyout formula might even contain a downward price adjustment for a shareholder who has attempted to transfer shares in contravention of the shareholders' agreement.

Voiding Transfers: The shareholders' agreement should provide that, in the event of any transfer of shares that would automatically terminate S corporation status (that is, to a nonqualified shareholder or to a thirty-sixth shareholder), the transfer will be void *ab initio* (from the beginning) and will be ignored for all purposes. Such a provision might avoid a problem with IRS if such a transfer were actually made. Of course, the inadvertent-termination provisions are also available. (See Questions 4:6–4:8.)

Q. 6:11 Is a shareholders' agreement binding on IRS?

A shareholders' agreement is not binding per se on IRS. However, to the extent that the shareholders' agreement fixes rights under state law, IRS generally will respect the ownership rights determined by state law. Federal law governs the tax results; however, state law will usually govern the determination of the ownership rights that are subject to federal taxation.

Q. 6:12 Are there any means, other than shareholders' agreements, of protecting the election against shareholders' disqualifying acts?

The shareholders' agreement may be coupled with a requirement that all of the corporation's stock be held in escrow, by an escrow agent. Also, a voting trust might be used. (See Question 1:19.)

Even if there is an enforceable shareholders' agreement, the shareholders of an S corporation might consider transferring possession of their shares to an escrow agent (escrowee), who could be one of their number. In this way, no transfer of stock by any shareholder can be effected without prior consultation with the escrow agent. The other shareholders can then be alerted to any proposed transfer and would be able to assess the effects of that transfer on the corporation's continuation as an S corporation. (At that point, the provisions of the shareholders' agreement might come into play.)

There does not seem to be any specific authority that would cast doubt on the effectiveness of the use of an escrow agent to hold all of the corporation's stock in these circumstances. For example, a question might be raised: When the stock is held in escrow, is it deemed to be "in trust," thus destroying a previously valid S corporation election? One Tax Court case touched briefly on this problem, but never decided the issue, since it was held that the escrowee in that case was, in no event, a shareholder in the S corporation. (See *Hoffman,* 47 TC 218 (1966).) It would also appear that IRS has, informally at least, approved the use of an escrow arrangement for the purpose of policing and protecting the S corporation election.

One private ruling presented a situation in which title to the shares of an S corporation would be transferred to a bank to assist in the enforcement of a shareholders' stock purchase agreement. The agreement was designed to prevent any of the shareholders from transferring shares to a nonqualifying shareholder, or to one who would terminate the S corporation status. Since the sole duty of the bank would be to transfer ownership of the stock on the happening of certain events, the bank would be a mere agent with certain ministerial duties. Therefore, the proposed arrangement would not be an ordinary trust that would terminate the election. It would be a custodial account that would not terminate the election. (*Letter Ruling 8010028*)

Failure to Protect the Election

Q. 6:13 What problems will the corporation have if its S corporation status is terminated despite all attempts to protect the election?

If the S corporation election terminates, the corporation will:

1. Be subject to all of the provisions of Subchapter C of the Code—including double taxation; and
2. Generally have to wait five years to reelect S corporation status.

If S corporation status is lost in the middle of a taxable year, the corporation will need to file two income tax returns. (See Questions 4:17–4:24.) It may also have estimated tax problems. (See Questions 4:25–4:26.)

Double Taxation: C corporations are subject to double taxation, at both the corporate level and the shareholder level. The corporation pays tax on its own income. When distributions are made to shareholders, the shareholders pay tax again on dividend distributions.

Reelection: Once the election is lost, by termination or revocation, the corporation must wait until the fifth taxable year following the last S corporation year before it or a successor corporation may reelect S corporation status, unless it obtains permission from IRS. (Section 1362(g)) (See Questions 2:17–2:18.)

Invalid Elections

Q. 6:14 What happens if the original election was invalid?

Most of the discussion in this chapter has centered around protecting the election against terminating events. Another problem, however, is that the original election may have been invalid. This might have occurred because one of the eligibility requirements was not met, the shareholders failed to consent, the election was never filed, or the election contained insufficient information to be a valid election. (See Chapters 1 and 2.)

The principal result of an improper S corporation election is that the corporation remains taxable on its own income. It obtains none of the advantages inherent in an S corporation election.

The "tragedy" of an S corporation election that is invalid from the beginning lies in the fact that its invalidity is usually not discovered until sometime later—two or three years after the "mistake" was made. A revenue agent might discover the defect in the course of a routine examination and surprise the shareholders by asserting deficiencies against the corporation for years remaining open under the statute of limitations. Or the agent might assert deficiencies against the shareholders for claiming the benefits of the corporation's previous net operating losses on their own tax returns, when they were not otherwise entitled to such deductions.

Planning Pointer. It is important to determine why the election was not effective. If all of the technical requirements were met but the election was filed late, the corporation does not attain the election in the year filed. However, a later filing is effective for the following year. (See Questions 2:2–2:3.) The same result would follow if the election was filed on time but the shareholder consents were late and IRS did not extend the time for filing the consents. (See Questions 2:12–2:13.)

■ **Example.** An election is filed on March 30, 1990, with the intent that it be effective for calendar year 1990. It will *not* be effective for 1990, but it *will be* effective for 1991. Thus, the impact of the failure to have an effective election is limited to one year.

On the other hand, if the S corporation election is ineffective because of a fatal defect in the election process, then no election ever occurred, and the corporation was never an S corporation to begin with.

■ **Example.** If an election was filed but shareholder consents were never included, there was never a valid election unless IRS granted an extension for the consents. (See Questions 2:12–2:13.) Or, if the election and consents were properly prepared, but never mailed because office procedures were not followed, the election was never made. (See Question 2:4.)

Q. 6:15 Can an invalid election be cured?

Another point to keep in mind about invalid elections is that they never went into effect. So, even if the defect making the election ineffective was inadvertent, there is no way to "cure" the situation for the period of time that the election was ineffective. An inadvertent *termination* may be curable, with the S corporation's status retained during the period that it would otherwise be terminated. (See Questions 4:6–4:7.) But if the S corporation election never went into effect, it cannot terminate. Hence, there is no statutory basis for making it effective, even though the cause of the ineffectiveness was inadvertent.

Q. 6:16 How long must a corporation making an invalid election wait before reelecting S corporation status?

An S corporation whose elective status has been terminated usually must wait five full years before it can commence to operate, once again, under Subchapter S. (See Question 2:17.) Must it wait five full years, however, after it is discovered that its original S corporation election was invalid from the beginning? The answer is clearly no. An election deemed never to have been made—that is, *validly* made—cannot be deemed to have been terminated. Hence, it is not a bar to a new election in the following year, and there is no need to wait five years. (*Rev. Rul. 71-549*, 1971-2 CB 319)

Q. 6:17 If the taxpayer mistakenly believes that an S corporation election is valid, will the filing of an S corporation tax return provide any protection against back taxes?

As previously noted (see Question 6:14), an invalid S corporation election is often discovered in the course of a routine audit, leading to assessments of back taxes for "open" years—that is, those for which the statute of limitations on assessment of deficiencies has not yet run. This period is generally three years from the later of (1) the due date of the return or (2) the date it is actually filed. (Section 6501) (See also Questions 14:23–14:24.)

In the absence of fraud, the filing of Form 1120S will start the statute of limitations running, even if the corporation was mistaken in the belief that it validly elected Subchapter S in the first place. (Reg. §1.6037-1(c); *Benderoff*, 398 F.2d 132 (8th Cir. 1968)) However, the fact that Forms 1120S were filed and not challenged by IRS will not prevent IRS from challenging the validity of the S corporation election for all open years. (*Leslie Combs II*, TC Memo 1989-206)

Chapter 7

Passive Investment Income

Basic Considerations

Q. 7:1 What is passive investment income?

Basically, passive investment income is what the term suggests—receipts from royalties, rents, dividends, interest, annuities, and sales and exchanges of stock and securities. (Section 1362(d)(3)(D)) IRS takes the position that tax exempt interest is included as passive investment income. (Reg. §1.1375-1A(f), Ex. 2; Prop. Reg. §1.1362-3(d)(5)(vi).)

It should be noted, for purposes of clarity, that the concept of *passive investment income* as discussed in this chapter *applies at the corporate level* and is separate and distinct from the concept of *passive income* under the *passive activity loss rules,* which *apply at the shareholder level.* Passive activity loss and income under the passive activity loss rules is a new concept introduced by the Tax Reform Act of 1986 (TRA '86) because Congress was concerned that the tax laws appeared unfair to the average taxpayer. Tax shelters created an imbalance not only in the payment of a fair share of taxes, but also in the rationale behind certain Code provisions. Many enterprises were created not for sound business reasons, but for motives of tax avoidance, thereby undercutting, in some instances, the established tax-favored reasons Congress had for giving special treatment to certain items. TRA '86 therefore established the concept of passive activities—businesses in which investors do not materially participate—and decreed that loss from passive activities generally may be set off only against income from such activities. (Section 469)

The passive activity loss rules are discussed at Questions 10:10–10:50.

Q. 7:2 When can passive investment income create problems for an S corporation?

An S corporation will have passive investment problems only if:

1. It has C corporation earnings and profits (E&P) from years when it was a C corporation or from a tax-free reorganization with a corporation that had C corporation E&P (see Questions 12:3 and 12:6–12:9); and

2. More than 25% of its *gross receipts* are attributable to passive investment income.

In such a case, the corporation may have both added tax liabilities and problems with its S corporation election. (See Question 7:3.)

If the corporation (1) has been an S corporation for all of its existence or (2) has no accumulated C corporation earnings and profits, there is no limit on the amount of passive investment income it can receive, and passive investment income will not present problems.

Q. 7:3 What problems can passive investment income cause?

A corporation that has accumulated C corporation earnings and profits and exceeds the 25% limitation on passive investment income may:

1. Be subject to a tax on its excess passive investment income at the corporate level at the highest corporate rate (Section 1375; see Questions 8:10–8:14); and

2. Lose its S corporation status if it exceeds the 25% limitation for three consecutive years (Section 1362(d)(3); see Question 6:7).

Planning Pointer. A C corporation contemplating an S corporation election should take these problems into account before making the election and monitor E&P and passive investment earnings after the election is made. (See Questions 6:7 and 7:27.)

Q. 7:4 When and how is the S corporation taxed on passive investment income?

A tax will be imposed on excess *net* passive investment income whenever an S corporation has (Section 1375(a)):

1. Accumulated C corporation earnings and profits at the end of an S corporation taxable year; and

2. Passive investment income (calculated as described at Question 8:10, without regard to certain built-in gains and losses) in excess of 25% of its *gross receipts*.

Basically, excess net passive investment income is net passive income multiplied by a fraction. Net passive income is passive investment income (as defined at Questions 7:1 and 7:5–7:26) less allowable deductions that are directly incurred in producing that passive income. The numerator of the fraction is the amount by which the gross passive income exceeds 25% of gross receipts. The denominator of the fraction is the total passive investment income for the taxable year. (Section 1375(b)) (See Question 8:11 for further information.)

"Gross Receipts"

Q. 7:5 Are the "gross receipts" used to measure passive investment income synonymous with "gross profits"?

The key measure for purposes of both the termination provision and the tax provision (see Questions 7:3 and 7:4) is *gross receipts* of passive investment income. (Sections 1362(d)(3) and 1375(a)) Gross receipts are not gross profits.

Q. 7:6 How is the term "gross receipts" defined?

The Code does not define "gross receipts" beyond indicating that only the gain from the sale or exchange of stocks and securities will be counted (Section 1362(d)(3)(D)(i); see Question 7:12), and that only the capital gain net income from the sale or exchange of capital assets other than stocks and securities will be included (Section 1362(d)(3)(C); see Question 7:11).

However, definitions were developed under the law prior to the Subchapter S Revision Act of 1982 (Revision Act) and, although the Revision Act made radical (and ameliorative) changes in the consequences of having excess passive investment income, the definitions developed under the old law (by regulations, rulings, and cases) would still seem to be pertinent.

Under prior law, IRS defined gross receipts as follows (Former Reg. §1.1372-4(b)(5)(iv)):

Q. 7:6

> Gross receipts. (a) The term "gross receipts" as used in [former] section 1372(e) is not synonymous with "gross income." The test under [former] section 1372(e)(4) and (5) shall be made on the basis of total gross receipts, except that, for purposes of [former] section 1372(e)(5), gross receipts from the sales or exchanges of stock or securities shall be taken into account only to the extent of gains therefrom. The term "gross receipts" means the total amount received or accrued under the method of accounting used by the corporation in computing its taxable income. Thus, the total amount of receipts is not reduced by returns and allowances, cost, or deductions. For example, gross receipts will include the total amount received or accrued during the corporation's taxable year from the sale or exchange (including a sale or exchange to which [former] section 337 applies) of any kind of property, from investments, and for services rendered by the corporation. However, gross receipts does not include amounts received in nontaxable sales or exchanges (other than those to which [former] section 337 applies), except to the extent that gain is recognized by the corporation, nor does that term include amounts received as a loan, as a repayment of a loan, as a contribution to capital, or on the issuance by the corporation of its own stock.

This definition in the regulations is further illustrated by a series of examples, one of which provides for inclusion, as a gross receipt, of the face amount (not the fair market value) of a note payable at a future time, received in partial payment for goods sold or services rendered. Proposed regulations under current law would generally apply a similar set of rules. (Prop. Reg. §1.1362-3(d)(4))

> **Planning Pointer.** Although inclusion of the face amount of such note in "gross receipts" may be debatable, it generally will be to the taxpayer's advantage to inflate as much as possible all gross receipts that are not passive investment income.

Q. 7:7 How are gross receipts calculated?

Gross receipts are calculated using the total amount received or accrued under the accounting method the corporation uses in computing its taxable income, without any reduction for returns, allowances, costs, or deductions. (Former Reg. §1.1372-4(b)(5)(iv); see also Prop. Reg. §1.1362-3(d)(4).) Gross receipts from sales or exchanges of capital assets other than stock and securities are taken into account only to the extent of net capital gains. (Section 1362(d)(3)(C); Prop. Reg. §1.1362-3(d)(4)(ii)(A))

There are several revenue rulings and cases that further define what items are included in gross receipts.

Commissions: Commissions earned with respect to credit life insurance for which the taxpayer acted as broker (the premium being billed directly by the insurer to the debtor), plus total premiums received thereon with respect to the taxpayer's direct billing of premiums to debtors, constituted part of the taxpayer's gross receipts. (*Valley Loan Association*, 258 F. Supp. 673 (D. Colo. 1966) (government did not appeal)) (See also *Rev. Rul. 69-192*, 1969-1 CB 207.)

Option Payment: Nonrefundable payments received for an option to acquire real property, when the payments were to be applied to the total purchase price if the option were exercised in a subsequent taxable year, were held to be part of the taxpayer's gross receipts in the year actually received. (*Branch et al.* (D. Ga. 1967), *vacating a prior adverse decision* (D. Ga. 1967))

The first *Branch* opinion had held that option payments were not gross income when received, since it could not be determined at the time whether they would be applied to the purchase price if the option were exercised (in which case they would enter into capital gain computation), or would be forfeited if the option lapsed (resulting in ordinary income).

In the second *Branch* opinion, however, the court relied on the fact that the taxpayer was on the cash receipts and disbursement method of accounting and had to account for the option payments in the year of receipt, not in a later year when the option was either exercised or allowed to lapse. On a somewhat dubious theory, the court gave a liberal interpretation of gross receipts in order to favor the taxpayer.

Liabilities Transferred Upon Sale: The amount of indebtedness (for example, a mortgage) on property sold by an S corporation and assumed by the buyer as part of the purchase price was includible as part of the selling corporation's gross receipts for the year of sale under Former Section 1372(e)(5). (*Rev. Rul. 68-364*, 1968-2 CB 371) Presumably, the same rule would apply if the buyer merely acquired the property "subject to" the existing indebtedness.

Principal Payments on Sales of Property: In interpreting the definition of gross receipts in the regulations (see Question 7:6), the Tax Court has held that a cash-basis taxpayer is entitled to take into account only the payments on principal actually received for the purpose of calculating its gross receipts. (*Sieh*, 56 TC 1386 (1971), *aff'd* (8th Cir. 1973)) But these principal payments related to payments for property the corporation had sold.

Like-Kind Exchanges: In *Helis v. Usry* (D. La. 1971), the court held that nontaxable exchanges (under Section 1031) of property held for productive use in a trade or business for like-kind property did not constitute gross receipts. The Fifth Circuit affirmed this holding (464 F.2d 330 (5th Cir. 1972)), while reversing in part on other grounds.

Q. 7:8 What impact do deductions have on gross receipts?

As previously noted, gross receipts are not gross profits. They are calculated without any allowances for, among other things, deductions. (See Questions 7:6 and 7:7.) Deductions become relevant only in calculating the tax on excess net passive investment income. (See Question 7:4.)

Thus, gross receipts are not to be reduced by *any* deductible expense. In *Llewellyn*, 70 TC 370 (1978), the S corporation had $4,206.69 of interest income and $2,372.49 of interest expenses in its first taxable year. The Tax Court held that the election was automatically terminated under pre-Revision Act law, stating: "We hold that interest expense may not be netted against interest income for purpose of section 1372(e)(5)(B)." *Llewellyn* was followed in *Sanborn*, TC Memo 1983-579.

Q. 7:9 When are installment-sale proceeds included in gross receipts?

If an S corporation reports gain on the sale of property under the installment method of accounting, the installment payments actually received in a given taxable year of the corporation are included in gross receipts for such year. (Former Reg. §1.1372-4(b)(5)(iv)(b), Ex. 3; Prop. Reg. §1.1362-3(d)(4)(iv), Ex. 3)

Q. 7:10 How is partnership income treated for gross receipts purposes?

When an S corporation is a participant in a joint venture or owns an interest in a partnership, it includes its pro rata share of all of the venture's (or partnership's) gross receipts. This inclusion procedure is based on Section 702(b), which provides that the character of any item of partnership income, gain, loss, deduction, or credit allocated to a partner will be treated as though such item was received directly by, or paid directly by, the partner.

IRS indicated its agreement with this conclusion in a situation in which an S corporation was a participant in a joint venture that had gross receipts of $40,000 and deductible expenses of $50,000, resulting in a net loss of $10,000. IRS held that the corporation's share of the $40,000 was to be used in the calculation of its gross receipts. (*Rev. Rul. 71-455,* 1971-2 CB 318)

IRS also followed this approach in a later private ruling. (*Letter Ruling 7743074*)

Q. 7:11 What special rules apply to calculating gross receipts from the sale of capital assets?

In the case of a disposition of capital assets that are not stocks or securities, gross receipts include only the capital gain net income therefrom. (Section 1362(d)(3)(C))

There is an important distinction between the treatment of capital gains from the sale or exchange of stocks and securities (which usually produce passive investment income) and of gains from the disposition of capital assets other than stocks and securities (which usually do not). In the case of stocks and securities, only gains are taken into account in calculating the gross receipts. (See Question 7:12.) In the case of other capital assets, the Code refers to capital gain net income as the amount to be included in gross receipts. Capital gain net income is the excess of capital gains over losses. (Section 1222(9)) So, losses from sales or exchanges of capital assets that are not stocks or securities do offset gains from such sales or exchanges and reduce the amount of gross receipts. This provision is intended to prevent "churning" of assets to produce additional nonpassive gross receipts.

Q. 7:12 Are all gross receipts from sales of stock used to calculate passive investment income?

For Subchapter S purposes, only the gain realized from the sale of stock or securities is included in passive investment income. Thus, it is the amount realized (selling price) less the adjusted basis, or gain, that is included in the passive investment income. (Section 1362(d)(3)(D)(i))

IRS took the position under the law prior to 1983 (which had an identical provision regarding gains from the sale or exchange of stocks or securities) that each transaction giving rise to gain or loss on the sale or exchange of stocks or securities must be separately considered. Since only the gain transactions constitute passive investment income, this position means that loss transactions cannot be used to offset gains for these purposes. (Former Reg. §1.1372-4(b)(5)(x)) This position presumably still governs, because when Congress enacted the Revision Act, it chose to adopt language identical to that of prior law relating to gain from the sale or exchange of securities, and regulations proposed under the Revision Act would also adopt it. (Prop. Reg. §1.1362-3(d)(4)(ii)(B))

The application of this position is illustrated as follows:

■ **Example.** X Corporation realizes the following gains and losses on sales of stock during the year 1989:

100 shares A Corporation	
Selling price	$15,000
Basis	10,000
Gain	$ 5,000
100 shares B Corporation	
Selling price	$10,000
Basis	15,000
(Loss)	($ 5,000)

X Corporation will have to include $5,000 of gain on the sale of A Corporation shares in computing its passive investment income. According to the regulations, X Corporation is not permitted to offset this gain by the loss on the sale of B Corporation shares.

Income Characterization

Q. 7:13 Is rental income always passive investment income?

When significant services are performed for the occupant, tenant, or lessee, rental income is not considered passive investment income. Rents received for the use or occupancy of rooms or other space in hotels, motels, apartment hotels (furnishing hotel-type services), and tourist and boarding homes usually do not constitute rents for S corporation purposes. Regulations under pre-Revision Act law provided in part that "Payments for the use or occupancy ... of offices in an office building, etc. are generally 'rents' under Section 1372(e)(5)." (Former Reg. §1.1372-4(b)(5)(iv); Prop. Reg. §1.1362-3(d)(5)(iv))

Much has been written about, and many cases have been fought over, the issue of whether particular establishments are more like hotels or more like office space. The question seems to revolve around the nature and extent of services performed for the recipient.

Q. 7:14 What level of services is required to make rental income active instead of passive?

The key question in almost all of the cases and rulings involving rent has been: Did the S corporation render significant services? If so, the payments received were not treated as rent (that is, passive investment income). Otherwise, the rents did constitute passive investment income. The S corporation can exclude payments from passive investment income by providing those significant services. IRS has not specifically enumerated what services, other than maid services, will be deemed significant services. Nor has it prescribed any rules with respect to the amount or extent of such services, in order that they may be deemed significant.

However, an S corporation that owned a bungalow colony for summer vacationers *failed to establish that the following services were substantial or significant:*

- Providing a common lighted recreation area equipped with tables, chairs, decks of cards, and bingo games, where children played ball during the day and their parents could play cards or bingo in the evening;
- Running occasional bingo games and parties for children of vacationing tenants; and
- Sponsoring and operating two or three parties for the adult vacationing bungalow tenants.

Hence, the taxpayer's gross receipts were deemed passive investment income. (*Feingold,* 49 TC 461 (1968)) (See also *City Markets, Inc.,* TC Memo 1969-202, *aff'd,* 443 F.2d 1240 (6th Cir. 1970); *H. & L. Reid, Inc.,* 375 F.

Q. 7:14   The S Corporation Answer Book

Supp. 1099 (E.D. Mich. 1973); *McIlhenney,* TC Memo 1979-43; *Lausmann,* TC Memo 1979-420; *Lillis,* TC Memo 1983-42.)

Q. 7:15   Is income from hotels, motels, and the like passive or active?

Rents received for the use or occupancy of rooms or other space in hotels, motels, apartment hotels (furnishing hotel-type services), and tourist and boarding homes usually do not constitute rents for S corporation purposes. These establishments generally provide significant services to their tenants or occupants over and above the mere rental of space. Such services would include maid service, but would not include providing ordinary heat and light; cleaning public entrances, exits, stairways, hallways, and lobbies; or collecting trash. (Prop. Reg. §1.1362-3(d)(5)(iv)) Apparently, even if the hotel or motel bills the tenant separately for "pure rent" and for the personal services (for example, maid service) rendered, neither payment will be considered rent so as to constitute passive investment income. (TIR 113 (Question 1) (11/26/58))

Suppose that an apartment hotel (furnishing hotel-type services) provided daily maid service to occupants upon the payment of an additional fee, and suppose that none of the tenants or occupants elected to take such maid service. Two questions are obvious:

1. Could the apartment hotel consider the amounts received from the tenants as being other than passive investment income?
2. Conversely, suppose that such apartment hotel provided maid service at no additional cost, but only once per week. Would these be significant services?

Since IRS makes no distinction between maid services that are billed separately and those included in the charge for the room, suite, or apartment, and since it has not prescribed any amount of maid services as being significant, it would seem that the answer to both questions is yes.

Q. 7:16   What about income from mobile-home and trailer parks?

This is an unclear area. IRS took the position in one private ruling that the various services rendered by the corporation to the lot owners in its mobile-home park with respect to the use and maintenance of the recreational facilities and other common areas, when considered in the aggregate, constitute significant services that are primarily for the convenience of the lot owners and are other than those usually or customarily rendered in connection with the rental of space for occupancy only. Thus it was held that payments received for the use and maintenance of the recreational areas and other common areas are not rents. (*Letter Ruling 7718007*)

Q. 7:17 Will income from office building rentals be treated as active or passive?

A corporation renting out office space in an office building (or renting out apartments or other personal residences) that does not render specific personal services to the tenants will ordinarily receive rents that are considered passive investment income. Regulations under pre-Revision Act law provided in part that "Payments for the use or occupancy ... of offices in an office building, etc., are generally 'rents' under Section 1372(e)(5)." (Former Reg. §1.1372-4(b)(5)(iv)) Proposed regulations under current law do also. (Prop. Reg. §1.1362-3(d)(5)(iv))

In what appears to be the first decision involving the gross receipts of an S corporation from its ownership of an office building, the Tax Court held (*Bramlette Bldg. Corp., Inc.*, 52 TC 200 (1969), *aff'd*, 424 F.2d 751 (5th Cir. 1970)):

> In our opinion the mere leasing of space to a third party (barbershop, drugstore, lunch counter), who performs services for the other tenants of the office building, does not constitute the providing of services within the meaning of the regulations. Nor do the services which may have been rendered to the tenants of the office building by the operators of the barbershop, drugstore, and lunch counter qualify as services rendered by petitioner.

Furthermore, the Tax Court held that providing a storage area and lounge for the convenience of the building's tenants does not constitute the rendition of services; that the services performed for tenants by the building's three maids, two porters, and two elevator operators, as well as the remodeling and painting of portions of the building, were the type of services "usually or customarily rendered" in connection with the ownership and operation of an office building; and that there was no evidence to show that the service provided by the building's maintenance engineer in repairing machines, furniture, and fixtures belonging to individual tenants was significant.

Q. 7:17   **The S Corporation Answer Book**

In another case, *H. & L. Reid, Inc.*, 375 F. Supp. 1099 (E.D. Mich. 1973), the taxpayer claimed that there were substantial services rendered to its office building tenants. Although the court found the services "exemplary," they were still the type customarily rendered by a landlord and were held not substantial or significant enough to remove the receipts from classification as passive investment income.

Q. 7:18 Can rental of buildings before an intended demolition create a passive investment income problem?

Rental income from dwellings purchased with the intention of demolishing them has been held to be passive investment income. (*Greene*, 70 TC 534 (1978)) The petitioners argued that the rental income received by the corporation prior to the actual demolition of the dwellings constituted "proceeds from demolition" that, under Reg. §1.165-3(a)(1), would constitute an adjustment to the basis of the underlying land and therefore would not be gross receipts. After stating that there appeared to be an absolute absence of authority on the question of what constitutes "from demolition" within the meaning of Reg. §1.165-3(a)(1), the Tax Court held that the rental income in this case did not constitute proceeds from demolition. It did not decide the question of whether the rents would have avoided classification as gross receipts of passive investment income if they had been characterized as proceeds from demolition.

Q. 7:19 Is income from parking facilities and airfields passive investment income?

Income from the operation of parking lots or garages, where cars are left by the customers with an attendant who parks them in whatever space is available, does not result in passive investment income from rents for Subchapter S purposes. (*Rev. Rul. 65-91*, 1965-1 CB 431; see also Prop. Reg. §1.1362-3(d)(5)(iv).)

IRS has held in a private ruling that various services rendered in connection with the operation of a public airfield and a related two-way aircraft radio station were significant services. Thus, amounts received for the hangars and tie-down fees were not passive rents. (*Letter Ruling 7752040*)

Q. 7:20 Do storage and warehousing activities create passive investment income from rents?

Ordinarily, providing storage or warehouse space alone will give rise to passive rental income. However, when the storage or warehousing company is required to perform significant services with respect to the property stored (for example, loading, unloading, inspection to prevent spoilage, refrigeration services, and the like), the storage or warehousing fees do not constitute rents. (*Rev. Rul. 65-91,* 1965-1 CB 431; see also Prop. Reg. §1.1362-3(d)(5)(iv).)

Q. 7:21 If the S corporation operates a recreational facility, will it have passive investment income from rents?

The answer seems to depend on the level of services rendered. (See Questions 7:13 and 7:14.) IRS has held that income from operation of tennis and handball courts by an S corporation employing a full-time janitor to clean and maintain the courts, locker rooms, and showers, did not result in passive investment income. (*Rev. Rul. 76-48,* 1976-1 CB 265) The ruling held that significant services were rendered by the corporation. Further, it held that lesson fees and receipts from the sale of sports items from the shop on the premises were not passive investment income.

Q. 7:22 Do farming operations present passive income problems?

A corporation owning farms that it leases to individuals on a "sharefarming" or "sharecropping" basis is not deemed to receive rents if the corporation's employees participate materially in production of the farm commodities through physical work or management decisions or both. (*Rev. Rul. 61-112,* 1961-1 CB 399) But if the corporation merely collects its share of the profits without participating in operations, this will be passive rental income. (*Kennedy et al.,* TC Memo 1974-147)

Q. 7:23 How are receipts from renting or leasing personal property classified as active or passive?

This is an area in which the level of services provided (see Questions 7:13 and 7:14) seems a particularly significant indicium. The following activities have been found to result in active income, rather than passive rental income:

- The rental of various items of household equipment (for example, tables, chairs, linens, glassware, silverware) to various individuals to be used generally for private parties, if the S corporation lessor delivers and picks up these items and washes, polishes, repairs, and stores them prior to renting to the next customer (*Rev. Rul. 64-232*, 1964-2 CB 334);
- Short-term automobile rentals, if the S corporation lessor furnishes normal maintenance (*Rev. Rul. 65-40*, 1965-1 CB 429);
- Long-term leasing of automobiles, if the S corporation lessor provides services and supplemental transportation (*Rev. Rul. 76-469*, 1976-2 CB 252);
- Truck or crane rentals, if the S corporation lessor furnishes the driver or operator (*Rev. Rul. 65-83*, 1965-1 CB 430);
- Television set rentals for hospital patients, if the S corporation lessor unlocks, locks, adjusts, and repairs these sets for each separate use (*Rev. Rul. 70-206*, 1970-1 CB 177);
- Leasing electronic video games, if the S corporation lessor is responsible for all maintenance and repair of the games (*Letter Ruling 8221053*);
- Leasing a computer system, if the S corporation lessor is obligated to pay for maintenance and repairs (*Letter Ruling 8225141*); and
- Distributing motion pictures, if the S corporation distributor renders significant services to ensure proper promotion and exhibition (*Rev. Rul. 75-349*, 1975-2 CB 349).

It would seem to follow from these rulings that the rental of coin-operated clothes washing and drying equipment, to be used in apartment house laundry rooms, ordinarily would not constitute rents if the S corporation lessor has to provide maintenance and repair services.

In contrast, the Tax Court has held that an S corporation that rented recorded videocassettes of motion pictures to cable television stations received passive rents. The taxpayer contended that the rental agreement resulted in a sale because the lessees did not return the cassettes. Alternatively, it contended that the corporation rendered significant services in connection with the rental income. Both arguments were rejected. (*Thompson*, 73 TC 878 (1980))

Similarly, income from the leasing of construction equipment by a construction company that was idle because of lack of construction activity was held to be passive rental income because no significant services were rendered. (*Letter Ruling 7731004*)

Q. 7:24 How is income from charters classified?

A charter is a lease of transportation equipment—with or without personal services. An analysis similar to that for other personal property rentals (see Question 7:23) seems to apply.

IRS has formally considered two situations concerning aircraft (*Rev. Rul. 81-197,* 1981-2 CB 166):

■ **Situation 1.** The tenant arranged for licenses, repairs, and hangar facilities, but was reimbursed by the corporation that owned the aircraft. IRS took the position that the arrangement resulted in passive rental income because the tenant made all arrangements for the services performed.

■ **Situation 2.** The S corporation arranged for licenses, repairs, and hangar facilities itself. It also supplied the pilots, who retained primary responsibility for the safety and operation of the planes. Thus, the owner-corporation retained possession, command, and control of the chartered planes. Therefore, the payments it received were "compensation for transportation services" and not passive rental income.

IRS applied a similar analysis in a private ruling that involved the question of whether income from chartering a jet aircraft was passive rental income. Mainly because the pilot of the plane was the owner's employee, IRS held that the owner retained "possession, command, and control" of the plane. Therefore, the charter fees received by the owner were held to be "compensation for transportation services rendered and not payments for the use of aircraft." Thus, they were not passive rental income. (*Letter Ruling 8114094*)

Similar results have been reached with regard to boat charters:
- The Tax Court has held that income from a "bare boat" charter of barges—when complete control and possession were turned over to the lessees—was rental income from a passive investment because it was received for the right to use the barges, and the services performed in connection with this arrangement were not significant enough to remove the rental income from the forbidden type of passive income (*Winn,* 67 TC 499 (1976), *aff'd on this point,* 595 F.2d 1060 (5th Cir. 1979)); and

- IRS, in a private ruling, held that significant services were rendered in connection with the chartering of a yacht when the S corporation owner was to bear all costs of dockage, maintenance, repair, insurance, operation, and advertising (*Letter Ruling 7718003*).

Q. 7:25 Can a "sale" ever be construed as a rental that creates a passive investment income problem?

Yes, apparently a "sale" can be viewed as a rental—and thus might give rise to a passive investment income problem. In one private ruling, IRS took the position that income from a timber contract was passive rental income. Although the contract provisions seemed to refer only to the purchase and sale of timber, IRS held that the payments were not for the sale of timber, but were really rental payments for the use of the land. (*Letter Ruling 8116081*)

In another private ruling, however, sale, installation, and operation of a fully computerized residential alarm system were held not to produce passive investment income. (*Letter Ruling 7732053*)

Q. 7:26 Is interest income ever excluded from the definition of passive investment income?

There are two situations in which interest will not be treated as passive investment income:

1. Interest on obligations received in connection with the sale of inventory or other property held for sale to customers in the ordinary course of business (Section 1362(d)(3)(D)(ii); Prop. Reg. §1.1362-3(d)(5)(vi)); and
2. Interest income received by certain lending and finance companies (Section 1362(d)(3)(D)(iii); Prop. Reg. §1.1362-3(d)(5)(ix)).

Lending and Finance Companies: Interest income of lending and finance companies is eligible for this exception to the passive investment income definition if, during the taxable year in question (Sections 1362(d)(3)(D)(iii) and 542(c)(6)):

1. At least 60% of the corporation's ordinary gross income is derived from the active conduct of the lending or finance business;
2. Passive investment income (calculated excluding interest income defined above) is 20% or less of ordinary gross income;

3. Deductions allocable to the lending or finance business equal at least 15% of the first $500,000 of gross income from the business plus 5% of such gross income in excess of $500,000; and
4. The principal amount of loans to a person directly or indirectly owning 10% or more of the corporation's stock does not exceed $5,000 at any time.

Interest income exempt from the definition of passive investment income under this rule is limited to income "derived directly from the active and regular conduct of a lending or finance business"—that is (Sections 1362(d)(3)(D)(iii) and 542(d)(1)):

1. From making loans;
2. From purchasing or discounting accounts receivable, notes, and installment obligations; and
3. From rendering services or making facilities available in connection with its lending, purchasing, and discounting activities.

(For unsecured loans and purchasing and discounts of secured receivables, notes, and obligations to qualify, the term must be 144 months or less, unless credit is extended under a line-of-credit arrangement permitting repayment both in full and in installments.)

Corporate Planning

Q. 7:27 What can be done to reduce a corporation's passive investment income?

The corporation can try to change the character of its income by changing the nature of the assets bringing in the income. Assets can be distributed to shareholders or sold. Alternatively, an active business may be conducted by the corporation in order to reduce the percentage of passive investment income gross receipts. (See Question 6:7.)

Planning Pointer. If an S corporation with C corporation earnings and profits wants to avoid problems with passive investment income, it must cleanse itself of any remaining C corporation earnings and profits. (See Questions 12:4–12:6 and 12:18–12:20.) Once the corporation has distributed those earnings and profits, it will no longer be subject to the passive investment income problems for the year of distribution or any future year. (This topic is discussed in more detail at Question 6:7.)

Chapter 8

S Corporations' Taxable Income and Losses; Taxation of the S Corporation

Fundamental Principles

Q. 8:1 How is S corporation income generally taxed?

Generally speaking, the corporation is not subject to tax, and the shareholders pay tax on the corporation's income. (See the discussion of the pass-through rules in Chapter 9.)

Q. 8:2 How, generally speaking, is the S corporation's taxable income computed?

The taxable income of an S corporation is computed on Form 1120S in the same manner as that of an individual, with certain exceptions (Section 1363(b)):

- All items that have a special tax significance must be separately stated (so that they can pass through to the shareholders) rather than being combined on page 1 of the Form 1120S;
- The S corporation does not deduct (1) taxes paid to foreign countries and to U.S. possessions, (2) charitable contributions, (3) net operating losses, and (4) depletion of oil and gas wells under Section 611;
- An S corporation can amortize organizational expenses under Section 248;

- Corporate tax preferences of Section 291 may apply if the S corporation or its predecessor was a C corporation for any of the three taxable years immediately preceding the year in question;
- Fringe-benefit deductions are available to the extent they are for benefits provided to employees other than shareholders owning more than 2% of the corporation's stock (Section 1372; see Questions 13:2–13:5); and
- To state the obvious, the personal exemption and itemized deductions available only to individuals cannot be claimed.

Q. 8:3 How does the S corporation treat dispositions of capital assets?

The general rule is that all items of income retain their special character as they pass through to the shareholders of an S corporation. (Sections 1363(b) and 1366(b)) Therefore, such items as long-term capital gains and losses, short-term capital gains and losses, and Section 1231 gains and losses on trade or business property that pass through to shareholders will retain their special status.

In some cases, a corporate-level tax—on passive investment income (see Questions 8:10–8:14) or on either long-term capital gain or "built-in gain"—will apply. (See Questions 8:15–8:33.)

Q. 8:4 Is the S corporation's taxable income affected if the corporation distributes appreciated property to its shareholders?

The distribution of appreciated assets—assets with a fair market value that is higher than the corporation's basis in them—is treated as though the S corporation had sold the assets. The S corporation recognizes gain represented by the difference between the fair market value and the basis, and passes the gain through to its shareholders, just as any other gain on a sale would pass through to the shareholders. (See Section 311(a). The Technical and Miscellaneous Revenue Act of 1988 (TAMRA) repealed, retroactive to taxable years beginning in 1987, Former Sections 1363(d) and 1363(e), which specifically applied the appreciated property rule to

S corporations, with exceptions for tax-free spinoffs and similar transactions under Sections 354, 355, and 356. These sections were deadwood because *General Utilities* repeal provides a general rule for distribution of appreciated assets.)

■ **Example 1.** A corporation that has an S corporation election in effect distributes as a dividend 500 shares of AT&T stock that has a basis of $25,000 and a fair market value of $30,000. The corporation will realize a gain of $5,000 on the distribution. If the stock is a capital asset and the holding period is long term, the gain will be long-term capital gain.

However, there is no corresponding rule permitting recognition of loss when assets for which the corporation's basis exceeds fair market value are distributed to shareholders.

■ **Example 2.** Assume the same facts, except that the basis of the AT&T stock is $50,000 and the fair market value is $40,000. In this case, since the basis is greater than the fair market value, there would be no gain. The loss would not be recognized.

The gain created on the distribution of appreciated property is subject to the income pass-through rules. (See Chapter 9.) Thus, for example, if appreciated property is distributed to any one shareholder, all of the shareholders, not just the one who received the property distribution, are taxed on their pro rata shares of the corporation's gain.

Planning Pointer. Instead of distributing property that has a tax basis in excess of its value, the S corporation should sell it to an unrelated party and distribute the proceeds. In that way, the corporation will be able to recognize the loss and pass it through to its shareholders, who may be able to deduct the loss on their own tax returns.

Q. 8:5 Are losses from transactions with "related parties" recognized in computing the S corporation's taxable income?

Losses from transactions between S corporations and related entities that are more than 50% owned (directly or indirectly through attribution) by the same persons are disallowed. (Section 267(a)(1)) For this purpose, related entities include the following:

- Two S corporations with more than 50% common ownership (Section 267(b)(11));

Q. 8:5

- An S corporation and a partnership with more than 50% common ownership (Section 267(b)(10));
- An S corporation and a C corporation with more than 50% common ownership (Section 267(b)(12)); and
- An S corporation and an individual who owns more than 50% of its shares (Section 267(b)(2)).

Q. 8:6 Can an S corporation deduct accrued expenses that are payable to its shareholders?

An S corporation can deduct expenses owed to a shareholder only at the time payments are made. (Section 267(a)(2)) This rule has the effect of putting an accrual-basis S corporation on the cash basis for expense payments to shareholders.

Q. 8:7 What limitations on deductions apply to the S corporation?

The following limitations apply at both the corporate level and the shareholder level:

1. The yearly dollar limitation on property that can be "expensed" instead of depreciated (Section 179(d)(8)); and
2. The yearly dollar limitation on the amortization of reforestation expenses (Section 194(b)(2)(B)).

Limitations for excluding income from the discharge of indebtedness contained in Sections 108(a), 108(b), and 108(c) are applied at the corporate level.

Q. 8:8 Which elections affecting the computation of an S corporation's income, deductions, and credits are made by the corporation, and which are made by the shareholders?

The general rule is that the S corporation makes all elections affecting the computation of its income, deductions, and credits. (Section 1363(c)(1)) Examples of such elections include opting out of installment-sale treatment and choosing to avoid income from the discharge of indebtedness by reducing the basis of assets. The elections made by the corporation are binding on all the shareholders.

Exceptions to the general rule are made for the following elections, which are made by each shareholder separately (Section 1363(c)(2)):

1. Elections concerning deductions for a recapture of certain mining exploration expenditures under Section 617; and
2. Elections to claim deductions or credits for taxes paid to foreign countries and possessions of the United States under Section 901.

(See also Prop. Reg. §1.1363-1(c).)

Q. 8:9 Under what circumstances may the S corporation itself be subject to income taxes?

As a general rule, the S corporation itself is not subject to income taxes. (See Question 8:1.) However, there are several exceptions to this rule for S corporations that were formerly C corporations (or that are successors of C corporations). These are:

1. Tax on excess passive investment income of Section 1375 (see Questions 8:10–8:14);
2. Long-term capital gains tax (see Questions 8:15–8:20);
3. Built-in gains tax (see Questions 8:21–8:33); and
4. Investment credit recapture (see Questions 8:34–8:35).

In these cases, the corporation must pay the tax directly.

C corporations becoming S corporations may also be subject to LIFO recapture. (See Questions 8:36–8:39.)

Tax on Excess Passive Investment Income

Q. 8:10 When is an S corporation subject to the tax on excess passive investment income?

The tax on excess passive income applies when (Section 1375(a)):

1. The corporation has C corporation earnings and profits at the end of its taxable year; and
2. Its passive investment income exceeds 25% of its gross receipts.

Q. 8:10 The S Corporation Answer Book

The definitions of passive investment income and gross receipts are reviewed in detail in Chapter 7. However, if the corporation is subject to built-in gains tax (see Question 8:22), recognized built-in gain or loss (as defined at Question 8:26) is not taken into account in calculating passive investment income subject to tax. (Section 1375(b)(4))

The rule about the interaction of the passive investment income tax and built-in gain was added by TAMRA but, as a technical correction to the Tax Reform Act of 1986 (TRA '86), is retroactive to 1987 years.

Planning Pointer. If the Subchapter C earnings and profits are not too high, it may be advisable to pay them to the shareholders. Then the S corporation would no longer be subject to the tax on excess passive income. (This and other ideas for dealing with passive income are discussed more thoroughly at Question 6:7.)

Q. 8:11 How is excess passive investment income taxed?

The tax on excess passive investment income is imposed at the highest corporate income tax rate—currently 34%. (Section 11(b)) This tax rate is multiplied by excess net passive income. Excess net passive income (ENPI) is net passive income (NPI) multiplied by a fraction. (Section 1375(a)) The numerator of the fraction is the amount by which the gross passive investment income (PII) exceeds 25% of gross receipts (GR). The denominator of the fraction is the total passive investment income (PII) for the taxable year. (Section 1375(b)) Reg. §1.1375-1A(b)(1)(i) expresses the definition of excess net passive income as:

$$\text{ENPI} = \text{NPI} \times \frac{\text{PII} - (.25 \times \text{GR})}{\text{PII}}$$

(See Chapter 7 for a discussion of passive investment income and gross receipts. See Question 8:12 for a discussion of a limitation on this tax.)

■ **Example.** Muart Corporation, a former C corporation, elected S corporation status effective in 1989. It had accumulated earnings and profits from years prior to the S election. For its calendar year 1989, it had total gross receipts of $260,000; gross passive income of $100,000; and allowable deductions directly connected with earning the passive income in the amount of $20,000. It had no built-in gains. Here is how the tax is computed:

Taxable Income and Losses — Q. 8:12

1. *Compute Net Passive Income:*
Gross passive income	$100,000
Less: Expenses of earning the passive income	20,000
Net passive income	$ 80,000

2. *Determine the Fraction to Apply to Net Passive Income:*
   (a) *Numerator:*
Gross passive income	$100,000
Less: 25% of gross receipts of $260,000	65,000
Numerator	$ 35,000

   (b) *Denominator:*
   Equals gross passive income of $100,000

   (c) *Fraction:*
   $$\frac{\$35,000}{\$100,000} = 35\%$$

3. *Determine Excess Passive Income:*
   Net passive income × Fraction = Excess passive income
   $80,000 × 35% = $28,000

4. *Determine Tax on Excess Passive Income:*
   Excess passive income × Highest corporate rate = Tax on excess passive income
   $28,000 × 34% = $9,520

Net Passive Income: Net passive income is passive investment income (see Chapter 7) less allowable deductions that are directly incurred in producing that passive income. (Sections 1375(b)(2) and 1375(b)(3)) The regulations state that deductions are directly connected with the production of income when they "have proximate and primary relationship to the income. Expenses, depreciation, and similar items attributable solely to such income qualify for deduction." The regulations go on to state that if any deduction is attributable partly to passive investment income and partly to other income, the deduction will be allocated between the two types of income on a reasonable basis.

Impact on Shareholders: The tax computed will be payable by the corporation and will reduce the amount of passive investment income passing through to the shareholders. (Section 1366(f)(3))

Q. 8:12 Is there any limit on the amount of excess net passive income that can be taxed?

Yes, there is one very important limit. The amount of excess net passive income subject to tax for any taxable year may not exceed the cor-

Q. 8:12   The S Corporation Answer Book

poration's taxable income for that year, determined without regard to the net operating loss deduction and the dividends-received deduction. (Section 1375(b)(1)(B))

Q. 8:13 Can IRS waive the tax on excess passive investment income?

Yes, the Code authorizes IRS to waive the corporate tax on passive investment income of an S corporation if it is established to IRS's satisfaction that the S corporation (Section 1375(d); Reg. §1.1375-1A(d)(1)):

1. Determined in good faith (albeit erroneously) that it had no C corporation earnings and profits at the close of a taxable year, and
2. Distributed the C corporation earnings and profits to the shareholders (resulting in ordinary income to them) during a reasonable period of time after it was determined that the earnings and profits existed.

Q. 8:14 How does an S corporation request a waiver of the tax on excess passive investment income?

The request must be made in writing to the District Director for the district in which the corporation's tax return is filed. It should contain all relevant facts to establish that the requirements for a waiver have been met. (See Question 8:13.) On the date the waiver is to become effective, all C corporation earnings and profits must have been distributed. (Reg. §1.1375-1A(d)(2)) The request may be in the form of a letter and must contain the following information:

1. A description of how and on what date the S corporation determined erroneously—in good faith and using due diligence—that it had no C corporation earnings and profits at the close of the taxable year;
2. A description of how and on what date it was determined that the S corporation actually did have C corporation earnings and profits at the close of the year;
3. A description of any steps taken to distribute earnings and profits and the dates on which such steps were taken; and
4. If the earnings and profits is not yet completely distributed at the time the request is made, a timetable for the proposed distribution and an explanation of why that timetable is reasonable.

Gains and Dispositions—An Overview

Q. 8:15 Can long-term capital gains or other gains and dispositions trigger a corporate-level tax?

Generally, capital gains (and losses) are passed through and taxed to the shareholders. (See Question 8:3.) In some circumstances, however, the S corporation itself may become liable for corporate income tax on the long-term capital gains. (Former Section 1374) (See Questions 8:16–8:20.) In other cases, a built-in gains tax may apply to various dispositions. (See Questions 8:21–8:33.)

Note on Statutory Reference: There are two versions of Section 1374. The first applies to S corporations that made S corporation elections prior to January 1, 1987 (transitional rules extended this date to January 1, 1989, for certain small corporations; see Questions 8:32–8:33) and imposes the "capital gains tax" or "long-term capital gains tax." The second version of Section 1374, enacted by TRA '86, applies to corporations that made the S corporation election after 1986 (or after 1988 if the transitional rules apply) and imposes the "built-in gains tax." (See Questions 8:21–8:33.)

Technically, Section 1374 imposing the built-in gains tax replaced Section 1374 imposing the capital gains tax, but the Conference Committee Report on TRA '86 makes it clear that the capital gains tax still applies in appropriate circumstances (see Questions 8:16–8:18), a position that TAMRA also adopts, with the clarification that current corporate tax rates apply. For purposes of clarity, the discussion of the capital gains tax will cite "Former Section 1374," and that of the built-in gains tax "Section 1374."

Long-Term Capital Gains

Q. 8:16 Must all S corporations be concerned with the corporate-level capital gains tax?

No, the capital gains tax applies only if long-term capital gains during a taxable year exceed $25,000 and certain other tests are met. (See Question 8:18.) In addition, the capital gains tax does not apply if (1) the S corporation is subject to the built-in gains tax with regard to its capital gains (see Question 8:22) or (2) either of the following applies (Former Section 1374(c)):

- The S corporation election has been in effect for the three taxable years preceding the year in which the gains in question occur; or
- The corporation has not been in existence for the entire three-year period preceding the year in question, but it has been an S corporation during its entire existence.

Q. 8:17 Can an S corporation subject to the capital gains tax avoid the tax by transferring assets to one that is not?

A special rule prevents an S corporation that does not meet the three-year test (see 8:16) from avoiding the tax by transferring assets to one that does meet the three-year test. If an S corporation acquired property during the three years before the taxable year in question, or within that taxable year, from a corporation that was not an S corporation during the prior three years and the basis of the acquired property is a substituted basis (determined in whole or in part by reference to the basis of property in the hands of the other corporation), the corporate-level tax on long-term capital gains will be imposed if the corporation meets the income tests. (See Question 8:18.) But in those situations, the total capital gains tax cannot be more than the alternative capital gains tax on the property that has the substituted basis. (Former Section 1374(c)(3))

Q. 8:18 What level of capital gain, and level of income, trigger the corporate-level capital gains tax?

The tax may be imposed only if all three of the following facts are present (Former Section 1374(a)):

1. The corporation's *net* long-term capital gain exceeds $25,000;
2. Its net long-term capital gain is more than 50% of its taxable income; and
3. Its taxable income exceeds $25,000.

For purposes of computing taxable income of the corporation in making these calculations, the rules of Subchapter C for regular corporations apply, with two exceptions. Neither the net operating loss deduction of Section 172 nor the dividends-received deductions of Section 243 *et seq.* is allowed.

In computing taxable income, the capital gains are combined with whatever ordinary income or loss the corporation may have. So, if the corporation has ordinary income, that ordinary income must be less than the long-term gain(s) for the tax to apply; otherwise the long-term gain(s) will not be more than half the taxable income. Also, if the corporation has ordinary losses within $25,000 of its long-term gain(s), after combining them the total taxable income will not be more than $25,000 and the corporate tax will not apply.

Planning Pointer. Because an S corporation that has not had S corporation status for three years may be taxed on its long-term gains, the corporate capital gains tax may be avoided by making the sale of corporate assets an installment sale. The idea is to limit the gain reportable under the installment method in any one year to $25,000 or less. If the gain realized by the corporation each year under the installment method is $25,000 or less, the corporation will not be taxed. Yet, that gain will pass through to the shareholders as capital gain under the rules for S corporations. (*Rev. Rul. 65-292*, 1965-2 CB 319)

If the installment-sale approach is used in order to avoid the corporate tax on capital gains, the corporation will probably not be active in the years following the sale. Actual or imputed interest will be realized because there is an installment sale. If the corporation has earnings and profits accumulated while it was a C corporation, close watch must be kept on the amount of interest realized each year in order to keep it below 25% of the corporation's gross receipts for that year. Otherwise there may be tax on the passive investment income (see Question 8:10), and the corporation's S corporation election may be lost (see Question 6:7).

Q. 8:19 How is the corporate-level capital gains tax computed?

The tax imposed is the lower of the following amounts (Former Section 1374(b) as amended by TAMRA, Section 1006(g)(1)):

1. 34% of net long-term capital gain in excess of $25,000; or
2. The regular corporate income tax amount that the corporation would pay on its entire taxable income if it were not an S corporation (for this purpose, taxable income is determined without regard to the net operating loss deduction and the dividends-received deduction). (Former Section 1374(d))

Options and Commodities Dealers: For purposes of this tax, net capital gains of any options dealer or commodities dealer are determined without taking into account gain or loss from "Section 1256 marked-to-market" contracts in connection with the normal course of the taxpayer's activity of dealing in or trading these options or commodities contracts. (Former Section 1374(c)(4)) An options dealer is a person registered on a national securities exchange (or on any exchange approved by IRS) as a market maker or specialist. (Section 1256(g)(8)) A commodities dealer is a person who is actively engaged in trading Section 1256 contracts and is registered with a domestic board of trade that is designated as a contract market by the Commodities Futures Trading Commission. (Former Section 1374(c)(4)(B)(ii))

Impact on Shareholders: The tax computed will be payable by the corporation. It will first reduce the amount of long-term capital gain passed through to the shareholders; any excess of tax over long-term capital gains will then reduce the amount of gain from sales or exchanges of trade or business property that is passed through to the shareholders. (Former Section 1366(f)(2))

Q. 8:20 Do gains already taxed as excess passive investment income enter into this corporate-level capital gains tax computation?

Some of the S corporation's capital gains may result in passive investment income subject to the tax on excess passive investment income. (See Question 8:10.) Any portion of net long-term capital gain that is subject to the passive investment income tax will not be subject to the capital gains tax. (Section 1375(c)(2))

The following formula is used to determine what portion of the excess net passive income is attributable to net long-term capital gain (Reg. §1.1375-1A(c)(2)): Excess net passive income is multiplied by a fraction, the numerator of which is net capital gain reduced by expenses attributable thereto and the denominator of which is total net passive income—that is, total passive investment income less allowable deductions directly attributable thereto. (See Question 8:11.)

Built-in Gains

Q. 8:21 What are "built-in gains"?

In order to answer this question, it is first necessary to ask and answer another question: Why is there a built-in gains tax?

TRA '86 generally repealed the rules allowing nonrecognition treatment to a corporation distributing or selling appreciated property in complete or partial liquidation (the *"General Utilities"* doctrine). However, S corporations—although they recognize a corporate-level gain (see Question 8:18)—will still avoid the "double tax" on this gain.

So that C corporations eligible for S corporation status will not convert in order to evade the new tax liabilities imposed by the *General Utilities* repeal, a corporate-level built-in gains tax is imposed on any gain that arose prior to the conversion and is recognized by the S corporation within 10 years after the effective date of the S corporation election.

A built-in gain is the excess of an asset's fair market value on the date an S corporation election becomes effective over the corporation's adjusted basis in the asset on that date. (Section 1374)

Planning Pointer. Upon electing S corporation status, it may be advisable for a former C corporation to obtain appraisals of some or all of its assets as of the effective date of the election.

Q. 8:22 Which S corporations are subject to the built-in gains tax?

As previously indicated (see Question 8:21), the built-in gains tax was imposed so that C corporations could not escape the *General Utilities* repeal by electing S corporation status and then distributing or disposing of assets in a liquidation or other tax-recognition event while incurring only one level of tax.

The built-in gains tax therefore applies to taxable years beginning after December 31, 1986, if the S corporation both:

1. Was previously a C corporation, and
2. Made its S corporation election after December 31, 1986.

Even if the election was made after December 31, 1986, certain transitional rules may apply. If the transitional rules apply, a corporation might avoid part of the impact of the built-in gains tax if it made the election before January 1, 1989. (See Questions 8:32–8:33.)

However, these rules are not quite as cut and dried as they appear. *IRS will consider how an S corporation acquired an asset, not just the corporation's technical status, in determining whether built-in gains tax applies.* Thus a corporation that does not appear to be covered by these rules may be—at least with regard to certain assets. (See Question 8:30.)

Q. 8:23 Which S corporations are not subject to the built-in gains tax?

Corporations that have been S corporations for their entire existence will not be subject to the built-in gains tax. Nor will S corporations whose elections were made by filing a Form 2553 before January 1, 1987—*even though* the elections became effective after January 1, 1987. (TRA '86, Section 632(b)) (For more on making the election, see Chapter 2.)

In addition, corporations that qualify under transitional rules may avoid some or all of the impact of the built-in gains tax if they elected S corporation status before January 1, 1989. (See Questions 8:32–8:33.)

Again, keep in mind that these rules are not as simple as they appear on their face. Even if the built-in gains tax does not, on the basis of these rules, apply to an S corporation, IRS will consider how a corporation acquired an asset—not just the corporation's technical status—in deciding whether built-in gains tax applies. (See Question 8:30.)

Also note that if the built-in gains tax does not apply—either because of the general effective date or because of the transitional rules—the long-term capital gains tax may apply. (See Questions 8:15–8:20.)

Q. 8:24 What types of dispositions trigger the built-in gains tax?

The built-in gains tax, like the *General Utilities* repeal itself, encompasses far more than liquidation and partial liquidation situations. Income and deduction items properly taken into account during the 10-year recognition period (see Question 8:25) but attributable to periods before the first taxable year for which the S corporation election was effective are included in the calculation of recognized built-in gain (discussed more fully at Question 8:26) (Section 1374(d)(5)) This provision, added by TAMRA, provides statutory authority for the IRS position that the tax covers "not only sales or exchanges but other income-recognition events that effectively dispose of or relinquish the taxpayer's right to claim or receive income." (*Ann. 86-128*, 1986-51 IRB 22) Such events (which are to be reflected in regulations) include:

- Collection of accounts receivable by a cash-basis taxpayer;
- Completion of a long-term contract performed by a taxpayer using the completed-contract method of accounting; and
- The sale of inventory in the ordinary course of business. (The taxpayer's method of tax accounting will determine whether inven-

tory is deemed held at the time of conversion to S corporation status. LIFO recapture rules, discussed at Questions 8:36–8:39, apply to elections made after December 17, 1987.)

Q. 8:25 How are built-in gains taxed?

A built-in gain is the excess of an asset's fair market value on the date an S corporation election becomes effective over the corporation's adjusted basis in the asset on that date. A C corporation that elects S corporation status after 1986, except to the extent transitional rules apply (see Question 8:32), is subject to a corporate-level tax on any built-in gain realized within 10 years of the first day of the first year in which the S corporation election is effective. (The "recognition period.") Also included are income items earned during the C corporation period that are reflected in taxable income during the 10-year recognition period. (See Question 8:24 for examples.)

Once a disposition triggers the tax, the tax itself is equal to the highest corporate tax for the particular type of income (ordinary or long-term capital gain—currently both 34%) times net recognized built-in gain for the taxable year (see Question 8:26). (Section 1374(b))

As in the case of the capital gains tax (see Question 8:19), therefore, the rate may be either the regular rate under Section 11 or the long-term capital gain rate under Section 1201(a).

Impact on Shareholder Pass-Through: The amount of any tax on built-in gains reduces the income that passes through to the shareholders by their proportionate shares of the tax. (Section 1366(f)(2))

Q. 8:26 What is net recognized built-in gain?

The built-in gains tax is based on *net recognized* built-in gain. Net recognized built-in gain is limited to the lesser of two amounts (Section 1374(d)(2)(A)):

1. The amount that would be the corporation's taxable income for the taxable year if taxable income consisted only of recognized built-in gains and recognized built-in losses, reduced by any net operating loss carryforwards from C corporation years; or
2. The corporation's taxable income determined as if the corporation

were a C corporation but without giving effect to the dividends-received deduction, net operating loss deduction, or credits.

However, some S corporations can use the taxable income limitation only to defer—not to avoid—built-in gains tax. (See Question 8:27.)

Recognized Built-in Gain: Recognized built-in gain is any gain the corporation recognizes on the disposition of any asset during the 10-year period beginning with the first day of the first taxable year in which the S election is effective *if* the corporation held the asset at the beginning of this period. Income items that are taken into account during the 10-year recognition period but that are attributable to C corporation periods are also treated as recognized built-in gains for the taxable years in which they are properly taken into account. (Section 1374(d)(5)) (See Question 8:24 for a discussion of what transactions are considered dispositions.)

If, however, the corporation can show that the asset appreciated during this 10-year recognition period, the recognized built-in gain is limited to the gain that was built in at the beginning of the recognition period, that is, the fair market value on the first day of the first taxable year in which the S election is effective, less the corporation's adjusted basis on that date. (Section 1374(d)(3))

■ **Example.** Corporation A, which has done business as a C corporation, elects S corporation status on March 15, 1990. The election is effective as of January 1, 1990, which is the beginning of A's taxable year. On January 1, 1990, A holds an asset with a fair market value of $500,000 and an adjusted basis of $200,000. On August 2, 1991, A disposes of this asset for $600,000. Assuming that A can prove appreciation of $100,000 between the effective date of the election and the date of the sale, A's built-in gain is $300,000 ($500,000 minus $200,000). (Of course, if A cannot establish that $100,000 of its realized gain is due to post-recognition-period appreciation, A's recognized gain will be the same as the realized gain: $400,000, or $600,000 less $200,000 basis.)

Planning Pointer. In light of the significant burden the built-in gains tax can impose, it is advisable to obtain competent independent appraisals of corporate assets as of the effective date of the election. A complete inventory of all assets—including cash and receivables—is also advisable.

Recognized Built-in Loss: The definition of recognized built-in loss parallels that of recognized built-in gain. A recognized built-in loss is a loss, recognized during the recognition period, of an asset the S corporation owned while it was a C corporation. However, as built-in losses reduce the built-in gains tax, the burden is on the S corporation to establish what assets it owned, as well as their value, when its election became effective. (Section 1374(d)(4))

Items that are deductible during the 10-year recognition period, but that are attributable to C corporation periods may also be treated as recognized built-in losses for the taxable years in which they are allowed as deductions. (Section 1374(d)(5)(B))

Planning Pointer. It may be advisable to have corporate minutes reciting that certain expenses that will be paid in the first S corporation year, such as compensation to shareholder-officers, are in payment for services rendered during the period prior to the S election. Again, to take advantage of built-in loss, a complete inventory and appraisal are advisable.

Q. 8:27 Can losses from S corporation years be used to minimize built-in gains tax?

Built-in gains tax is based on the lesser of two amounts: (1) net recognized built-in gain; or (2) corporate taxable income, subject to certain modifications. (See Question 8:26.) If this were the only basis for the tax, S corporations could time losses to decrease taxable income and thus avoid or significantly reduce built-in gains tax.

However, S corporations with elections made on or after March 31, 1988, have a limited ability to manipulate the taxable income limitation. To the extent the recognized built-in gains less recognized built-in losses exceed the corporation's taxable income, the excess is treated as a recognized built-in gain in the succeeding taxable year. (Section 1374(d)(2)(B)) Thus, the built-in gains tax will not apply to loss years, but the potential for tax will be carried forward to future years.

Planning Pointer. If the S corporation can carry the excess forward long enough, the 10-year recognition period will expire, and no tax will ever be imposed on the excess.

Q. 8:28 Is there any overall limitation on the amount of built-in gains tax?

The net recognized built-in gains rule (see Question 8:26) limits imposition of the built-in gains tax to the situation the tax is supposed to control, the avoidance of corporate-level tax by conversion to S corporation status. However, there is another limitation on the taxation of built-in gains. It provides additional protection for a corporation that converts to S corporation status and takes with it built-in losses as well as built-in gains.

The amount of built-in gain taken into account in any taxable year cannot exceed *net unrealized built-in gain* less net recognized built-in gain for prior taxable years. (Section 1374(c)(2)) Net unrealized gain is the amount by which the fair market value of all of the corporation's assets at the beginning of the 10-year recognition period exceeds the aggregate adjusted bases of those assets at that time. (Section 1374(d)(1)) Proper adjustments are made for recognized built-in gains and losses. (Section 1374(d)(5)(C))

The principles used in applying this limitation are similar to those used in determining recognized built-in gain.

■ **Example.** Again assume (as at Question 8:26) that Corporation A elects S corporation status, effective for its taxable year beginning January 1, 1990. At that time, A has:

1. An asset with a fair market value of $500,000 and an adjusted basis of $200,000—a built-in gain of $300,000;
2. An asset with a fair market value of $200,000 and an adjusted basis of $100,000—a built-in gain of $100,000; and
3. An asset with a fair market value of $100,000 and an adjusted basis of $150,000—a built-in loss of $50,000.

A's assets have an aggregate fair market value of $800,000, and A's aggregate adjusted basis in these assets is $450,000. Therefore, A has a net unrealized built-in gain of $350,000 (aggregate fair market value of $800,000 less aggregate adjusted basis of $450,000).

On August 2, 1991, A disposes of the asset in which it has an adjusted basis of $200,000 and recognizes a built-in gain of $300,000. This is the only recognized built-in gain in 1991, and A has no recognized built-in losses, so this is also the net recognized built-in gain.

In 1992, A disposes of the asset with a fair market value of $200,000 and an adjusted basis of $100,000. A's recognized built-in gain on that disposition is $100,000. However, A's net unrealized built-in gain in excess of built-in gain recognized in previous years is only $50,000 ($350,000 less $300,000). Therefore, the recognized gain taken into account is only $50,000, regardless of whether A actually disposes of the loss asset.

Q. 8:29 Can a corporation's shareholders contribute "loss" property before electing S corporation status and thus lower this "net unrealized built-in gain" limitation amount?

If a corporation could receive a contribution of built-in loss assets—assets with a fair market value less than adjusted basis—shortly before a conversion to S corporation status, the built-in gains tax would be limited because the contributed losses would reduce net unrealized built-in gain. (See Question 8:28.) However, IRS has anticipated this tactic. Special rules are provided for corporations that receive contributions of built-in loss assets and then elect S corporation status. The contribution of such property will not reduce the net unrealized built-in gain unless (*Ann. 86-128, 1986-51 IRB 22*):

- The property was contributed to the corporation more than two years before the earlier of (1) the beginning of the first taxable year as an S corporation or (2) the filing of the corporation's S corporation election; or
- The taxpayer can show non-tax-avoidance reasons such as a clear and substantial relationship between the contributed property and the conduct of the corporation's current or future business enterprises.

TAMRA in effect ratifies this provision by authorizing whatever regulations are necessary to carry out the purposes of the built-in gains tax. (Section 1374(e))

Q. 8:30 How does the built-in gains tax apply to property the corporation has received in a tax-free transaction?

Taxpayers might be tempted to use the tax-free reorganization and carryover basis provisions of the Code to attempt to circumvent the built-in gains tax. Therefore, in TAMRA, Congress effectively endorsed a preexisting IRS position concerning antiabuse rules. (*Ann. 86-128*, 1986-51 IRB 22) The application of the transitional rule discussed at Questions 8:31–8:32 to these transactions is not clear and presumably will be spelled out in forthcoming regulations. In the meantime, in light of the general thrust of IRS rulings and announcements in the area, it is probably safe to assume that the transitional relief discussed at Question 8:32 will be available to the extent it is available to the transferor.

S Corporation–C Corporation Carryover Basis Transactions: When an S corporation disposes of appreciated property received from a C corporation or former C corporation in a transferred-basis transaction such as a tax-free merger of a C corporation into an S corporation, the disposition will be subject to built-in gains tax. In other words, the acquisition of the property will be treated as a conversion to S corporation status with respect to the assets so transferred, regardless of whether the transferee is otherwise subject to the built-in gains tax. With respect to this property, net unrealized gain (see Question 8:28) will be measured at the time of receipt, and the 10-year recognition period during which the built-in gains tax can apply (see Question 8:26) will begin on the date the property is received. (Section 1374(d)(8), added by TAMRA)

■ **Example.** X is a C corporation. Y has been an S corporation during its entire corporate existence and therefore is not subject to the built-in gains tax. On July 1, 1990, X merges into Y in a statutory merger exempt from tax under Section 361. X's assets, in which X has a net unrealized gain of $10 million, are transferred to Y. Y takes X's net unrealized gain with regard to these assets, as well as the built-in gain (or loss) with regard to each of them, as of July 1, 1990. The recognition period will run through June 30, 2000.

S Corporation–S Corporation Carryover Basis Transactions: When an S corporation already subject to the built-in gains tax transfers property in a tax-free reorganization with another S corporation, the built-in gains tax will again apply to the transferee with regard to the assets received—the transferee S corporation again is treated as converting to S corporation status as of the date of the transfer with regard to the assets involved. In this case, however, the recognition period with regard to the assets is the recognition period remaining in the hands of the transferor. (Section 1374(d)(6))

■ **Example.** Assume the same facts as above, except that X is an S corporation subject to the built-in gains tax and its recognition period began January 1, 1989. Y's net unrealized built-in gain in the assets transferred from X will still be $10 million, but the recognition period will run through December 31, 1999, only.

Carryover-Basis Transactions: When an S corporation subject to the built-in gains tax receives property exchanged in a tax-free carryover-basis transaction (such as a like-kind exchange (Section 1031) or an involuntary conversion (Section 1033)), the net unrealized built-in gain inherent in assets transferred by the corporation subject to the built-in gains tax will be preserved in the assets received by that corporation. The rules in this situation are basically the same as those in a merger involving two S corporations—the recognition period for the property transferred out by the corporation subject to the tax carries over to the property received, as does the built-in gain inherent in the property. Thus the corporation's net unrealized built-in gain is unchanged.

Q. 8:31 Are gains subject to tax as excess passive investment income also subject to tax as built-in gains?

Dispositions of property that generate built-in gains may also generate the type of passive investment income subject to the tax on excess passive investment income. However, recognized built-in gains and loss are not taken into account in calculating passive investment income. (See Question 8:10.)

This rule, adopted by TAMRA, reverses the former rule that any portion of built-in gain subject to the tax on passive investment income would not be subject to the built-in gains tax. (Former Section 1375(c)(2))

Q. 8:32 What transitional relief is provided from the built-in gains tax?

Transitional rules under TRA '86 provide that the built-in gains tax will not fully apply to qualified small corporations (see Question 8:33) that filed S corporation elections before January 1, 1989. (TRA '86, Section 633(d)(8), as amended by TAMRA)

However, this transitional relief is not total. It does not apply to items of ordinary income and short-term capital gain. In other words, relief from the built-in gains tax will apply only to net long-term capital gains for corporations making elections during this transitional period. (TRA '86, Section 633(d)(2))

However, to the extent that the long-term capital gains are not subject to the built-in gains tax, they may still be subject to the capital gains tax. (See Questions 8:15–8:20.)

Additionally, relief from the built-in gains tax on long-term capital gains may be only partial—depending on the corporation's value. (See Question 8:33.)

Q. 8:33 Which corporations are eligible for this built-in gains tax transitional relief?

A corporation is a qualified corporation eligible for the transitional relief from the built-in gains tax only if it meets both of the following conditions (TRA '86, Sections 633(d)(5) and 633(d)(6), as amended by TAMRA):

1. More than 50% of its stock is owned by 10 or fewer individuals, estates, or trusts (for S elections made on or after March 31, 1988, these owners must be a "qualified group" that, with limited tacking or look-through exceptions for estates and trusts, must have held the stock for five years or, if less, the entire period of the corporation's existence); and
2. Its value, as measured by the value of its stock on August 1, 1986, or on the date a valid S corporation election is made (whichever value is higher), does not exceed $10 million.

To the extent the corporation's value exceeds $5 million, relief will be phased out at the rate of 1% for each $50,000 in value.

Family members (within the meaning of Section 318(a)) are treated as one individual.

Investment Tax Credit Recapture

Q. 8:34 When will the S corporation itself be liable for investment tax credit recapture?

Even though an S corporation is generally not subject to corporate income tax, and even though the investment tax credit has been repealed, an S corporation that was formerly a C corporation may continue to remain subject to recapture of the investment tax credit.

Investment credit recapture is required if a taxpayer disposes of property on which the credit has been claimed before the end of one full year after the period—generally three years or five years—on which the credit is based. In other words, part of the credit on three-year property must be recaptured if a disposition occurs within four years of the date it was placed in service; for five-year property, recapture is required if a disposition occurs within six years. A percentage, determined by the period that the property remained in service, of the credit amount that actually reduced income taxes must be paid as income tax. (Section 47)

If a corporation acquired an asset while it was a C corporation, used the investment tax credit to reduce corporate income taxes, and then elected S corporation status, disposition of the asset triggers a corporate-level recapture tax. (Section 1371(d)(2))

However, no corporate-level tax results from the disposition of assets acquired after an S corporation election became effective. The corporation's shareholders will incur any liability. (Other questions relating to investment credit for S corporations are discussed at Questions 9:6–9:7.)

Q. 8:35 Will the election (or the termination) of S corporation status cause investment tax credit recapture?

No, the election of S corporation status is not treated as a disposition of assets that causes investment credit recapture. It is treated as a mere change in the form of conducting business. (Section 1371(d)(1)) Neither will the termination of S corporation status have any effect upon investment credit recapture. (Reg. §1.47-4(d))

LIFO Recapture

Q. 8:36 Will the S corporation election itself ever trigger a corporate-level tax?

Yes, it may. Under the Revenue Act of 1987, a C corporation that uses the LIFO method for its last taxable year before an S corporation election becomes effective must "recapture" a LIFO amount and include it in income for the last C corporation taxable year. (Section 1363(d))

The LIFO recapture provision applies to S corporation elections made after December 17, 1987. In the case of elections made after December 17, 1987, and before January 1, 1989, the provision will not apply if the corporation's board of directors adopted a resolution to make an S corporation election by December 17, 1987, or if a ruling request with respect to the business was filed with IRS on or before December 17, 1987, expressing an intention to make such an election. The transitional rule applies to a ruling request concerning eligibility for S corporation status that was filed on or before December 17, 1987, by the corporation itself or by a former parent corporation that was subsequently merged into the S corporation.

Q. 8:37 What is the LIFO recapture amount?

The LIFO recapture amount is the amount by which the inventory's FIFO value exceeds its LIFO value as of the close of the last C corporation taxable year. Appropriate adjustments to the basis of inventory are made to take into account the amount included in gross income.

Q. 8:38 How is the total LIFO recapture tax computed?

The tax is computed by comparing (1) the amount due for the final C corporation year (as calculated on Schedule J to Form 1120), including the LIFO recapture amount (see Question 8:36); and (2) the amount due for the final C corporation year, excluding the LIFO recapture amount. The excess of the first amount over the second is the LIFO recapture tax liability, which is payable over a four-year period. (See Question 8:39; see also *Ann. 88-60*, 1988-15 IRB 47.)

Note that in making these comparative calculations, items such as any foreign tax credit may have to be recalculated.

Q. 8:39 When is the LIFO recapture tax payable? How is it reported?

The tax attributable to the inclusion of the LIFO recapture amount in the income of the corporation is payable in four equal installments. The first installment is to be paid on the due date for the last C corporation year return (including extension). The other installments are due on the respective due dates of the corporation's returns for the three succeeding taxable years. No interest is payable on these installments if they are paid on time.

To report the amount for the last C corporation year, the corporation shows (1) the tax calculation, including the entire LIFO recapture amount, on Schedule J of Form 1120 and (2) the tax calculation, excluding the LIFO recapture amount, on a worksheet in Schedule J format. As the total of the amount actually shown on Schedule J will include all additional tax due on LIFO recapture, the three-quarters of the LIFO tax that is deferred should be subtracted before tax due is entered on the final line of Schedule J, and the deferral amount should be noted on the dotted line preceding the entry: "Section 1363(d) deferral—$ (amount)." (See *Ann. 88-60*, 1988-15 IRB 47 and the Instructions to Forms 1120 and 1120-A.)

For the three subsequent years, the tax is to be included in the total tax reported on the Form 1120S). To the left of the total, the amount and "LIFO tax" are to be written. (See instructions to Form 1120S)

The remaining three deferral installments must be paid by the due dates of the S corporation returns of the three succeeding taxable years. (The Form 1120S instructions for these years will describe how to report these amounts.)

Chapter 9

Taxation of S Corporation Shareholders—Basic Pass-Through and Allocation Principles

Pass-Through of Income, Losses, and Other Items

Q. 9:1 How do income, losses, and other specific items affecting shareholder tax liability pass through to the shareholders of an S corporation?

The shareholders treat all of these items as if they received them directly. In other words, the S corporation is treated as a mere conduit. Its shareholders are treated in a manner similar to the way that partners in a partnership are treated. All items retain their special tax significance. (Sections 1366(a) and 1366(b).)

Q. 9:2 When do these items pass through to shareholders?

Each shareholder generally reports his or her share of the S corporation's income, loss, deductions, and credits in his or her taxable year in which the taxable year of the S corporation ends. (Section 1366(a)) A special rule covers shareholders who die before the end of the corporation's taxable year. (See Question 9:13.)

Currently, allowability of deductions and losses may also be limited by specific statutory provisions (see Question 9:15), by the taxpayer's basis or investment in the corporation (see Questions 10:1–10:2 and Chapter 11), by the at-risk rules (see Questions 10:3–10:9), and by the passive activity loss rules (see Questions 10:10–10:50).

Q. 9:3 Does the characterization of items passing through to shareholders of an S corporation ever change in the process?

No, the character of all items passed through to the shareholders of an S corporation is determined just as if such items were realized by the shareholders directly from the source from which the corporation realized them. (Section 1366(b)) The nature of the pass-through item (e.g., the type of gain) is usually determined without regard to the shareholder's activities.

Q. 9:4 Is passed-through S corporation income simply reported as an aggregate on the shareholder's tax return?

No, it is not. Various items arise at the corporate level but may affect the tax liability of a shareholder because of their character. They must be separately stated and passed through to the shareholders. Some of the items that must be separately stated are described below.

Capital Gains and Losses: Long-term and short-term capital gains and losses pass through as separate items of income or loss. These gains are not offset by losses at the corporate level.

Section 1231 Gains and Losses: Gains and losses that result from the sale or exchange of property used in the S corporation's trade or business are passed through separately and are then aggregated by each shareholder with his or her other gains or losses. (These Section 1231 gains and losses are not aggregated with capital gains at the corporate level and then passed through to the shareholders as capital gains.)

Charitable Contributions: The limit on corporate charitable contributions (10% of taxable income) does not apply to contributions made by an S corporation. Instead, the contributions pass through to the shareholders, who add them to their own contributions, which are then subject to the 50% or 30% limitations that apply to individuals. (See Section 170.)

Tax-Exempt Interest: Tax-exempt interest passes through to the shareholders and increases their bases in their S corporation stock. (Section 1367(a)(1)(A)) (See Question 11:6.) Subsequent corporate distributions will not result in the taxation of tax-exempt income, but if the corporation has earnings and profits (E&P), the taxable E&P must be distributed before the tax-exempt basis can be distributed. (See Question 12:17.)

Tax Credits: Tax credit items pass through to shareholders under the general per-share, per-day rule that applies to all other pass-through items. (Section 1366(a)(1)(A))

Foreign Taxes: Foreign taxes paid by an S corporation pass through to the shareholders, who may treat such taxes as credits or deductions (subject to the applicable limitations). Rules concerning the source of income and the amount of creditable taxes apply at the shareholder level.

Depletion: For purposes of the oil and gas depletion allowances, S corporations pass through the depletion allowance in the same manner that partnerships do—i.e., the percentage or cost depletion allowance is computed separately by each shareholder.

Travel and Entertainment Expenses: Travel and entertainment expenses incurred (or reimbursed to employees) by the corporation are not generally separately stated items. However, there is a complication because of the Tax Reform Act of 1986 (TRA '86) changes to the travel and entertainment rules. Effective for taxable years beginning after December 31, 1986, meal and entertainment expense deductions are subject to an 80% limitation on deductions. (Section 274(n)) When the 80% limitation is applied to tickets, it must be applied only to face value (plus, IRS says, agents' commissions), and not to any premiums such as scalpers' fees, which are totally nondeductible. Subject to a three-year phase-in, the deduction for luxury skybox rentals is limited to 80% of the face value of the highest priced regular seats. IRS will apply the rules only to expenses paid or incurred by the corporation after December 31, 1986. As a result, *fiscal*-year S corporations that have taxable years beginning before January 1, 1987, and ending within shareholders' taxable years beginning on or after January 1, 1987, must separately state travel and entertainment expenses affected by these rules. (See Reg. §1.1366-2.)

Miscellaneous Itemized Deductions: TRA '86 limited the miscellaneous itemized deductions of individuals, trusts, and estates to the amount that exceeds 2% of adjusted gross income. Expenses so limited include (Section 67; Temp. Reg. §1.67-1T(a)):

- *Unreimbursed* employee business expenses;
- Expenses for the production or collection of income that are deductible only under Section 212;
- Expenses related to tax determinations and the like that are deductible only under Section 212; and
- "Hobby losses" deductible only under Section 183.

Q. 9:4

The 2% limitation applies at the *shareholder* level—taking into account all miscellaneous deductions from all sources—in *shareholder* taxable years beginning after December 31, 1986. Thus, each such item that passes through must be separately stated. (Temp. Reg. §1.67-2T(b)(1))

If expenses relate to both a trade-or-business activity and the production of income or the like, they must be allocated on a reasonable basis. (Temp. Reg. §1.67-1T(c)) Apparently, although the only statement is an inference in an example, the characterization and allocation of S corporation expenses is made at the corporate level.

■ **Example.** An S corporation incurs $1,000 in expenses to which Section 212 applies. A pro rata share of $200 of these expenses passes through to shareholder A, an individual. A may deduct his miscellaneous itemized deductions, including his $200 share of S's Section 212 expenses, to the extent that the total amount exceeds 2% of his adjusted gross income.

Passive Activity Loss Rule Items: The shareholder must also separately state certain items of deduction, loss, and credit that are treated under the passive activity loss rules. (See also Questions 10:36–10:38.)

Q. 9:5 Are any elections concerning the items that are passed through made by shareholders?

Generally, any elections regarding the S corporation's income are made by the corporation. (See Question 8:8.) However, the shareholder makes (Section 1363(c)(2); Prop. Reg. §1.1363-1(c)):

1. Elections under Section 617, concerning predevelopment mining expenditures and recapture thereof; and
2. Elections under Section 901, to claim a deduction or a credit for foreign taxes.

Q. 9:6 How is the pass-through affected by dispositions of property on which the S corporation has claimed the investment tax credit?

When an S corporation disposes of property on which it has claimed an investment tax credit prior to the end of the investment tax credit term, there will be a recapture of the investment tax credit.

If the investment credit property was acquired and the credit used while the corporation was a C corporation, the corporation itself will pay the recapture tax. (Section 1371(d)(2)) (See Question 8:34.) This is an exception to the general rule that S corporations do not pay taxes.

However, if the corporation acquired the property while the S corporation election was in effect (and the credit has passed through to the shareholders), the shareholders will be deemed to have disposed of the property, and they will be subject to the investment tax credit recapture. (Reg. §1.47-4(a))

Effect of S Corporation Election or Termination: The election of S corporation status will not be treated as a disposition of assets that will cause investment credit recapture. It will be treated as a mere change in the form of conducting business. (Section 1371(d)(1)) Neither will the termination of S corporation status have any effect on investment credit recapture. (Reg. §1.47-4(d))

Changes in Ownership

Q. 9:7 Do changes in ownership of S corporation stock cause recapture of the investment tax credit?

When the shareholder of an S corporation disposes of a substantial portion of his or her stock in the S corporation, the shareholder is deemed to be disposing of a portion of the investment credit property. (Reg. §1.47-4(a)(2); *Rainier* (6th Cir. 1989); *Charbonnet*, 455 F.2d 1195 (5th Cir. 1972)) Recapture occurs when the shareholder's proportionate stock interest is reduced below 66⅔%. Once such a reduction has been made, no additional recapture of investment credit will occur because of a disposition of S corporation stock until the proportionate stock interest goes below 33⅓%. For purposes of determining these percentages of ownership, both indirect and direct ownership are counted, but the burden is on the taxpayer to prove indirect ownership.

Q. 9:8 When S corporation stock changes hands, how are these pass-through items generally allocated among the shareholders?

The general rule is that each shareholder's pro rata share of all items of income, deductions, credits, and the like for the corporation's taxable year is calculated as follows (Section 1377(a)(1)):

1. First allocate a proportion of all such items to each day of the taxable year; and
2. Then divide the daily amount by the number of shares outstanding on each day.

The shareholder then multiplies this result:

1. First by the number of shares he or she holds; and
2. Then by the number of days during the year that he or she held the shares.

■ **Example.** On January 1, 1989, an S corporation (a calendar-year corporation) is owned by two shareholders, Able and Baker. Able owns 80 shares, and Baker owns 20 shares. On July 1, 1989, Baker sells his 20 shares to Charlie. The corporation has taxable profit of $365,000 for 1989. The computations are as follows:

Profit per day = $365,000 ÷ 365 days = $1,000 per day
Profit per share per day = $1,000 per day ÷ 100 shares
= $10 per share per day

	Number of Shares	Number of Days	Per Share Daily Profit	Allocation
Able	80	365	$10	$292,000
Baker	20	181	$10	36,200
Charlie	20	184	$10	36,800
Total				$365,000

In actuality, because S corporation items maintain their character as they pass through (see Question 9:1), this type of calculation must be made for each type of income—for example, long-term capital gains, ordinary income, and Section 1231 income from the sale or exchange of business and income-producing assets—as well as each type of loss and deduction—for example, Section 1231 losses, ordinary losses, and charitable contribution deductions.

Q. 9:9 Must shareholders always use this pro rata method of allocating S corporation items?

When one or more shareholders terminate all interests in the corporation, the shareholders may—instead of prorating income, loss, and all

Pass-Through and Allocation Principles   Q. 9:11

other items on a purely mathematical daily basis (see Question 9:8)—want to use the corporation's books to determine which items should be allocated to which shareholders. The corporation may elect an alternative method of allocation for all items, but only with consent of *all* persons who were shareholders during the taxable year. (Section 1377(a)(2)) (Note that this differs from the consent requirement, described at Question 4:22, which applies if the election is revoked or terminated during a year.)

Q. 9:10 What is the alternative allocation method that may be used if a shareholder terminates his or her interest in the S corporation?

The alternative method is applied as if the taxable year consisted of two taxable years—the first of which ended on the date of the termination of the shareholder's interest. Income, expenses, credits, and the like are allocated to each portion of the year, based on when they actually occurred according to the corporation's books and records. (Section 1377(a)(2)) For this purpose, books and records include work papers.

Q. 9:11 How much of a difference does the method of allocating income, deductions, and the like make?

When the identity of S corporation shareholders changes in the middle of the year, the corporation may use either the mathematical pro rata daily method (see Question 9:8) or the alternative actual method (see Question 9:10) to decide which S corporation items each shareholder reports. The difference between the two methods depends on whether the items of income, loss, deduction, and the like have occurred more or less evenly throughout the year, or primarily in one particular part of the year. The following example shows how dramatically different the results of the pro rata daily method and the alternative actual method can be in a particular case, and shows the type of analysis that must be applied in determining which method to use (in practice, of course, the calculations must be made separately for each separately characterized item).

> ■ **Example.** At the beginning of its taxable year, an S corporation is owned by two shareholders, A and B. A owns 80%, and B owns 20%. Exactly at the midpoint of the taxable year, B sells all of her shares

to C. The corporation has a $100,000 profit for the taxable year, of which $75,000 is earned during the first half of the year and $25,000 is earned during the second half of the year. The results of the two allocation methods are:

Shareholder	Pro Rata Daily Method	Alternative (Actual) Method
A	$ 80,000	$ 80,000
B	10,000	15,000
C	10,000	5,000
Total	$100,000	$100,000

Q. 9:12 How does the S corporation make the election to use the alternative (actual) method of calculating pass-through allocations?

The S corporation makes the election by filing a statement with its return for the taxable year, signed by a person authorized to sign the tax return. The statement must (Temp. Reg. §18.1377-1T):

1. Say that the corporation elects under Section 1377(a)(2) to have the rules provided in Section 1377(a)(1) applied as if the taxable year consisted of two taxable years;

2. Set forth the fact that the sale of a shareholder's stock is the reason for treating the year as if it had terminated, and state the date of sale; and

3. Have attached to it a statement of consent—signed by *each person who was a shareholder of the corporation at any time during the taxable year*—indicating that each shareholder consents to the election to treat the year as if it consisted of two taxable years.

Q. 9:13 Do these allocation rules apply if a shareholder dies during the S corporation's taxable year?

Under the general rule, the shareholders report their shares of S corporation items in their taxable years in which the taxable year of the S corporation ends. (See Question 9:2.) But when a shareholder dies before the end of the corporation's taxable year, the deceased shareholder's shares of all S corporation items are included in his or her final income tax return. (Section 1366(a)(1)) Any S corporation items with respect to the portion of the corporation's taxable year after the shareholder's death are reported on the income tax return of the shareholder's estate or the income tax return of whoever acquires the stock on his or her death. These items may be allocated between the two portions of the year, using either the pro rata daily method (see Question 9:8) or the alternative (actual) method (see Question 9:10).

Other Concerns

Q. 9:14 Can allocated amounts be affected if members of shareholders' families perform services for, or lend money to, an S corporation?

Allocations can be affected if there is inadequate consideration. IRS has the authority to make adjustments in the S corporation items taken into account by shareholders and members of their families, in order to reflect the value of services or capital furnished by family members. (Section 1366(e)) Family members include (Section 704(e)(3)):

- A spouse;
- Ancestors;
- Lineal descendants; and
- Any trusts for the primary benefit of the foregoing persons.

Were it not for this authority, taxpayers could supply services at no charge in order to inflate the income of an S corporation that was owned by family members in lower income tax brackets.

Q. 9:15 Is the shareholder limited in the amounts of allocated deductions he or she can claim?

The following limitations will apply at both the corporate and the shareholder levels, similar to treatment of partnerships (where the limitations apply at the partnership level and the partner level):

- The dollar limitations in Section 179(b)(1) relating to the expensing of certain depreciable business assets. (Section 179(d)(8))
- The $10,000 limitation of the amortization of reforestation expenses. (Section 194(b)(2)(B))

The rule for excluding income from the discharge of indebtedness under Section 108 is treated in a manner different from the partnership rule. In the case of a partnership, the limitations of Sections 108(a), 108(b), and 108(c) are applied at the partner level. In the case of an S corporation, these sections are applied at the corporate level.

There are also certain limitations on losses and deductions S corporation shareholders may claim based on their investment in the S corporation. (See Questions 10:1–10:2 and Chapter 11.) The at-risk and passive activity loss rules may limit the losses that some shareholders can claim. (See Question 10:3–10:50.)

Chapter 10

Taxation of S Corporation Shareholders—Limitations on Losses

Basis Limitations

Q. 10:1 How does basis limit losses and deductions passing through to S corporation shareholders?

Shareholders may deduct S corporation losses and deductions passing through to them in the year reportable by the corporation only to the extent that they have sufficient basis in their S corporation stock and/or basis in loans made by them to the S corporation. (Section 1366(d)) Shareholders do not have basis for loans to the corporation that they have guaranteed unless they actually make payments on the guaranteed amounts. (See Chapter 11, particularly Questions 11:4–11:10, for the manner of calculating basis.)

Impact on Worthless Stock and Worthless Debt Deductions: Shareholders are entitled to deductions for worthless S corporation stock and worthless corporate indebtedness to them. (Sections 165(g) and 166(d)) However, the pass-through provisions (and the basis adjustments of Section 1367; see Questions 11:5–11:9) apply before these deductions are taken. (Section 1367(b)(3)) Thus, S corporation losses and deductions pass through first—even if the stock or debt becomes worthless before the pass-through losses and deductions are incurred.

This rule is generally advantageous to the shareholders, because worthless stock and debt generally generate capital losses, for which only limited deductibility is available.

Responsibilities of a Tax Return Preparer: At least one court has imposed a return preparer penalty for a tax return preparer's failure to take the basis limitations into account when deducting S corporation losses. Meyer Papermaster had prepared both an S corporation return and the individual shareholder's tax return. The corporation showed a loss, and Papermaster deducted the entire loss on the shareholder's return even though it exceeded the shareholder's basis in the S corporation stock. A district court in Wisconsin held that this amounted to disregard of the express limitations on the loss deductions passing through to shareholders and imposed a $100 tax preparer penalty on him. (*Papermaster* (E.D. Wis. 1980))

Q. 10:2 What happens to losses that are disallowed because of the basis limitation?

Shareholders who lack sufficient basis to deduct their full shares of the S corporation's deductions and losses in the year in which the losses and deductions are incurred may be able to deduct their previously nondeductible shares of losses and deductions in subsequent taxable years. Losses and deductions that have previously been disallowed because of inadequate basis are treated as having been incurred in the first subsequent year in which such basis does exist. (Section 1366(d)(2))

Impact of Termination: If the S corporation election is terminated, the previously disallowed losses and deductions may still be deducted during a post-termination transition period. (Section 1366(d)(3)) But the basis must have been restored prior to the end of the post-termination transition period in order to be deductible. (See Questions 12:23–12:25 for a discussion of the post-termination transition period.)

At-Risk Rules

Q. 10:3 What are the "at-risk" rules, and how do they differ from the basis limitation?

The at-risk rules (Section 465) limit the net losses that S corporation shareholders, among others, may deduct for an activity to the amounts at risk. The amount deemed at risk is generally the sum of:

1. Cash contributions to the activity; and
2. Borrowed amounts used in the activity for which the taxpayer is personally liable (that is, for which the lender has "recourse" against the taxpayer), provided the lender has no interest in the activity other than as a creditor, or to the extent permitted by regulations.

Special rules exist with regard to arrangements under which guarantees, stop-loss agreements, and the like protect the investor against loss.

Basically, the at-risk rules require that a taxpayer subject to them bear a real economic risk of loss before claiming deductions related to the activity. For example, if the taxpayer's interest in the property is acquired through a "nonrecourse" loan—one in which the lender can foreclose against the property but not move against the taxpayer or any of the taxpayer's other assets—the taxpayer does not have such a risk. Thus, in function, the at-risk rules are similar to the basis limitation rules. (See Questions 10:1–10:2.) This similarity may be why little attention has been paid to them in the S corporation context, even though they have applied since 1979 to all activities engaged in by a taxpayer subject to the rules to carry on a trade or business or produce income. (Section 465(c)(3)(A)) As far as individual taxpayers (including S corporation shareholders) were concerned, the only significant exception was the exclusion for the activity of holding real estate. (Former Section 465(c)(3)(D), repealed by the Tax Reform Act of 1986 (TRA '86))

However, although many S corporation activities may be aggregated for purposes of meeting these requirements—leaving them virtually indistinguishable from the basis limitation rules of Section 1366(d)—certain activities may not be aggregated for at-risk rule purposes. (See Questions 10:4–10:5.)

Level at Which the Rules Apply: The at-risk rules apply only at the shareholder level, which has been true since the Subchapter S Revision Act of 1982, despite the fact that IRS has never withdrawn proposed regulations referring to old corporate-level at-risk requirements. (See Prop. Reg. §1.465-10.)

Priority Rules: The at-risk rules apply *after* the basis limitations and *before* the passive activity loss rules. (Temp. Reg. §1.469-2T(d)(6); *Uri*,

Q. 10:3 The S Corporation Answer Book

TC Memo 1989-58) In other words, losses are not tested under the at-risk rules until the shareholder has sufficient basis to deduct them. (See further discussion at Question 10:36.)

Q. 10:4 When can S corporation activities be aggregated for purposes of the at-risk rules?

S corporation shareholders have to be personally at risk to claim S corporation losses and credits. The general rule is that each activity must be treated separately, and an appropriate portion of basis allocated to each activity, unless certain aggregation requirements are met.

Aggregation of all activities constituting a trade or business is permitted, and income from one activity may be used to offset a loss from another in arriving at a net loss under the at-risk rules, if (Section 465(c)(3)(B)):

1. The shareholders actively participate in management; or
2. At least 65% of losses are allocated to shareholders who actively participate in management.

Planning Pointer. Note that there is a two-pronged test. All shareholders may aggregate if the 65% test is satisfied. Even if it is not satisfied, an individual shareholder may still aggregate if he or she actively participates in management. Both these tests should be applied to calculate loss deductions. They should be applied before year end to determine whether the shareholder should increase equity or make additional loans to the corporation to increase his or her basis for losses.

Q. 10:5 What activities constitute a trade or business for at-risk rule purposes?

The listing of activities covered by the at-risk rules is divided into two parts. The first, Section 465(c)(1), designates the following five specific activities: (1) leasing of Section 1245 personal property, (2) film and videotape ventures, (3) farming, (4) oil and gas ventures, and (5) geothermal ventures. The second, Section 465(c)(3), adds the category of all other activities constituting a trade or business or designed for the production of income. Clearly, the shareholder may aggregate losses from enterprises falling into this catchall Section 465(c)(3) category if one of the participation standards discussed above is met. But what about the activities listed in Section 465(c)(1)?

The statute specifically provides that leasing activities may be aggregated for equipment placed in service during one tax year. A lease not entered into in the same year, and each activity in the other four designated categories, is to be treated as a separate activity unless IRS provides to the contrary in regulations. (Sections 465(c)(2)(A) and 465(c)(2)(B)(ii))

In temporary regulations originally designed for 1984 only, but that have been extended every year since (see, for example, *Ann. 88-58*, 1988-15 IRB 46), IRS has provided that in the case of film and videotape, farming, oil and gas, and geothermal activities, the shareholder may aggregate all corporate ventures of the same type. For example, two farms may be aggregated, and two film and/or videotape distribution ventures may be aggregated. Two ventures of different types may be aggregated if one of the active participation standards is met. (Temp. Reg. §1.465-1T) Additional limitations may be imposed by amendment of the temporary regulations.

However, Section 1245 leasing is not mentioned in the temporary regulations. Thus it appears that the more restrictive statutory standard applies, and leases may not be aggregated except insofar as property is placed in service in the same year. Nor does it appear that leasing may be aggregated with other activities. The statutory rule about participation applies only to activities brought under the at-risk rules by virtue of Section 465(c)(3) as "other activities" and to activities to which IRS chooses to extend the rule by regulation. (Sections 465(c)(3)(B) and 465(c)(3)(C)) Leasing is in neither category.

Q. 10:6 How and when is the amount at risk calculated?

The shareholder's amount at risk is the sum of: (1) the cash and property actually contributed to the activity, (2) borrowed funds for which the shareholder is actually liable, and (3) property, other than assets of the S corporation, pledged by the shareholder as security for the debt. (Section 465(c)(1); Prop. Reg. §1.465-10(c)) Basically, these rules are the same as those used to determine basis under Section 1366(d): If a shareholder borrows money from a third party and invests it in the S corporation, his or her basis includes the investment made with the borrowed

Q. 10:6 The S Corporation Answer Book

money. Conversely, if the corporation borrows directly, the shareholder's basis is not increased—even if the shareholder personally guarantees the loan. (See Questions 11:13–11:14.) However, the shareholder may have to calculate separate amounts at risk for separate corporate activities.

Nonrecourse Debt: In calculating the amount that a shareholder has at risk, only recourse debt—that is, an obligation that the shareholder is personally liable to repay or that is secured by the shareholder's pledge of property other than assets of the corporation—is included. Nonrecourse debt—borrowed funds that the shareholder is not obligated to repay—is not considered an amount at risk.

Other Excluded Debt: Also excluded from the amount at risk are funds borrowed from a person, or any related person within the meaning of Sections 267(b) and 707(b), who has an interest (other than as a creditor) in the corporation. (Section 465(b)(3))

However, an amount borrowed from a person related to the *shareholder* whose amount at risk is being calculated will not be excluded (unless that person also has an interest in the activity).

Related persons are spouses, parents, grandparents, children, grandchildren, and siblings. Partnerships in which the shareholder has a more-than-10% interest and corporations in which the shareholder holds more than 10% of the stock are also related persons.

In addition, the shareholder is not at risk to the extent that he or she is protected from economic loss by insurance, guarantees, or stop-loss agreements. (Section 465(b)(4))

Q. 10:7 What happens to losses disallowed under the at-risk rules?

Losses that are disallowed are carried over indefinitely. The unused loss may be deducted in the next succeeding year in which the at-risk rules are satisfied. (See Section 465(a)(2).)

Q. 10:8 Do loss deductions decrease the amount at risk?

The amount a shareholder has at risk is reduced by the portion of the loss that is deductible. (Section 465(b)(5)) Withdrawals—for example, distributions—reduce the amount at risk. To the extent that the shareholder reports income from the activity, the amount at risk is increased.

Q. 10:9 What happens if a shareholder has a negative amount at risk?

The amount at risk *can* be reduced below zero, which might occur if a recourse loan were converted into a nonrecourse loan. A distribution might also reduce the amount at risk below zero. (See Prop. Reg. §1.465-3.)

To the extent that the amount at risk falls below zero, the shareholder must recapture the negative amount and report it as income. The amount of recapture income is the extent by which the negative amount exceeds the excess of losses previously allowed over losses previously recaptured. The recapture income is treated as a deduction attributable to the activity in the following year. The shareholder will not, however, benefit from the deduction unless the shareholder is again at risk. (Section 465(e))

■ **Example.** A shareholder is at risk for $100. During the year, she receives a distribution of $120. Her amount at risk is reduced to a *negative* figure ($-$$20). Assuming she has previously deducted losses from the corporation of $20 or more, she will have to report the $20 as income. The $20 will be deductible the following year, subject to the at-risk limits. If, in a subsequent year, her allocable share of corporate loss is $40, she will not be able to deduct the entire loss unless she has increased her amount at risk by $60.

Passive Activity Loss (PAL) Rules—Overview

Q. 10:10 How do the PAL rules limit a shareholder's deductions?

Effective for taxable years beginning in 1987, the passive activity loss (PAL) rules restrict the ability of S corporation shareholders—as individuals, estates, and trusts—to claim losses and credits from passive trade-or-business activities. (Section 469(a)) These rules apply to all S corporation items passed through to the shareholders. They apply to deductions (but not credits) for alternative minimum tax (AMT) purposes as well as for regular tax purposes, except to the extent that the taxpayer is insolvent. (Sections 58(b) and 58(c)(1)) However, for regular tax but not for AMT purposes, the impact of the rules on "preenactment" interests acquired on or before October 22, 1986, is phased in over a five-year period, becoming fully effective in 1991. (Sections 469(m)(3) and 58(b)(3)) (See Questions 10:50–10:51.)

In general, losses and credits from a business *activity* (not a particular investment) (see Questions 10:12–10:22) in which the taxpayer does not "materially participate" for the taxable year in question are not allowed to shelter other income—including salary, active business income, and "portfolio" income such as dividends, interest, royalties, and nonbusiness capital gains. These losses and credits are carried forward indefinitely until offsetting passive income exists or until, in the case of losses, there is a fully taxable disposition of the entire interest in the activity in which they arose. (See Question 10:48.)

Rental activities are given special treatment; they are viewed as inherently passive. However, special rules apply to rental real estate activities in which the taxpayer "actively participates" for a particular taxable year. (See Questions 10:41–10:42.)

Planning Pointer. Congress did not intend that taxpayers be able to circumvent the operation of the PAL rules by selecting the form in which they do business. Therefore, the rules extend to personal service corporations in which owner-employees directly or indirectly own 10% or more of the corporation's stock. (Section 469(a)) Other closely held C corporations that are subject to the at-risk rules may not use losses or credits from passive activities to offset portfolio income (as defined in Question 10:29).

Q. 10:11 To what types of activities do the PAL rules apply?

The PAL rules apply to activities involving the conduct of a trade or business by a taxpayer (such as an S corporation shareholder) subject to the rules. The Code broadly defines the term "trade or business" as applying to investments, insofar as provided in regulations, as well as to trades or businesses in the traditional sense. (Sections 469(c)(1) and 469(c)(6)) The temporary regulations, however, limit covered activities to (Temp. Reg. §1.469-1T(e)):

1. Those considered trades or businesses for purposes of Section 162;
2. Those for which research and experimentation expenses can be deducted under Section 174; and
3. Rentals of tangible property.

The temporary regulations generally use the term "trade-or-business" to refer to the first two types of endeavors. The activities that encompass them are active or passive, depending upon whether or not the taxpayer materially participates. (Temp. Reg. §1.469-1T(e)(1)(i))

Rentals, which are inherently passive, are generally called "rentals." Under the temporary regulations, an activity is a "trade-or-business activity" only if it (1) is not a rental activity and (2) involves the conduct of business or rental operations that are not treated as incidental to an activity of holding property for investment. (Temp. Reg. §1.469-1T(e)(2)) (The nature of a rental activity is discussed more thoroughly at Questions 10:39–10:40.)

Planning Pointer. The definition of trade or business assumes a going concern. Start-up expenses are not subject to the PAL rules.

PAL Rules—Definition of Activity

Q. 10:12 Why is it important to define the scope of an activity?

The determination of the scope of an "activity" is important for several reasons, the most important of which are:

- The material participation test (see Question 10:25);
- The active participation test for rental real estate (see Question 10:42); and
- The disposition-of-an-entire-interest test (see Question 10:48).

All of these tests apply to the *entire activity*, rather than to specific undertakings or investments.

Q. 10:13 Is the S corporation itself a discrete activity?

The S corporation may, or may not, constitute a single activity of a shareholder. The characterization depends on the facts, and the determination may vary from shareholder to shareholder depending on each individual's facts and circumstances.

The temporary regulations provide rules for determining when those endeavors to which the passive loss and credit limitations apply—that is, trade-or-business endeavors and rental endeavors—are treated as one or more activities for purposes of the limitations. In general, these rules are divided into three groups (Temp. Reg. §1.469-4T(a)(2)):

Q. 10:13

1. The *undertaking rules* identify the business and rental operations that constitute an undertaking. (Temp. Reg. §1.469-4T(a)(3)) (See Question 10:14.)
2. The *activity* rules identify the undertaking or undertakings that constitute an activity. (Temp. Reg. §1.469-4T(a)(4)(i)) (See Questions 10:15–10:22.)
3. The *special circumstance* rules apply to the business and rental operations of consolidated groups of corporations and publicly traded partnerships. (Temp. Reg. §1.469-4T(a)(5)(i)) A group filing a consolidated return for the taxable year is treated as one taxpayer in determining its activities and those of its members. (Temp. Reg. §§1.469-4T(m)(1) and 1.469-1T(h)(2)(ii)) A taxpayer's interest in business and rental operations held through a publicly traded partnership is viewed as if the taxpayer had no interest in any other business and rental operations. (Temp. Reg. §1.469-4T(n)) This rule means business and rental operations owned through a publicly traded partnership cannot be aggregated with operations that are not owned through the partnership. (Temp. Reg. §1.469-4T(a)(5)(i))

For taxable years ending before August 10, 1989, a taxpayer's business and rental operations could be organized into activities under the above rules or under any other reasonable method. (Temp. Reg. §1.469-4T(p))

Planning Pointer. Aggregating activities makes it easier to establish material participation—for example, to satisfy the more-than-500-hours-a-year test discussed at Question 10:25. Conversely, treating activities as separate enables the owner to treat the sale of any such activity as a complete disposition.

Q. 10:14 How does the S corporation shareholder identify an undertaking?

The general rule is any trade-or-business operations—or any rental operations—are treated as part of the same undertaking if they are (1) conducted at the same location and (2) owned by the same person (i.e., legal entity). Conversely, trade-or-business—or rental—operations constitute separate undertakings if they either are conducted at different locations or are not owned by the same person. (Temp. Reg. §§1.469-4T(a)(3)(ii) and 1.469-4T(c)(2)) All operations conducted through the S corporation would meet the second, or ownership, test for a single undertaking, but they would not necessarily meet the location test. In addition, special rules (discussed below) apply to the combination of rental and nonrental operations.

Operations Not at Fixed Location or at Customer's Location: Operations that are not conducted at a fixed location, or that are conducted at the customer's place of business, are treated as part of the undertaking with which they are most closely associated. (Temp. Reg. §1.469-4T(c)(2)(iv))

Support Operations: Operations conducted at a specific location that do not relate to the business conducted at the location are treated as part of the undertaking that they support. (Temp. Reg. §§1.469-4T(a)(3)(iii), 1.469-4T(c)(2)(ii)(A)(1), and 1.469-4T(c)(2)(ii)(A)(2))

Rental and Nonrental Operations: Generally, rental operations and nonrental operations must be treated as separate undertakings. (Temp. Reg. §1.469-4T(d)(1)) However, there is an exception—the 80/20 rule.

80/20 Rule: If operations of one class (rental or nonrental) that are merely incidental to operations of the other class are conducted at the same location, no segregation (or "fragmentation") into separate rental and nonrental activities is required. This rule applies if more than 80% of the income from the combined operations is attributable to either the rental or the nonrental operations. (Temp. Reg. §1.469-4T(d)(2)) For this rule to apply, ownership of both operations must be identical. It cannot apply if, for example, shareholders use an S corporation to conduct a medical practice and, in proportion to their shareholdings, directly own the building in which the practice is housed.

Oil and Gas Wells: Special rules also apply to working interests in oil and gas wells that the statute makes active regardless of the nature of the taxpayer's participation. (See Temp. Reg. §1.469-4T(e)(1)(ii)).

Q. 10:15 How does the S corporation shareholder identify an activity?

As a starting point, each undertaking (see 10:14) constitutes a separate activity. (Temp. Reg. §1.469-4T(a)(4)(i)) However, special rules may either require or permit aggregation of two or more undertakings or the fragmentation of a single activity into two or more activities. The rules depend on whether the undertakings involve a trade or business (see Questions 10:16–10:21), professional services (see Question 10:22), or rental real estate (see Question 10:23).

Q. 10:16 When are trade-or-business undertakings aggregated in determining a shareholder's activities?

Trade-or-business undertakings—which include all undertakings other than rental undertakings, oil or gas wells treated as separate undertakings, and professional service undertakings (Temp. Reg. §1.469-4T(f)(1)(ii))—are subject to two mandatory aggregation rules.

The first aggregation rule treats trade-or-business undertakings that are both controlled by the same interests (see Question 10:17) and similar (see Question 10:18) as part of the same activity. (Temp. Reg. §1.469-4T(a)(4)(ii)(B)) These interests are treated as part of the same activity of the taxpayer for any taxable year in which the taxpayer:

1. Owns interests in each trade-or-business undertaking through the same pass-through entity (partnership, S corporation, estate or trust) (Temp. Reg. §§1.469-4T(b)(2)(i) and 1.469-4T(f)(2)(i));
2. Owns a direct or substantial indirect interest (i.e., at any time during the taxable year owns more than 10% of a pass-through entity that directly owns the undertaking) in each trade-or-business undertaking (Temp. Reg. §§1.469-4T(f)(2)(ii) and 1.469-4T(f)(3)(i)); or
3. Materially or significantly participates in the activity that would result if the trade-or-business undertakings were treated as part of the same activity (Temp. Reg. §1.469-4T(f)(2)(iii)).

Trade-or-business undertakings (including undertakings that have been aggregated because of their similarity and common control) are subject to a second aggregation rule under which undertakings that are controlled by the same interests (see Question 10:17) and constitute an integrated business (see Question 10:19) must be treated as part of the same activity. (Temp. Reg. §1.469-4T(a)(4)(ii)(C))

Thus, the aggregation rules generally do not apply to small interests passive investors hold in trade-or-business undertakings, except to the extent they hold the interests through the same pass-through entity. (Temp. Reg. §1.469-4T(a)(4)(ii)(B))

Q. 10:17 When are trade-or-business undertakings controlled by the same interests for purposes of these aggregation rules?

Control is a facts-and-circumstances test. (Temp. Reg. §1.469-4T(a)(4)(ii)(B)) In general, there is a rebuttable presumption that undertakings are controlled by the same interests if a group of five or fewer persons owns more than 50% of each of the undertakings. (Temp. Reg. §1.469-4T(j))

A shareholder's interest in an S corporation and share of any interest in a pass-through entity or undertaking held through an S corporation is determined on the basis of the shareholder's stock ownership. (A partner's ownership percentage is the greater of the capital interest or the partner's largest distributive share of any item of partnership income or gain, disregarding guaranteed payments under Section 707(c). Neither a beneficiary's interest in a trust or estate nor a share of any interest in a pass-through entity or undertaking held through a trust or estate is taken into account. (Temp. Reg. §1.469-4T(j)(3)) There is an attribution rule for related parties. (See Temp. Reg. §1.469-4T(j)(3)(iii)(A).)

Q. 10:18 When are undertakings similar for purposes of the first trade-or-business aggregation rule?

The temporary regulations provide that businesses are similar if they are engaged in similar trades or businesses or if they are vertically integrated.

Similar Trade or Business: Undertakings are similar if more than 50% (by value) of their operations are in the same line(s) of business. The definition of a line of business generally follows the Standard Industrial Classification (SIC) Codes. (See Temp. Reg. §§1.469-4T(f)(4)(i) and 1.469-4T(f)(4)(ii); *Rev. Proc. 89-38*, Sec. 4, 1989-24 IRB 75.) The aggregation into activities by line of business includes only trade-or-business undertakings and not any similar rental undertakings. (Temp. Reg. §1.469-4T(f)(1)) If, for example, an S corporation has a real estate development undertaking (which is a trade-or-business undertaking) and a real estate rental undertaking, the two undertakings are not similar for purposes of this rule. (See Temp. Reg. §1.469-4T(f)(5), Ex. 7.)

Vertical Integration: Undertakings are vertically integrated if they consist of different stages in the production or distribution of the same product or group of products. Operations conducted at different locations because of nontax business reasons (such as economies of scale or transactions among interrelated undertakings) may constitute a single activity under this rule.

Q. 10:19 When is there an integrated business for purposes of the second trade-or-business aggregation rule?

Under the second, or integrated business, aggregation rule, all the facts and circumstances are taken into account in determining whether the operations of two or more trade-or-business activities constitute a single integrated business. The following factors are generally the most significant (Temp. Reg. §1.469-4T(g)(3)):

1. Whether the operations are conducted at the same location;
2. The extent to which other persons conduct similar operations at one location;
3. Whether the operations are treated as a unit in the primary accounting records reflecting the results of the operations;
4. The extent to which other persons treat similar operations as a unit in the primary accounting records reflecting the results of the similar operations;
5. Whether the operations are owned by the same person;
6. The extent to which the operations involve products or services that are commonly provided together;
7. The extent to which the operations serve the same customers;
8. The extent to which the same personnel, facilities, or equipment are used to conduct the operations;
9. The extent to which the operations are conducted in coordination with or reliance upon each other;
10. The extent to which the conduct of any such operations is incidental to the conduct of the remainder of the operations;
11. The extent to which the operations depend on each other for their economic success; and
12. Whether the operations are conducted under the same trade name.

Q. 10:20 Can, and should, a trade-or-business activity ever be disaggregated or fragmented?

Yes, taxpayers can elect to treat a nonrental undertaking as a separate activity even if the undertaking would be treated as part of a larger activity under the aggregation rules applicable to the undertaking. (Temp. Reg. §1.469-4T(a)(4)(v))

The election applies to a taxpayer's interest in any undertaking (other than a rental real estate undertaking that would otherwise be treated as part of an activity that includes the taxpayer's interest in any other undertaking). (Temp. Reg. §1.469-4T(o)(1)) However, a shareholder of an S corporation conducting two or more trade-or-business undertakings must treat these undertakings as a single activity if the corporation does so on its return. (Temp. Reg. §1.469-4T(o)(5))

The effect of the election is to permit the taxpayer to realize a suspended PAL loss on disposition of the interest in the separate business activity (see Question 10:48) but not to require recharacterization of the taxpayer's level of participation during the period he or she holds an interest in the activity (see Questions 10:24–10:25). Once filed, the election precludes further fragmentation of the activity in a later year. (Temp. Reg. §§1.469-4T(o)(3) and 1.469-4T(o)(4))

For existing interests, this election must be made on the first return filed after August 9, 1989. It is too late to make a disaggregation election upon disposition of one of the undertakings.

Planning Pointer. This rule imposes on the taxpayer the burden of assuming from the outset the accounting costs that result from maintaining separate records on each undertaking. Thus, unless the shareholder anticipates losses from an undertaking of which he or she might dispose before disposing of similar ones, a disaggregation election is not advantageous.

Election Mechanics: The election is made by attaching a written statement to the taxpayer's return for the taxable year for which the election is made. (Temp. Reg. §1.469-4T(o)(7)(i)) The written statement must (1) state the name, address, and taxpayer identification number of the person making the election; (2) contain a declaration that the taxpayer is making an election under Temp. Reg. §1.469-4T(o); (3) identify the undertaking with respect to which the election is being made; and (4) identify the remainder of the activity in which the undertaking would otherwise be included. (Temp. Reg. §1.469-4T(o)(7)(ii))

Q. 10:21 How does a fragmentation election impact the level of participation in a trade-or-business activity?

If a taxpayer elects to treat a nonrental undertaking as a separate activity (see Question 10:20), the taxpayer's level of participation (material, significant, or otherwise) in the separate activity is the same as the taxpayer's level of participation in the larger activity in which the undertaking would be included but for the election. (Temp. Reg. §1.469-4T(a)(4)(v)) This rule means the taxpayer will be treated as materially participating for the taxable year in the separate activities if and only if the taxpayer would, without making the election, be treated as materially participating for the taxable year in the larger or original activity. (Temp. Reg. §1.469-4T(o)(6)(i))

Likewise, the taxpayer will be treated as significantly participating for the taxable year in the separate activities if and only if the taxpayer would, without making the election, be treated as significantly participating for the taxable year in the original activity. (Temp. Reg. §1.469-4T(o)(6)(ii))

(Material participation and significant participation are discussed at Questions 10:24–10:25.)

Q. 10:22 What special aggregation rule applies to a professional service undertaking?

An undertaking is treated as a professional service undertaking for any taxable year in which the undertaking derives more than 50% of its gross income from providing services performed in the fields of health, law, engineering, architecture, accounting, actuarial science, performing arts, or consulting. (Temp. Reg. §1.469-4T(h)(1)(ii))

In general, a taxpayer's professional service undertakings are treated as part of the same activity if they are (Temp. Reg. §§1.469-4T(a)(4)(iii) and 1.469-4T(h)(2)):

1. Similar—i.e., if more than 20% of operations (by value) are in the same field;
2. Related—i.e., if one derives more than 20% of its gross from persons who are customers of the other; or
3. Controlled by the same interests (see Question 10:17).

Q. 10:23 What special rules apply in determining which rental real estate undertakings constitute an activity?

A rental real estate undertaking is a rental undertaking in which at least 85% of the unadjusted basis of the property made available for use by customers is real property. (Temp. Reg. §1.469-4T(k)(1)(ii)) In general, the rules for aggregating rental real estate undertakings are elective. They permit taxpayers to treat any combination of rental real estate undertakings as a single activity. Taxpayers may also (1) divide their rental real estate undertakings and treat portions of the undertakings as separate activities or (2) recombine the portions into activities that include parts of different undertakings. (Temp. Reg. §1.469-4T(a)(4)(iv)(A))

However, there are two "consistency" rules and an anti-abuse rule, which are discussed below. (There is also a special rule that applies when the activity is rental of a dwelling unit covered by Section 280A; see Temp. Reg. §1.469-4T(k)(7).)

All rental real estate undertakings (or portions thereof) that are treated as part of the same activity under these rules for a taxable year ending after August 9, 1989, must be treated as part of the same activity in each succeeding taxable year. (Temp. Reg. §1.469-4T(k)(3))

Consistency Rules: One consistency rule is partially aimed at ownership through S corporations and other pass-through entities. A taxpayer may *not* fragment rental real estate in a manner that is inconsistent with the treatment of the property by an S corporation (or any other pass-through entity through which the taxpayer holds the interest) or with the taxpayer's treatment of that property in earlier taxable years. (Temp. Reg. §1.469-4T(a)(4)(iv)(B)) Therefore, an S corporation shareholder must treat two or more rental real estate undertakings as a single rental real estate undertaking if the S corporation does on its applicable return, which is the return reporting the S corporation's income, gain, loss, deductions, and credits taken into account by the taxpayer for that taxable year. (Temp. Reg. §§1.469-4T(k)(2)(ii) and 1.469-4T(k)(4))

Additionally, a taxpayer cannot fragment a portion of leased property (including a ratable portion of any common areas or facilities) unless that portion of the leased property can be separately conveyed under applicable state and local law (including any limitations imposed by any special rules or procedures, such as condominium conversion laws, that restrict the separate conveyance of parts of the same structure). (Temp. Reg. §§1.469-4T(k)(2)(iii)(A) and 1.469-4T(k)(2)(iii)(B))

Anti-Abuse Rules: If the income or gain from a rental real estate undertaking is subject to recharacterization under anti-abuse rules for rental of nondepreciable property, the undertaking is treated as a separate activity. A taxpayer cannot aggregate or fragment a rental real estate undertaking if less than 30% of the unadjusted basis of property used or held for use by customers in that undertaking during the taxable year is subject to the allowance for depreciation under Section 167. (Temp. Reg. §§1.469-4T(a)(4)(iv)(B)) and 1.469-4T(k)(6))

PAL Rules—Material Participation

Q. 10:24 How does a shareholder "participate" in an S corporation activity?

Unless an activity is inherently passive—i.e., unless it is a rental activity (see Questions 10:39–10:41)—it is passive with regard to a taxpayer unless the taxpayer materially participates in the activity for the taxable year in question. (Sections 469(c)(1)(B) and 469(h)) To materially participate, the shareholder must first participate.

Participation for purposes of the material participation test is a concept that applies only to the owner (shareholder) and his or her spouse. (A nonowner employee, other than the spouse of an owner, cannot participate.) Generally, participation is any work performed by an individual in connection with a trade-or-business activity in which he or she owns an interest. (Temp. Reg. §1.469-5T(f)(1)) Participation of spouses is aggregated without regard to whether (1) both spouses own interests or (2) a joint return is filed. (Temp. Reg. §1.469-5T(f)(3))

Participation can include work performed by an investor (shareholder) who is not an employee if the individual is directly involved in day-to-day management or operations. (Temp. Reg. §1.469-5T(f)(2)(ii)) However, the investor may have some difficulty meeting the material participation tests discussed below.

However, when all is said and done, there is an important limitation on all of the above: Work not customarily performed by an owner will *not* constitute participation if one of the principal purposes is to avoid disallowance of losses or credits under Section 469. (Temp. Reg. §1.469-5T(f)(2)(i))

Q. 10:25 What makes a shareholder's participation "material"?

The temporary regulations set forth seven tests for material participation. These tests apply only to individuals. Rules for trusts and estates will appear in Temp. Reg. §1.469-5T(g). The seven ways in which an individual may meet the material participation test are (Temp. Reg. §1.469-5T(a)):

1. The individual participates in the activity for more than 500 hours during the taxable year.
2. The individual's participation is substantially all of the participation by all individuals, including nonowners, in the activity during the taxable year.
3. The individual participates in the activity for more than 100 hours during the taxable year, *provided* that no one other individual—owner or nonowner—participates more.
4. The activity is a "significant participation activity"—that is, a trade-or-business activity in which the individual participates for more than 100 (but less than or equal to 500) hours during the year—and the individual's aggregate participation in all significant activities is more than 500 hours during the taxable year.
5. The individual materially participates in the activity for any five of the ten taxable years immediately preceding the year in question without regard to this test (e.g., a shareholder who has retired as company president might continue to materially participate under this test), provided that for taxable years beginning before January 1, 1987, material participation must consist of participation of more than 500 hours in each taxable year. For purposes of this participation test, an individual has materially participated in an activity for a preceding taxable year if the activity includes an undertaking involving substantially the same business and rental operations as an undertaking that was included in an activity in which the taxpayer materially participated (Temp. Reg. §1.469-5T(j)(1)). If an individual takes into account any item of gross income or deduction from an S corporation (or a partnership) that is characterized as an item of gross income or deduction from an activity in which the individual materially participated, the individual is treated as materially participating in the activity for purposes of applying this test to any later taxable year of the individual. (Temp. Reg. §1.469-5T(h)(3))

6. The activity is a personal service activity (health, law, engineering, architecture, accounting, actuarial science, performing arts, consulting, or any other trade or business in which capital is not a material income-producing factor) and the individual materially participated for any three preceding years (again, the more-than-500-hours test must be met for years beginning before 1987). For purposes of this participation test, an individual has materially participated in an activity for a preceding taxable year if that activity includes an undertaking involving substantially the same business and rental operations as an undertaking that was included in an activity in which the taxpayer materially participated (determined without regard to the participation test at (5) for the preceding taxable year. (Temp. Reg. §1.469-5T(j)(1)). If an individual takes into account any item of gross income or deduction from an S corporation (or a partnership) that is characterized as an item of gross income or deduction from an activity in which the individual materially participated, the individual is treated as materially participating in the activity for purposes of applying this test to any later taxable year of the individual. (Temp. Reg. §1.469-5T(h)(3))

7. The individual can show material participation in operations and/or management based on the facts and circumstances.

Facts-and-Circumstances Test: Material participation based on the facts and circumstances must be regular, continuous, and substantial. (Temp. Reg. §1.469-5T(a)(7)) The first two sets of temporary regulations reserved the general discussion of the facts-and-circumstances test, and it is far from clear that any showing of material participation based on the facts and circumstances will be honored before regulations are issued. However, participation must be for more than 100 hours, and management activities are taken into account only under limited circumstances. (See Temp. Reg. §1.469-5T(b)(2).)

Q. 10:26 Which taxable year is used to measure material participation, the shareholder's or the S corporation's?

The existence of material participation is determined at the *shareholder* level. However, if the corporation has a fiscal year (see Chapter 3), the *corporation's taxable year* is the year used to measure whether material participation exists. (Temp. Reg. §1.469-2T(e)(1))

■ **Example.** A, a calendar-year individual, is a shareholder in S corporation X, which has a January 31 year end. During the taxable year ending January 31, 1990, X engaged in a single trade-or-business activity. For the period February 1, 1989, through January 31, 1990, A did not materially participate in the activity. In A's calendar-year 1990 return, A's pro rata share of S corporation income and deductions must be treated as passive activity gross income and passive activity deductions, even if A meets the material participation standards for the period January 1, 1990, through December 31, 1990.

Q. 10:27 How should the shareholder substantiate participation?

Participation, of course, is something IRS can dispute at audit. According to the temporary regulations, contemporaneous daily time reports, logs, or similar documentation are not required—although there is no better proof than such records, if they are customarily maintained in the ordinary course of business. Proof can also include, but is not limited to, identification of services performed over a period of time, and approximate hours spent, through use of appointment books, calendars, and narrative summaries. (Temp. Reg. §1.469-5T(f)(4))

PAL Rules—Disallowed Losses and Credits

Q. 10:28 If the shareholder does not materially participate in an S corporation activity, how—and why—is passive activity gross income calculated?

If the S corporation is involved in an activity or activities that are encompassed by the PAL rules (see Question 10:11), and if the shareholder does not materially participate in any or all of them for a corporate taxable year (see Questions 10:24–10:26)—or if they are rental activities (see Questions 10:39–10:40)—it becomes necessary to determine if the shareholder has a passive activity loss. A passive activity loss—or loss disallowed by the PAL rules—for a taxable year is the amount, if any, by which the passive activity deductions (see Question 10:33) for the taxable year exceed the passive activity gross income for the taxable year. (Temp. Reg. §1.469-2T(b)) Passive activity gross income generally consists of items of gross income from *all* passive activities.

(Temp. Reg. §1.469-2T(c)) (Special rules apply to items from "publicly traded" partnerships.)

Any reasonable method may be used to allocate income between or among activities. Income from a trade-or-business activity is generally characterized by the nature of the taxpayer's participation for the year in which the income is received, unless it is for disposition of property or an interest in property (in which case the rules set forth at Question 10:43 apply). However, income from positive Section 481 adjustments is characterized by the nature of participation in the year of change. (Temp. Reg. §1.469-2T(c)(5)) Remember that if the S corporation has a fiscal year, the corporate year (not the shareholder's) is the year used to test participation. (See Question 10:26.)

Q. 10:29 Is income from S corporation investments passive activity gross income?

"Portfolio income" is not passive activity gross income. In the simplest sense, portfolio income includes income that can be expected to produce a positive cash flow. Thus it generally includes interest, dividends, royalties, and the like—*provided* that they are not received in the ordinary course of business. It also includes income from the disposition of such assets. (Section 469(e)(1); Temp. Reg. §1.469-2T(c)(3)) Income the corporation derives from property held for investment is portfolio income and maintains its character when it is passed through to the shareholder.

Likewise, when the S corporation disposes of investment property, the gain (or loss) on the disposition is portfolio gain (or loss). (See Temp. Reg. §§1.469-2T(c)(2) and 1.469-2T(d)(5)(i).) (Similar rules apply when the shareholder disposes of shares in the S corporation; see Questions 10:44–10:47.)

The upshot of these rules is that the portfolio income the shareholder derives from the corporation's investments cannot generally be sheltered by losses from the corporation's business activities (except to the extent of any directly related deductible expenses) unless the shareholder materially participates in those activities.

The rule applies to *all* investment income, even the return on assets set aside to produce working capital for the legitimate needs of the business. (Section 469(e)(1)(B))

Planning Pointer. The S corporation should segregate its portfolio income on its books.

Portfolio-Type Income Received in the Ordinary Course of Business: Income such as interest, royalties (other than those for literary, artistic, and musical works), and the like are not portfolio income if they are derived in the ordinary course of business. (Temp. Reg. §1.469-2T(c)(3)(ii))

For royalties to qualify for this rule, a special test must be met, and, in the S corporation context, this test applies at the corporate level. Royalties are derived in the ordinary course of business if the corporation either (1) created the property licensed or transferred or (2) performed substantial services or incurred substantial marketing costs. (Temp. Reg. §1.469-2T(c)(3)(iii)(B)) This rule enables shareholders who have borne the risk involved in the creation, development, or marketing of the activity to treat the income, if any, as trade-or-business income—instead of as passive income.

However, consonant with this purpose of recognizing economic risk, a shareholder acquiring an interest in the S corporation after the creation of the property, performance of services, or making of marketing expenditures generally cannot take advantage of the special royalties rule. Effective for 1988 taxable years, the shareholder must treat his or her pro rata share of royalty income as portfolio income (offset, of course, by deductions reasonably allocated to the property). (The shareholder is deemed to fall under the rule treating royalties as business income if the share of reasonably related expenses—including the full value of capital items—(1) is more than 50% of the share of gross royalty income for the year or (2) exceeds 25% of the shareholder's interest in the property generating the royalties, as valued at the time the shareholder acquired the shares.) (Temp. Reg. §1.469-2T(f)(7))

Q. 10:30 How are S corporation distributions treated?

Distributions out of C corporation-year earnings and profits that are taxed as dividends under Section 1368(c)(2) are portfolio income. (Temp. Reg. §1.469-2T(c)(3)(i)(B); see also *Letter Ruling 8752017.*)

Q. 10:31 How is the shareholder's pro rata share treated?

No portion of the shareholder's pro rata share of S corporation items is treated as compensation for services—even if the salary paid to the shareholder represents less than the fair market value of the shareholder's services. (Temp. Reg. §1.469-2T(c)(4)) The pro rata share items are either portfolio items or from a business activity. Compensation for personal services, which is always active, is limited to (Temp. Reg. §1.469-2T(c)(4)(i))

- Earned income (e.g., salary paid the shareholder);
- Property (e.g., stock options) transferred in connection with services;
- Retirement and deferred compensation benefits;
- Taxable Social Security benefits; and
- Other items that may be defined by IRS.

Planning Pointer. If the shareholder materially participates in the activity for which he or she is compensated, the question of salary versus pro rata share would generally seem to make no difference as far as the PAL rules are concerned. Both the compensation and the pro rata share attributed to the activity would be active income (or not be passive activity gross income). However, if the activity is an inherently passive rental activity, an opportunity to *create* passive income might exist. This is demonstrated by the following example based on the temporary regulations.

■ **Example.** C owns 50% of the stock of X, an S corporation. X owns and manages rental real estate. X pays C a salary for the services C performs in connection with the management of these properties. Although C's pro rata share of X's gross income is passive activity gross income, the salary—even if it is less than the fair market value of C's services—is not. (See Temp. Reg. §1.469-2T(c)(4)(ii).)

IRS has indicated that generally it will respect form here and not recharacterize the pro rata share so as to impute earned income.

Q. 10:32   Is the trade-or-business income from the S corporation always characterized by the nature of the shareholder's participation?

Income that is neither compensation nor portfolio income is trade-or-business income. However, not all trade-or-business income is passive merely because the shareholder (or other taxpayer) does not materially participate in the activity generating the income. The temporary regulations recharacterize some or all of certain categories of net income as active—that is, excludable from passive activity gross income—even if they are derived from a trade-or-business activity in which the taxpayer does not materially participate.

One of these categories is certain royalty income. (See discussion at Question 10:29.) Another is income from the rental of property (which is always a passive activity) by the shareholder to an S corporation activity in which the shareholder materially participates. (See Temp. Reg. §1.469-2T(f)(6).) These rules, and other "recharacterization" rules spelled out at Temp. Reg. §§1.469-2T(f)(3)–1.469-2T(f)(7), are effective for *1988* taxable years. (Temp. Reg. §1.469-11T(a)(2)) There is a binding contract exception for the rental of property to the S corporation.

In addition, active income can result from "significant participation" activities that do not, in the aggregate, produce material participation. (Temp. Reg. §1.469-2T(f)(2)) (The definition, and the material participation rule, are explained at Question 10:25.) This rule was effective in 1987 taxable years.

Q. 10:33 What deductions are "passive activity deductions"?

A passive activity loss exists to the extent that passive activity deductions for a year exceed passive activity gross income for that year. (Temp. Reg. §1.469-2T(b))

A passive activity deduction is a deduction that arises in connection with a passive activity for the taxable year or that has been carried over as a previously disallowed passive activity deduction. (Temp. Reg. §1.469-2T(d)(1)) The year in which it arises is the year in which it would be deductible but for operation of the PAL rules, the capital loss limitations of Section 1211, and the percentage depletion limitations of Section 613A(d). (Temp. Reg. §1.469-2T(d)(8)) Material participation is measured by the shareholder's activity for the corporate year in which the deduction arises under the PAL rules. (There is an exception for negative Section 481 adjustments, which are characterized according to the year of change; Reg. §1.469-2T(d)(7).)

■ **Example.** In 1990, A, a calendar-year individual, acquires shares in R, a calendar-year S corporation. R's only activity is a trade-or-business activity in which A materially participates for 1990. R incurs a loss in 1990. A's pro rata share of R's 1990 loss is $1,000. However, A's basis in the R shares at the end of 1990 (without regard to A's pro rata share of corporate loss) is $600; accordingly, Section 1366(d) disallows 1990 deductions for $400 of A's pro rata share of corporate loss. The remaining $600 of A's pro rata share of R's loss would be allowed as a deduction for 1990 if taxable income for all taxable years were determined without regard to Sections 469, 613A(d) and 1211. (See Questions 10:1–10:9 for a fuller discussion of the impact of the basis limitation and at-risk rules.)

A does not materially participate in R's activity in 1991. In that year, R again incurs a loss, and A's pro rata share of the loss is again $1,000. At the end of 1990, A's basis in the R shares (without regard to A's pro rata share of corporate loss) is $2,000; accordingly, in 1991, Section 1366(d) does not limit A's deduction for either A's $1,000 pro rata share of R's 1990 loss or the $400 loss carried over from 1990 under Section 1366(d). No Code provision other than Section 469, 613A, or 1211 blocks the deductions in 1991.

The $600 loss that was not disallowed in 1990 by virtue of Section 1366(d) is treated as arising in 1990 and is not a passive activity deduction because A materially participated in R's activity in 1990.

However, the $400 loss that was disallowed in 1989 by virtue of Section 1366(d), as well as the $1,000 loss from the activity in 1991, is treated as arising in 1991 (see Section 1366(d)(2)). These deductions are passive activity deductions because R does not materially participate in 1991. (See Temp. Reg. §1.469-2T(d)(1))

In the context of the S corporation, deductions maintain their character as they pass through to the shareholder. If they are attributable to a trade-or-business activity within the meaning of the PAL rules, they are generally characterized by the material participation, or lack of it, in the *corporate* taxable year with respect to which they are passed through. (Temp. Reg. §1.469-2T(e)(1))

The income-basket concepts (portfolio, compensation, and trade-or-business) that apply to characterizing income also apply in characterizing deductions. Thus deductions clearly and directly attributable to portfolio income and assets are active (see Temp. Reg. §1.469-2T(d)(2)(i)), as are deductions properly attributable to compensation (see Temp. Reg. §1.469-2T(d)(2)(vii)). Certain other deductions, according to the temporary regulations, are also never passive. (See Temp. Reg. §1.469-

2T(d)(2)) Note, however, that the temporary regulations speak in terms of exclusions and are tightly drawn to include as many items as possible in the passive activity deduction basket.

Special rules may also apply if the S corporation disposes of property used in, or an interest in, an activity or if a shareholder disposes of S corporation shares. (See Questions 10:43–10:47.)

Q. 10:34 How does the shareholder treat "self-charged interest" passed through on loans to the S corporation?

Expense items (other than interest) clearly and directly attributable to portfolio income are never passive. (Temp. Reg. §1.469-2T(d)(2)(i)) The same rule applies to loss from dispositions of assets that produce portfolio income. (Temp. Reg. §1.469-2T(d)(2)(iv)) Interest expense related to the corporation's investment activities is never passive (Temp. Reg. §1.469-2T(d)(2)(iii)), although the shareholder may be subject to the investment interest limitations of Section 163(d).

Similarly, interest a shareholder receives on a loan to the S corporation is normally portfolio income because it is not received in the ordinary course of a trade or business. What then happens to the shareholder's pro rata share of interest expense, which—assuming the loan proceeds are used in the course of a business activity—is a trade-or-business deduction subject to the PAL rules?

The legislative history of the PAL rules indicates a concern with such "self-charged" interest, which might lack economic significance because the shareholder is essentially paying himself or herself back; it also indicates that there should be an allocation of the interest expense.

Future regulations (in Temp. Reg. §1.469-7T) are to deal with this issue—and with the issue of corporate loans to the shareholder. They may also permit this type of netting in other appropriate circumstances, but are not to permit passive income to offset nonpassive income except to the extent of the shareholder's allocable share of the specific payment at issue.

Q. 10:35 What about interest on debt incurred to purchase or carry S corporation shares?

Interest expense is never a passive activity deduction unless it is allocable to a passive activity. (Temp. Reg. §§1.163-8T and 1.469-2T(d)(2)(iii))

Whether interest incurred to acquire S corporation shares will be treated as investment interest or trade-or-business interest will depend on the nature of the corporation's business. If the corporation's assets are used solely to conduct a trade or business, the interest will be trade-or-business interest. Of course, in this case, whether the taxpayer's interest expense deductions are limited by the PAL rules will depend on whether the taxpayer materially participates in the business. (*Ann. 87-4*, 1987-3 IRB 17)

Q. 10:36 How do the basis limitation and at-risk rules affect passive activity deductions?

The PAL rules come into play only after losses are no longer barred by the basis limitation rules of Section 1366(d) (see Questions 10:1–10:2) or the at-risk rules of Section 465 (see Questions 10:3–10:9). Items that are disallowed under the basis limitation or the at-risk rules are not treated under the PAL rules for the year. (Temp. Reg. §1.4692T(d)(6)(i))

For purposes of the PAL rules, these items arise in the taxable year in which they would be allowable as a deduction under all Code provisions other than Section 469, the percentage depletion rules of Section 613A(d), and the capital loss rules of Section 1211. (Temp. Reg. §1.469-2T(d)(8))

■ **Example.** X's pro rata share of an S corporation deduction is disallowed in 1990 under Section 1366(d). It is not disallowed in 1991 under Section 1366(d) (or any provision other than Sections 469, 613A(d), and 1211). The deduction arises in 1991 for purposes of the PAL rules. Thus 1991 is the year in which the PAL rules (including the material participation and active participation standards discussed at Questions 10:15 and 10:42) apply.

Thus, in order to determine what amounts may be subject to the PAL rules, it may become necessary to determine what portion of an item survives the basis limitation and/or the at-risk rules.

If any portion of an S corporation shareholder's pro rata share of loss is disallowed under Section 1366(d), a ratable portion of the shareholder's pro rata share of *each* item of *corporate* deduction or loss is deemed disallowed under Section 1366(d). (Temp. Reg. §1.469-2T(d)(6)(ii)(B))

The amount left to be tested under the PAL rules is the amount of the item less this ratable share.

Likewise, if any portion of a loss from an activity is disallowed under the at-risk rules of Section 465, a ratable portion of *each* item of deduction or loss from the *activity* is disallowed. (Temp Reg. §1.469-2T(d)(6)(iii)) The amount surviving to be tested under the PAL rules is the amount of the item less the ratable share.

Priority Rules: As further explained elsewhere (see Question 10:3), the basis limitation and the at-risk rules apply similar concepts but use different measures. The basis limitation rules apply to the shareholder's pro rata share of *all* S corporation losses. The at-risk rules apply to each activity (investment or business) of the S corporation, or to a permitted aggregation of corporate activities. Thus, although the basis limitation rules apply to the entire set of S corporation activities, the at-risk rules may apply to one or more discrete subsets.

If there is an overlap between the basis limitation and the at-risk rules, the basis limitation is applied first for purposes of the PAL rules. The portion of an item disallowed under the basis limitation is not taken into account in determining the loss under the at-risk rules. (Temp. Reg. §1.469-2T(d)(6)(iv))

Reporting Considerations: In identifying items of deduction and loss that are not disallowed under Sections 1366(d) and 465, the shareholder must separately identify items that would result in a different income tax liability if items were not taken into account separately. (See Temp. Reg. §1.469-2T(d)(6)(v).)

Q. 10:37 How do the PAL rules affect credits passed through by the S corporation?

For regular tax purposes, the PAL rules apply to credits as well as losses. (Section 469(a)(1)(B)) Except to the extent that the special $25,000 allowance for rental real estate applies (see Questions 10:41–10:42), credits (other than the foreign tax credit) attributable to passive activities may be used only to offset tax attributable to passive income. The credits affected are general business credits, the possessions corporation credit, credits for clinical testing of certain drugs, and credits for fuel from unconventional sources. (Section 469(d)(2); Temp. Reg. §1.469-3T(b)(1)(B)) The excess credit amount, which must be carried over, is referred to as the "passive activity credit" for the year.

The passive activity credit is thus defined as the sum of all credits subject to the PAL rules for the year, less the regular tax liability (if any) allocable to all passive activities for the year. (Section 469(d)(2); Temp. Reg. §1.469-3T(a))

When an S corporation passes a credit through to a shareholder, the character of the credit as active or passive is determined with regard to the shareholder's participation during the taxable year of the corporation in which the credit is subject to the rules.

Disallowed passive activity credits may be carried forward. (See Question 10:38.)

Once a credit is no longer subject to Section 469 it is allowed or disallowed, and disallowed portions are carried back and carried forward, under the ordinary rules of Section 39. (Temp. Reg. §1.469-3T(e))

Credits Subject to the PAL Rules for a Taxable Year: A covered credit is subject to the rules if it (Temp. Reg. §1.469-3T(b)(1)):

- Is attributable to the taxable year (that is, would be allowable if credits allowed for all taxable years were determined without regard to the limitations of Sections 26(a), 28(d)(2), 29(b)(5), 38(c), and 469) *and* arises in connection with the conduct of an activity that is a passive activity for the year; or
- Is a carryover of a credit previously disallowed under the PAL rules.

Special rules apply to qualified progress expenditures qualifying for a rehabilitation credit. (See Temp. Reg. §1.469-3T(b)(2).)

Pre-1987 Credits: Credits attributable (as defined above) to a pre-1987 taxable year of the shareholder are not subject to the PAL rules. (Temp. Reg. §1.469-3T(b)(4))

Calculation of Regular Tax Liability Allocable to Passive Activities: Regular tax liability is tax liability pursuant to Section 26(b). (Section 469(j)(3); Temp. Reg. §1.469-3T(d)(2)(i)) Thus, AMT liability is not considered in the calculation. Regular tax liability allocable to passive activities is calculated by comparing (Temp. Reg. §1.469-3T(d)(1)):

1. The taxpayer's regular tax liability for the year (before any credits are claimed), and

2. The regular tax liability (before any credits are claimed) on taxable income reduced by any excess of passive activity gross income over passive activity deductions.

To the extent that the amount in 1 exceeds the amount in 2, credits from passive activities are available for the year. The remainder is the disallowed passive activity credit. Note that if there is a passive activity loss, or if passive activity deductions offset passive activity gross income, no credits will be allowed; they will all be subsumed in the disallowed passive activity credit.

Q. 10:38 What must the shareholder do to account for disallowed losses and credits attributable to S corporation activities?

To the extent that passive income exists in any taxable year, losses arising from passive activities in that year generally may offset it. There need be no matching of income and deductions from specific activities. (Section 469(d)(1)) Or, in the terms of the temporary regulations, a passive activity loss occurs for a taxable year only to the extent that passive activity deductions exceed passive activity gross income. (Temp. Reg. §§1.469-2T(b) and 1.469-2T(c)) A similar rule applies to credits from passive activities. (Section 469(d)(2))

However, once a passive activity loss exists, or a credit is disallowed, the disallowed loss or the passive activity credit must be allocated among the taxpayer's passive activities for the succeeding taxable year in a manner that reasonably reflects the extent to which each activity continues the business and rental operations relating to the loss activity. The disallowed deductions or credits so allocated must be treated as deductions or credits from that activity for the succeeding taxable year. (Temp. Reg. §1.469-1T(f)(4)(i)) This is necessary so that proper accountings can be made if there is a taxable disposition of the entire interest or if the shareholder materially participates in a subsequent year.

(Note that the general rules permitting all passive activity deductions to offset all passive activity gross income, and all credits from passive activities to offset tax attributable to passive activities, do not apply to interests in publicly traded partnerships. Under the Revenue Act of 1987, each publicly traded partnership—if it is not taxed as a corporation—consists of a separate and discrete basket of income, deduction, and credit items that must be accounted for separately. (See Section 469(k).)

Presumably, this rule applies at the shareholder level to interests held by the S corporation. Regulations are to be promulgated in Temp. Reg. §1.469-10T.)

Planning Pointer. Because of these allocation rules, the taxpayer must be able to segregate all income, deduction, and credit items according to the activity in which they are incurred.

Loss Allocation: Allocation of losses is a two-step process. First, a ratable portion of the disallowed loss must be allocated among the taxpayer's passive activities for the year. Then the ratable portion of the loss from the activity must be allocated among the deduction items arising from the activity.

The loss from the activity is generally the amount by which passive activity deductions from the activity exceed passive activity gross income from the activity for the taxable year. However, any loss allowed under the special rules from active participation in rental real estate (see Questions 10:41–10:42) is subtracted from the loss from the activity. (Temp. Reg. §1.469-1T(f)(2)(i)(B)) Additionally, if net income from significant participation activities is recharacterized as active (see Question 10:32), those activities are treated as a single activity to which no loss is allocated. (Temp. Reg. §1.469-1T(f)(2)(i)(C))

Reporting Considerations: The shareholder may also have to separately identify these items if separate identification would result in a different tax liability. The general rules of Section 1366(a)(1)(A) apply. (See Question 9:4.) However, the temporary regulations point out certain items that fall under this rule: deductions arising in rental real estate activities in which the shareholder actively participates, deductions arising in rental real estate activities in which the shareholder does not actively participate, and losses taken into account under Sections 1211 and 1231. (Temp. Reg. §1.469-2T(f)(2)(iii))

Credit Allocation: Generally, if any or all of the credits from a passive activity are disallowed for a taxable year, a ratable portion of each credit arising from passive activities is disallowed.

Exceptions: This rule does not apply to credits allowed under the special rule for active participation in rental real estate, for which temporary regulations are forthcoming. (The temporary regulations are to be contained in Temp. Reg. §1.469-9T.)

The rule also does not apply to credits for which a basis increase is claimed upon a fully taxable disposition of the entire interest in the activity. (See Question 10:48.) (Temp. Reg. §1.469-1T(f)(3)(ii))

Reporting Considerations: Credits must generally be accounted for separately according to the rules of Section 1366(a)(1)(A). (See Question 9:4.) Separate accounting would generally be required for, inter alia, low-income housing credits, rehabilitation credits, other credits claimed with regard to rental real estate activities in which the taxpayer does not actively participate, other credits claimed with regard to rental real estate activities in which the taxpayer does actively participate, and credits subject to special credit allowance limitations (e.g., the general business credit). (Temp. Reg. §1.469-1T(f)(3)(ii))

Carryovers: Ratable portions of losses and deductions and of the passive activity credit are carried over and treated for PAL rule purposes in the taxpayer's immediately succeeding taxable year. (Temp. Reg. §1.469-1T(f)(4)) They continue to be carried over until they are allowed. (Section 469(b)) Suspended losses, but not credits, are also allowable upon a taxable disposition of the taxpayer's entire interest in the activity. (Section 469(g)(1); see Question 10:48.) Any cessation of use described in Section 47(a)(1), 47(a)(3), or 47(a)(5), or any change in use described in Section 47(a)(2) or 47(a)(4), means that credit allocations must be adjusted appropriately. (Temp. Reg. §1.469-3T(f))

PAL Rules—Rental Activities

Q. 10:39 What special rules apply to items from the S corporation's rental activities?

Rental activities are intrinsically passive (Section 469(c)(2)), although special rules apply to losses and credits from rental real estate activities (see the discussion below of the active participation standard). Therefore, a line must be drawn between rental and nonrental activities.

The determination of whether a rental activity exists, and of whether an exception to it applies, is a yearly one. In the S corporation context, it is made at the corporate level and according to the corporate year.

Definition of Rental Activity: Basically, a rental activity is an activity in which payments are principally for the use of tangible property. (Section 469(j)(8)) The temporary regulations provide the following test; an activity is a rental activity if (Temp. Reg. §1.469-1T(e)(3)(i)):

1. Gross income attributable to the conduct of the activity for the year represents amounts paid or to be paid principally from the use of tangible property; or
2. Expected gross income from the activity will consist of payments principally for use of tangible property held for rent.

Planning Pointer. The key factor is a holding for rent, and it does not matter whether the transaction is framed as a lease or something else (for example, a service contract).

There is an exception for property rented to a pass-through entity by an owner. (See Question 10:40.) The temporary regulations also provide five other exceptions to the definition of rental activity. These exceptions generally look to the nature of the rental and other services provided. (See Temp. Reg. §§1.469-1T(e)(3)(ii)(A)–1.469-1T(e)(3)(ii)(E).)

Q. 10:40 What happens if the S corporation rents property from a shareholder?

If an S corporation shareholder (in the capacity of a shareholder) makes property available to the S corporation for use in a corporate activity, the provision of the property is *not* a rental activity (and thus does not generate passive activity gross income). (Temp. Reg. §§1.469-1T(e)(3)(ii)(F) and 1.469-1T(e)(3)(vii); the same exception applies to partners and joint venturers.)

This rule does not apply when there are a bona fide lease and bona fide rent payments. However, a special recharacterization rule can still apply if a shareholder who materially participates in an S corporation activity rents property to the S corporation for use in that activity. (Temp. Reg. §1.469-2T(f)(6); see also Question 10:32.)

Q. 10:41 Is there an exception for the S corporation's rental real estate activities?

Relief from the "always passive" characterization is available to some shareholders who conduct rental real estate activities through the S corporation.

Although rental activities are inherently passive, a special rule permits individuals and some estates to use up to $25,000 in deductions and credits (calculated as deduction equivalent) to offset nonpassive income. (Married individuals filing separately who live apart from their spouses during the entire taxable year may claim half this allowance; Section 469(i)(5).) To qualify for this special rule, the taxpayer generally must "actively participate" in the rental activities for the taxable year in question. A special rule applies to rehabilitation credits and low-income housing credits. Temporary regulations on these rules are to be included in Temp. Reg. §1.469-9T; the following discussion, based on the statute and legislative history, is subject to the caveat that *there are no clear standards until regulations provide them.*

Q. 10:42 When and how does the shareholder "actively participate" in the S corporation's rental real estate activities?

Generally, the eligible individual or estate must meet the active participation standard for the taxable year in question. If the taxpayer owns the interest in the activity as an S corporation, the individual shareholder must meet the active participation test, and if the corporation has a fiscal year, the test period is the corporation's year. (Temp. Reg. §1.469-2T(e)(1); see the example in the material participation discussion at Question 10:26.)

To qualify, an individual must, in conjunction with his or her spouse, both:

- Own at least 10%, by value, of all interests in the activity (Section 469(i)(6)); and
- Participate in a significant and bona fide sense in such matters as management decisions and arranging for others to provide services such as repairs.

An estate is deemed to actively participate for taxable years ending less than two years following the death of the individual owner if the owner actively participated in the taxable year of his or her death. (Section 469(i)(4)) This provision is intended to give the executor or fiduciary breathing room to make decisions with respect to the appropriate disposition of the property.

Active participation is never presumed. It must be proven. When the taxpayer engages in more than one rental real estate activity, the 10% rule applies to each. However, only one $25,000 offset is allowed for all activities in which the taxpayer actively participates.

Planning Pointer. Keep in mind that active participation, unlike material participation, does not require regular, continuous, and substantial involvement in operations. Management decisions that can show active participation include:

- Approving new tenants;
- Deciding on rental terms; and
- Approving capital or repair expenditures.

A net lessor is unlikely to meet this standard. Services provided by an agent are not attributable to the principal, and a merely formal and nominal participation in management, in the absence of a genuine exercise of independent discretion and judgment, is insufficient.

Special Rule for Low-Income Housing and Rehabilitation Credits: When these credits are involved, individuals are in effect deemed to participate actively—and thus are eligible for the credit (subject to maximum income limitations)—whether or not they in fact participate actively. (Section 469(i)(6)(B))

PAL Rules—Dispositions of Property or Interests in Property

Q. 10:43 When does a shareholder recognize gain (or loss) from a corporate disposition of property? How is the gain (or loss) characterized?

Generally, when an S corporation disposes of property it uses in an activity, or an interest in property used in an activity, the characterization of items passed through to the shareholders follows the rules previously discussed unless there is a fully taxable disposition of the entire interest in the activity. (See Question 10:48.)

However, some special rules apply. They govern timing of gain and loss recognition. They also govern allocations with regard to property used in more than one activity, and recharacterization of gain from substantially appreciated property, if the property is acquired in a nonrecognition transaction and is not acquired for the purpose of dealing in the property. (See Temp. Reg. §§1.469-2T(c)(2)(iv) and 1.469-2T(c)(2)(v)) (Note that if the corporation disposes of an interest in a partnership or other pass-through entity, the disposition is treated as though the shareholders had directly sold the interest, and the rules discussed at Questions 10:44–10:47 apply.)

Timing Rules: Gain from the disposition is treated as gross income for PAL rule purposes in the taxable year(s) in which it is recognized. (Temp. Reg. §1.469-2T(c)(2)(i)(A)(*1*)) For example, gain on an installment sale would be recognized according to regular installment sale principles. (See Temp. Reg. §1.469-2T(c)(2)(i)(A), Ex. 2.) Any loss recognized in any year upon a disposition is a deduction from the activity in which the property or interest in property was used. (Temp. Reg. §1.469-2T(d)(5)(i)(A))

However, the *character* (as active or passive) of the gain or loss from the sale of trade-or-business property or interests is determined by the nature of the taxpayer's participation in the corporation's taxable year of disposition. (Temp. Reg. §§1.469-2T(c)(2)(i)(A)(*2*), 1.469-2T(c)(2)(i)(A)(*3*), and 1.469-2T(d)(5)(i)(B))

The rules for losses also apply to deductions for abandonment and worthlessness, with the operative date for characterization being the year when the event giving rise to the deduction arises.

Property Used in Different Activities: There are two ways in which property can be viewed as used in more than one activity:

1. The same "property," as one would normally define the term, can be used in two separate activities at the same time—for example, a corporation uses one floor of a two-story building it owns to conduct its trade or business and rents the other out to a commercial tenant. In such a case, the gain or loss—that is, the amount realized upon disposition and the adjusted basis of the property—must be allocated between (or among) the separate interests in a "reasonable" manner. (Temp. Reg. §§1.469-2T(c)(2)(i)(C)(*1*) and 1.469-2T(d)(5)(iii)(A))

2. The same property may have been used for different activities at different times. If the use has varied within the 12 months prior to the disposition, the gain or loss—that is, the amount realized upon disposition and the adjusted basis—must again, in general, be allocated among the activities in a way that "reasonably" reflects the use of the property during the 12-month period ending on the date of disposition. However, the amount realized and the basis may be allocated to the activity in which the property was used predominantly if the fair market value of the interest does not exceed

Q. 10:43

the lesser of (a) $10,000 or (b) 10% of the sum of the combined fair market value of the interest and of all other property used in the activity (as determined immediately before the disposition). (Temp. Reg. §§1.469-2T(c)(2)(ii) and 1.469-2T(d)(5)(ii))

Planning Pointer. Note that either or both of these allocation rules can apply in any given situation.

Characterization Rule for Dispositions of Substantially Appreciated Property: If the fair market value of the property (or interest in property) used in a passive activity exceeds 120% of the adjusted basis, the gain is treated as active unless the property was used in a passive activity for either (Temp. Reg. §1.469-2T(c)(2)(iii)):

1. 20% of the period during which the S corporation held the interest (the regulations refer to the "taxpayer," which in this case is apparently the corporation); or
2. The entire 24-month period ending on the date of disposition.

For these purposes, the date of disposition is not the closing date. It is the date on which an oral or written agreement creates either a binding obligation to transfer the property or an option to transfer the property for a fixed or otherwise determinable price. (Temp. Reg. §1.469-2T(c)(2)(iii)(B)) Thus the corporation cannot enter into an agreement and simply delay the closing date in order to avoid operation of this rule.

An interest in property is treated as an interest in property held for investment—not as used in a passive activity—during periods in which the interest is held through a C corporation or similar entity. (Temp. Reg. §1.469-2T(c)(2)(iii)(D))

This rule is applied after the allocation rule for property used in more than one activity during the preceding 12 months. (Temp. Reg. §1.469-2T(c)(2)(iii)(D))

Q. 10:44 How must the shareholder account for a disposition of S corporation shares?

If a shareholder sells, exchanges, or otherwise disposes of S corporation shares, the amount of gain or loss from *each* activity must be determined. (Temp. Reg. §1.469-2T(e)(3)(i)) The general rule is that a ratable portion of any gain or loss is treated as gain or loss from the disposition of each trade-or-business, rental, or investment activity in which the S corporation owns an interest. (Temp. Reg. §1.469-2T(e)(3)(ii)(A)) For purposes of these rules, all portfolio assets are treated as a single investment activity (Temp. Reg. §1.469-2T(e)(3)(v))—i.e., it is not necessary to make allocations to separate investment activities.

As a corollary, if the S corporation disposes of an interest it holds in a partnership, shareholder gain or loss is allocated among the partnership activities by applying the rules as though the shareholder were the direct holder of the partnership interest. (Temp. Reg. §1.469-2T(e)(3)(ii)(D)(3)) In such a case, references to the corporation should be read as references to the partnership.

Q. 10:45 What valuation date is used to account for shareholder dispositions?

Generally, the corporation may choose one of two dates (called "applicable valuation dates") on which to determine these ratable portion amounts (Temp. Reg. §1.469-2T(e)(3)(ii)(D)(*1*)(*i*)):

1. The beginning of the corporation's taxable year during which the disposition occurs, or
2. The date of disposition.

Note that this choice, *which is exercised at the corporate level,* leaves some room for maneuvering. There is, however, no choice *if one of three designated events occurs before the disposition of the shares but during the same corporate taxable year.* In these three cases, the applicable valuation date is the *date immediately preceding disposition* (Temp. Reg. §1.469-2T(e)(3)(ii)(D)(*1*)(*ii*)):

1. The corporation disposes of more than 10% (by value at the beginning of the taxable year) of its interest in any activity;
2. The corporation disposes of more than 10% of the property (by value at the beginning of the taxable year) that it uses in any activity; or
3. The shareholder contributes either substantially appreciated or depreciated property to the S corporation—that is, property with either (a) a fair market value that exceeds both 120% of adjusted basis and 10% of the shareholder's interest in the corporation as of the beginning of the taxable year *or* (b) an adjusted basis that

exceeds both 120% of fair market value and 10% of the shareholder's interest in the corporation as of the beginning of the taxable year.

Q. 10:46 What allocation methods can be used in accounting for shareholder dispositions?

The temporary regulations provide rules for determining ratable portions of gain or loss and a default rule for use in case insufficient information is available. In addition, a special, more liberal rule applied for certain dispositions in *corporate* taxable years beginning before February 19, 1988.

Ratable Portion Method: The temporary regulations provide the following formulas for the ratable portion, depending upon whether gain or loss is recognized on the transaction as a whole. (Temp. Reg. §1.469-2T(e)(3)(ii)(B))

If *gain is recognized,* the ratable portion is:

1. Net gain that would have been allocated if the S corporation had sold its entire interest in the activity for fair market value,
2. Divided by the sum of net gain amounts that would have been allocated if the corporation had sold its entire interest in each appreciated activity for fair market value.

If *loss is recognized,* the ratable portion is:

1. Net loss that would have been allocated if the S corporation had sold its entire interest in the activity for fair market value,
2. Divided by the sum of net loss amounts that would have been allocated if the corporation had sold its entire interest in each depreciated activity for fair market value.

(Note that the term "recognized" is used in this context without regard to the PAL rules. Passive losses may not be used to offset active income unless there is a disposition of the entire interest in the activity; see Question 10:48.)

For purposes of these rules, the following definitions apply (Temp. Reg. §1.469-2T(e)(3)(i)(E)):

1. An *appreciated activity* is one for which a net gain would have been allocated to the shareholder if the S corporation had sold its entire interest in the activity for fair market value on the applicable valu-

ation date (as discussed above), and a *depreciated activity* is one for which a net loss would have been allocated.

2. A *net gain* is the amount by which gains from the sale of all property used by, or representing the interest of, the S corporation in the activity exceed the losses from the same, and a *net loss* is the amount by which such losses exceed such gains.

■ **Example.** A owns 50% of S, a calendar-year S corporation. In 1993, A sells one-half of that interest—or 25% of the outstanding shares of S—for $50,000. S chooses January 1, 1993, as the applicable valuation date. A's adjusted basis in the shares sold is $30,000. Thus A recognizes $20,000 in gain from the sale.

S is engaged in three trade-or-business activities—X, Y, and Z—and owns marketable securities that are portfolio assets. For 1993, A materially participates in activity Z, but not in X or Y. The special rules for substantially appreciated property (see Question 10:37) do not apply. On January 1, 1993, the fair market values and adjusted bases of properties used in S's activities are:

	Adjusted Basis	Fair Market Value
X	$ 68,000	$ 48,000
Y	30,000	62,000
Z	20,000	80,000
Securities	2,000	10,000
	$120,000	$200,000

A's $20,000 gain is allocated by multiplying it by ratable net gain, that is:

1. Gain allocated as if S had sold the entire interest in each activity on January 1, 1993,
2. Divided by the sum of net gain amounts that would have been allocated to A if S had sold the entire interest in each appreciated activity on January 1, 1993.

If S had sold its entire interest in Y and Z and the marketable securities on January 1, 1993, A would have been allocated the following amounts of net gain:

Y	—	$ 8,000 [25% × ($62,000 − $30,000)]
Z	—	$15,000 [25% × ($80,000 − $20,000)]
Securities	—	$2,000 [25% × ($10,000 − $ 2,000)]
		$25,000

Thus, the ratable portions of gain allocated are:

Y	—	$6,400 [$20,000 × (8,000/25,000)]
Z	—	$12,000 [$20,000 × (15,000/25,000)]
Securities	—	$1,600 [$20,000 × (2,000/25,000)]

The gain allocated to Y is passive activity gross income. The gain allocated to Z and the securities is active income. (See Temp. Reg. §1.469-2T(e)(3)(viii), Ex. 1.) Since the adjusted basis of X exceeds its fair market value, there is a loss and the activity does not enter into the calculation.

Default Rules: If the allocation rules discussed above cannot be followed, gain or loss is to be allocated among activities in proportion to the respective fair market values of the corporation's activities. (Temp. Reg. §1.469-2T(e)(3)(ii)(C))

Disposition in Corporate Taxable Years Beginning Before February 19, 1988: Gain from dispositions in these years that is subject to the PAL rules may generally be allocated by any reasonable method—including, but not limited to, the ratable portion and default methods described above.

However, the ratable portion or the default method must be used if a shareholder who materially participates in the activity contributes (1) after February 19, 1988, and (2) during (a) the shareholder taxable year in which the corporate disposition occurs or (b) the immediately preceding shareholder taxable year, either substantially appreciated portfolio assets or substantially appreciated assets that the shareholder has used in a trade or business. (Temp. Reg. §1.469-2T(e)(3)(iv)) (Substantially appreciated assets are those with a fair market value that exceeds 120% of adjusted basis; Temp. Reg. §1.469-2T(e)(3)(vi)(B).)

Q. 10:47 Can a shareholder change the character of gain from a disposition of property by contributing the property to the S corporation?

Generally, under the PAL rules, gain on disposition of an interest in substantially appreciated property (i.e., property with a fair market value in excess of 120% of adjusted basis) is treated as active unless the interest in the property was used in a passive activity for either (1) 20% of the period during which the taxpayer held the interest, or (2) the entire 24-

month period ending on the date of disposition. (Temp. Reg. §1.469-2T(c)(2)(iii); see Question 10:43.)

If an S corporation shareholder personally owns appreciated property that, upon disposition, would generate active income under this rule, he or she might be tempted to contribute that property to an S corporation activity in which he or she does not materially participate, and thus generate passive activity gross income. Thus a special characterization rule applies, so that the shareholder cannot circumvent the general rule and generate passive income upon the sale or other disposition of S corporation shares. A portion of the gain will be recharacterized as active if (Temp. Reg. §1.469-2T(e)(3)(iii)):

1. Gain the shareholder recognizes on disposition of the S corporation shares is allocated to a passive activity;
2. Gain allocated to the shareholder would have been treated as active under the general rules discussed at Questions 10:17–10:18 and 10:44 if all of the property used in the activity had been sold immediately prior to the disposition for its fair market value on the applicable valuation date; and
3. The shareholder gain attributable to the substantially appreciated property formerly used in the nonpassive activity is more than 10% of the shareholder gain.

In such a case, the shareholder gain allocated to the interest in the activity is gain from a passive activity only to the extent it exceeds the gain attributable to the substantially appreciated property. Gain up to the amount attributable to the substantially appreciated property is active. This rule applies only to that part of the gain that is characterized as gain from a passive activity. (Temp. Reg. §1.469-2T(c)(iii)(E))

Q. 10:48 When does a disposition trigger suspended losses?

The type of disposition that triggers such recognition is a "fully taxable disposition of the taxpayer's entire interest in the activity" (Section 469(g)(1))—that is, a disposition of the interest held in all entities that are engaged in the activity, and to the extent held in proprietorship form, of all assets used or created in the activity. Temporary regulations have yet to define this standard, or how it is applied. These rules will be contained in Temp. Reg. §1.469-6T. If an S corporation is involved, a disposition of the entire interest can occur at either:

1. The shareholder level; or
2. The corporate level.

In other words, if the S corporation disposes of its interest in the activity, the shareholder need not dispose of his or her interest in the S corporation in order to deduct previously suspended losses.

Definition of "Fully Taxable Disposition": According to the legislative history, a fully taxable disposition generally includes a sale of the property to a third party at arm's length, presumably for a price reflecting fair market value. A mere change in form of ownership is not a disposition, although suspended losses may be used to offset any gain recognized. But abandonments and worthless securities deductions can qualify. In addition, special rules are provided for death and gifts (see Sections 469(g)(2) and 469(j)(6), respectively), as well as for related-party transactions and installment sales (see Sections 469(g)(1)(B) and 469(g)(3), respectively).

Impact of Disposition of the Entire Interest: Losses, but not credits, that have been suspended and carried over under the PAL rules are allowed in full when gain or loss is recognized upon a disposition of the entire interest in the activity. However, the capital loss limitation rules still apply in determining recognized loss.

After the capital loss limitations, to the extent relevant, are applied, both previously suspended losses and any loss realized on the sale are allowed to offset income in the following priority order (Section 469(g)(1)(A)):

1. Income or gain from the activity disposed of for the taxable year (including any gain realized on disposition);
2. Net income or gain for the taxable year for all other passive activities; and
3. Any other income or gain.

Note that, under this ordering rule, active income may be offset only after passive income is exhausted.

Credits: Unlike suspended losses, suspended credits are not allowed upon a disposition of the entire interest in an activity. However, when the entire interest in an activity is disposed of in a fully taxable disposition and a basis adjustment was made for a credit taken as a result of placing property in service (for example, the investment or rehabilitation credit), an election is available.

Upon such a disposition, the taxpayer may elect to increase the basis of the credit property (by an amount no greater than the amount of the original basis reduction) to the extent that the credit has not been allowed by reason of the PAL rules. At the time of the basis adjustment election, the amount of the suspended credit that may thereafter be applied against tax liability is reduced by the amount of the basis adjustment. (Section 469(j)(9))

The purpose of this election is to permit the taxpayer to recognize economic gain or loss, taking account of the full cost of property for which no credit was allowed.

Q. 10:49 What is the PAL impact of a revocation or termination of the S corporation election? Is it equivalent to a disposition?

Certain situations may not constitute dispositions, but may terminate application of the PAL rules. One instance is an individual's material participation in a trade or business in which he or she was passive before. In this case, disallowed losses and credits can be used in the year of the change to the extent they offset current income and tax liability. Remaining losses and credits must still be carried over under the PAL rules. (Section 469(f)(1))

The statute does not deal with the case of an S corporation that converts to C corporation status and thus (unless it is still a covered personal service corporation) escapes all or part of the application of the PAL rules. However, it does deal with the case of a corporation that ceases to be a personal service corporation or closely held C corporation subject to the at-risk rules. In such cases, deductions and credits arising after status changes are not subject to the PAL rules, and suspended losses and credits arising before the status change remain suspended indefinitely unless recognized under other provisions of the PAL rules. (See Section 469(f)(2).)

Regulations dealing with these issues will be promulgated as Temp. Reg. §1.469-1T(k).

PAL Rules—Effective Dates and Transitional Rules

Q. 10:50 When are the PAL rules effective? What phase-in rules apply?

The PAL rules apply to taxable years of the taxpayer (i.e., the shareholder) beginning after December 31, 1986. The temporary regulations are also retroactive to that date, with the exceptions for certain recharacterization rules that have been noted at appropriate points in the preceding discussion. (Temp. Reg. §1.469-11T(a))

Events occurring before 1987 taxable years are treated as though the PAL rules had been in effect for all taxable years. Thus, material participation could have occurred before the shareholder's 1987 taxable year if the test for retired owners applies. (Temp. Reg. §1.469-11T(a)(4)) (See Question 10:25.) If the corporation has a fiscal year, the shareholder's material participation in the corporation's 1986 fiscal year is considered for purposes of determining whether the shareholder materially participated with regard to items reported on the shareholder's 1987 return. (See Temp. Reg. §1.469-11T(a)(5), Ex. 1.)

Phase-in Rules for Preenactment Interests: Disallowances of losses or credits from interests acquired on or before October 22, 1986, and held at all times thereafter are phased in for regular tax (but not AMT) purposes according to the following applicable percentages (Sections 469(m)(1) and 469(m)(2); Temp. Reg. §1.469-11T(b)(2)): 35% of the passive activity loss and the passive activity credit are disallowed in 1987, 60% in 1988, 80% in 1989, 90% in 1990, and 100% in 1991. The same phase-in is permitted if, on October 22, 1986, the shareholder was under a binding written contract to purchase S corporation shares and the activities are qualified. To the extent that a shareholder owned shares in an S corporation (or was under a binding written contract to purchase them) on October 22, 1986, the phase-in rules also apply, as discussed below, if on that date the corporation was under a binding written contract to purchase an activity or an interest in one. (Section 469(m)(3)(B)(ii); Temp. Reg. §§1.469-11T(c)(7)(i) and 1.469-11T(c)(7)(ii)) However, the rule does not apply if the shareholder held stock in a C corporation that later elected S corporation status. (Temp. Reg. §1.469-11T(c)(2)(ii))

For the activity to qualify under the preenactment interest rule, either (1) any of the business and rental operations that are part of the activity continue business and rental operations that any person was conducting on October 22, 1986, or (2) at least 50% (by value) of the property used in the activity during the taxable year must have been (a) in existence or under construction on August 16, 1986, or (b) acquired or constructed pursuant to a binding contract in effect on August 16, 1986. (Section 469(m)(3)(B); Temp. Reg. §1.469-11T(c)(3)(i))

Calculation of Preenactment Loss and Preenactment Credit: If the interest is a preenactment interest under this definition, it does not matter whether the activity would have been active or passive with regard to the shareholder for any year of the shareholder beginning before January 1, 1987. (Temp. Reg. §1.469-11T(c)(3)(ii))

A loss from a preenactment interest (or, in the terms of the temporary regulations, a "preenactment loss") is the lesser of (Section 469(m)(3)(A); Temp. Reg. §1.469-11T(b)(3)):

1. The passive activity loss for the year, or
2. The passive activity loss for the year determined by taking into account only income and deduction items attributable to preenactment interests.

Likewise, the passive activity credit from preenactment interests (the "preenactment credit") is the lesser of (Section 469(m)(3)(B); Temp. Reg. §1.469-11T(b)(4)):

1. The passive activity credit, or
2. The passive activity credit for the year determined by taking into account only credits from preenactment interests.

Planning Pointer. To apply these rules, income—as well as losses and credits—must be traced and allocated to preenactment interests.

Q. 10:51 What happens under the phase-in rules if the shareholder's proportionate holding in a preenactment interest changes?

To the extent that the taxpayer's proportionate interest in the activity increases or decreases after October 22, 1986, adjustments must be made. (See Temp. Reg. §1.469-11T(c)(5).)

■ **Example.** A and B, calendar-year individuals, own all the stock of X, a calendar-year S corporation. On October 22, 1986, A and B own 50 shares of X stock each. On July 1, 1987, X issues an additional 100 shares of stock to B (but does not issue any additional stock to A).

Q. 10:51   The S Corporation Answer Book

On December 1, 1987, A purchases 70 shares of X stock from B. Thus, A and B have the following shares of items of income, gain, loss, deduction, and credit from activities of X:

Period	A's Share	B's Share
10/22/86–6/30/87	50%	50%
7/1/87–11/30/87	25	75
12/1/87 and thereafter	60	40

Both A and B have 50% shares of each item of X as of October 22, 1986. Since there are no increases or decreases in their shares before June 30, 1987, their 50% shares of items of X assigned to the period from January 1, 1987, through June 30, 1987, are attributable to their preenactment interests.

As a result of the decrease in A's share on June 30, 1987, only a 25% share of the items of X assigned to the period from July 1, 1987, through November 30, 1987, is attributable to A's preenactment interest. In addition, notwithstanding the increase in B's share, only a 50% share of such items (B's share as of October 22, 1986) is attributable to B's preenactment interest.

As a result of the decrease in B's share on November 30, 1987, only a 40% share of the items of X assigned to the period from December 1, 1987, through December 31, 1987, is attributable to B's preenactment interest. In addition, notwithstanding the increase in A's share, only a 25% share of such items (A's share as of October 22, 1986, reduced by the amount of the decrease in A's share on June 30, 1987) is attributable to A's preenactment interest. (Temp. Reg. §1.469-11T(c)(5)(iii), Ex. 7)

Chapter 11

Shareholders' Basis in S Corporation Stock and Loans

Functions of Basis

Q. 11:1 When and why must a shareholder determine his or her basis in an S corporation?

"Basis" is the concept that reflects a shareholder's investment in the S corporation.

It is necessary to know the shareholder's basis in an S corporation in three situations:
1. To determine gain or loss when the shareholder sells or exchanges the stock;
2. To ascertain whether the shareholder may claim deductions and losses passed through by the S corporation; and
3. To determine the tax treatment of corporate distributions to the shareholder. (See Chapter 12 for a discussion of distributions.)

Q. 11:2 How is basis used to determine a shareholder's gain or loss on sale or exchange of stock?

The determination of gain or loss on sale or exchange is made by subtracting the basis in the S corporation stock (see Questions 11:4–11:8) from the proceeds received from the sale or exchange. A positive result means a profit, and a negative result means a loss. Liquidation of the corporation is also considered a sale or exchange for this purpose, and it is necessary to know the basis in the stock to determine whether the liquidation resulted in a gain or loss.

Q. 11:3 How is basis used to impose a limitation on losses?

S corporation losses that a shareholder can claim are limited to the shareholder's basis in his or her stock (see Questions 11:4–11:8), plus the shareholder's basis in loans he or she has made to the S corporation (see Questions 11:9–11:19). The limitation is discussed in detail at Questions 10:1–10:2.

Return Preparer Penalty: A tax return preparer who ignores this basis limitation rule may face a return preparer penalty. (See Question 10:1.)

Determining Basis

Q. 11:4 How is a shareholder's basis in S corporation stock determined?

The shareholder's basis in stock of an S corporation is determined in the same manner as the basis in stock of a C corporation, except that certain yearly adjustments are made. Thus, a shareholder's initial basis in S corporation stock he or she buys is the cost of the stock.

A shareholder's initial basis in stock he or she inherits is the fair market value on the date of death (or on the alternate valuation date if the alternate valuation date election is made on the federal estate tax return). (Section 1014)

If the shareholder obtains stock in a tax-free incorporation under Section 351, the shareholder's initial basis in the stock is equal to his or her basis in the assets he or she transferred to the corporation in exchange for the stock, reduced by (1) any money and property received from the corporation and (2) any liabilities assumed by the corporation in connection with the transfer. (Section 358) If the liabilities to which the transferred assets were subject exceeded the shareholder's basis in the assets, the shareholder's basis in the stock is zero. (See *Wiebusch*, 59 TC 777 (1973).)

Q. 11:5 What yearly adjustments must be made to each shareholder's basis in his or her S corporation stock?

Annual adjustments—both increases (see Question 11:6) and decreases (see Question 11:7)—are made to the basis in S corporation stock to reflect transactions that occur at the corporate level. (These adjustments are similar to yearly adjustments made to a partner's basis in a partnership interest.)

Impact of Basis Adjustments on Worthless Stock Deductions: If the stock in the S corporation becomes worthless, the shareholder is entitled to a deduction for this worthless stock. The deduction is measured by the shareholder's basis in the stock. (Section 165(g))

The pass-through provisions (see Chapter 9) and the basis adjustments apply before the worthless stock deduction, even if losses incurred after the stock becomes worthless (but during the same taxable year) are passed through. (Section 1367(b)(3)) This priority rule means that the basis available to the shareholder for the worthless stock will be reduced.

This priority rule is advantageous to the shareholder because the S corporation may pass through ordinary trade-or-business losses and deductions, which—subject to the loss limitations discussed in Chapter 10—are deductible. Worthless stock deductions are generally capital losses, for which deductibility is limited.

■ **Example.** Assume that an S corporation's stock becomes worthless and the corporation files for bankruptcy. In the same taxable year, the corporation incurs losses of $10,000; some of these losses are incurred after the stock becomes worthless. Further assume that the S corporation has one shareholder, whose basis at the beginning of the year in question was $12,000. If the worthless stock deduction were taken first, the shareholder would have a capital loss of $12,000 (which he might not be able to deduct), reducing his basis in the stock to zero. With a zero basis in his stock, the shareholder would not be able to deduct the S corporation's net operating loss of $10,000, because the basis limitation discussed at Question 11:3 would apply (assuming for the moment that he had no additional basis in debt).

However, because the net operating loss deduction is deemed to be passed through first, the shareholder will be permitted an ordinary loss of $10,000 from a trade or business (which, subject to the limitations of the at-risk and passive activity loss rules, is fully deductible if the taxpayer has offsetting income). Only the remaining $2,000 would be a worthless stock capital loss.

Q. 11:6 Which items increase a shareholder's basis in his or her S corporation stock?

The basis in S corporation stock is increased by the following items:

1. S corporation taxable income, to the extent that it is actually included in the gross income of the shareholder (the gross income may be as originally shown on the shareholder's tax return or as later determined by an adjustment resulting from an audit) (Sections 1367(a)(1)(A), 1367(a)(1)(B), and 1367(b)(1)) (if a shareholder is spreading recognition of income from a short 1987 year over four years, as described in Question 3:2, basis is still increased in the first year by the entire amount of taxable income; there is no four-year spread for basis);
2. Nontaxable income of the corporation, subject to the same limitations and adjustments as taxable income (Sections 1367(a)(1)(A) and 1367(b)(1));
3. The excess of percentage depletion deductions over the basis in the property subject to depletion (as a result of this adjustment, the excess of percentage depletion over cost depletion will not decrease the basis in the S corporation stock) (Section 1367(a)(1)(C));
4. Increases in the basis in S corporation property caused by recapture of investment tax credits if the shareholder's basis in stock has previously been reduced because of the credit and is being restored to reflect the recapture (Section 48(q)(6); for more on recapture, see Questions 8:34–8:35 and 9:6–9:7); and
5. Actual distributions that a former domestic international sales corporation (DISC) subsidiary makes on or after January 1, 1985, of income derived before that date (see *Rev. Rul. 85-86,* 1985-1 CB 291).

The increase in basis in stock for corporate income is made only after any basis in loans that has previously been reduced is restored. (Section 1367(b)(2)(B)) (See Question 11:9.)

Q. 11:7 Which items decrease a shareholder's basis in his or her S corporation stock?

Basis is decreased, but never below zero, by the sum of the following items:

1. All losses and expenses, both deductible and nondeductible, other

than capital expenses (Sections 1367(a)(2)(B), 1367(a)(2)(C), and 1367(a)(2)(D));
2. Dividend distributions that are not taxable because they are distributions of previously taxed income (see Questions 12:21–12:22) or of the accumulated adjustments account (see Questions 12:10–12:19) (Section 1367(a)(2)(A));
3. The shareholder's deduction for oil and gas depletion under Section 611 to the extent that it does not exceed the proportionate share of his or her adjusted basis under Section 613A(c)(13)(B) (Section 1367(a)(2)(E)); and
4. Any adjustment required when the basis in corporate assets was reduced to reflect the reduction of basis in S corporation property for the investment tax credit (this credit generally applies only to property placed in service before 1987).

Q. 11:8 What happens if the adjustments would decrease the basis in stock to below zero?

Basis in stock is never reduced below zero. (Section 1367(a)(2)) If the basis reduction amounts reduce the basis in the stock to zero, any excess of these amounts (other than those for dividend distributions) will then reduce the shareholder's basis in any loans made by said shareholder to the S corporation. (Section 1367(b)(2)(A))

The increase in basis in stock for corporate income (see Question 11:6) is made only after any basis in loans that has been previously reduced is restored. (Section 1367(b)(2)(B))

Q. 11:9 What is the shareholder's basis in loans made to the S corporation?

The shareholder's initial basis in a loan that qualifies as one that can increase basis (see Questions 11:13–11:18) is the amount of the loan. Subsequently, two types of basis adjustments are required (Section 1367(b)(2)):
1. Basis must be reduced for losses and deductions passed through to shareholders to the extent that these losses and deductions exceed the shareholders' bases in their stock; and
2. Basis that has been reduced by pass-through losses and deductions

may be restored by profits of subsequent S corporation years (these profits are applied to restore the basis of reduced-basis loans before they are applied to increase the basis of stock).

Impact of Worthless Debt Deduction on Basis Adjustments: If an S corporation debt to a shareholder becomes worthless during a year, the shareholder is entitled to a deduction in the amount of his or her basis in the debt. (Section 166(d)) This deduction is similar to the deduction for worthless stock (see Question 11:5), and the priority rules are the same. In other words, basis adjustments for pass-throughs are made before basis in the worthless debt is determined (Section 1367(b)(3)), and the shareholder is therefore able to deduct passed-through ordinary trade-or-business losses before calculating the capital loss from the worthless debt.

Q. 11:10 Is basis in loans ever reduced below zero?

No, basis in loans is never reduced below zero. When basis in both stock and loans is exhausted, shareholder deductions for pass-through expenses and losses are suspended until the shareholder obtains sufficient basis for deductions. (See Questions 10:1–10:2.) This additional basis can come from restoration of basis from corporate income (see Question 11:6) or from additional loans and/or contributions to capital (see Questions 11:13–11:25).

Q. 11:11 What happens when the S corporation repays loans in which the shareholder's basis has been reduced?

When repayments are made on loans with basis that has been reduced, IRS takes the position that each repayment of principal is allocable partly to return of basis and partly to income. (See *Rev. Rul. 68-537*, 1968-2 CB 372.)

> ■ **Example.** A shareholder lent his S corporation $10,000, and the basis of the loan was reduced to $6,000 by the pass-through of losses. Subsequently, the corporation made a principal repayment of $1,000. This repayment would be a tax-free return only to the extent of $600 (and reduces basis accordingly). The other $400 would be considered income.
>
> If the loan is not evidenced by a note, the income element is ordinary

income. On the other hand, if the loan is evidenced by a note, then the redemption of a corporate obligation is a sale or exchange resulting in capital gain. (*Rev. Rul. 64-162*, 1964-1 (Part 1) CB 304, interpreting Former Section 1232, which is now Sections 1271–1275; Section 1271(a)(1) contains the provision that amounts received by the holder of a debt instrument (bond, debenture, note) will be considered received in an exchange, so *Rev. Rul. 64-162* should still apply to make the gain a capital gain.)

The restoration of basis to loans for profits in subsequent years (see Question 11:6) is made prior to the determination of the tax treatment of the repayment of loans, even if the repayment takes place earlier in the taxable year.

Q. 11:12 How are payments on more than one outstanding loan allocated between return of basis and income?

In a situation in which there was more than one note outstanding and repayments were made, the Tax Court held that the fraction of payments representing income should be added together for the computation.

Thus, the fraction of payments representing income "should have as its numerator the difference between the face amount of the total indebtedness to the shareholder and the shareholder's basis therein and as its denominator the total indebtedness." (*Novell*, TC Memo 1970-31) Or:

$$\text{Income} = \frac{\text{Total indebtedness less basis}}{\text{Total indebtedness}}$$

Structuring Loans to Increase Basis

Q. 11:13 What type of loan to the corporation gives the shareholder additional basis for losses and deductions?

Basically, the only type of loan that creates additional basis for the shareholder is a loan from the shareholder to the corporation. The courts have consistently vetoed various accommodation arrangements. (See Questions 11:14–11:18.)

In addition, there must be some business purpose for the loan. It must serve some purpose other than increasing the shareholder's basis. IRS has adopted a substance-over-form analysis in holding that a financing agreement lacked any commercial reality and therefore did not create basis. (*Rev. Rul. 80-236,* 1980-2 CB 240)

Planning Pointer. Because a loan should have the effect of increasing basis if there is a valid business reason for it, the business reasons should be documented in the corporate minutes that authorize the corporation to borrow the money.

The shareholder might also consider a contribution to capital instead of a loan. (See Question 11:23.)

Q. 11:14 Can a shareholder obtain basis for purposes of the limitation on losses and deductions by guaranteeing a loan the corporation obtains from a third party?

No, the shareholder cannot. Innumerable cases have held, uniformly, that a shareholder's personal guarantee of an S corporation's notes and/or loans does not provide basis for purposes of the loss and deduction pass-throughs. (See, for example, *Perry,* 47 TC 159 (1966), *aff'd,* 392 F.2d 458 (8th Cir. 1968); *Raynor,* 50 TC 762 (1968); *Neal,* 313 F. Supp. 393 (D. Cal. 1970); *Blum,* 59 TC 438 (1972); *Bader,* TC Memo 1987-30; *Estate of Daniel Leavitt,* 90 TC 206 (1988); *Edward R. Erwin, III,* TC Memo 1989-80; *Douglas D. Fear,* TC Memo 1989-211. But see *Selfe v. U.S.,* 778 F.2d 769 (11th Cir., 1985) for an apparent contradiction to this rule.)

Q. 11:15 Does the situation change if the shareholder-guarantor actually has to make payments on the loan?

Yes, it does. Despite the general rule that a guarantee of a corporate loan does not create basis for the purpose of the limitation on deductions and losses (see Question 11:14), if the shareholder makes payments on the guarantee, the corporation's indebtedness to the third party becomes the debt of the guaranteeing shareholder who makes the payments. (*Rev. Rul. 70-50,* 1970-1 CB 178)

However, these payments create debt that increases basis only in the year the shareholder pays the corporate debt under the guarantee. They do not relate back to the year the guarantee was made. (*Rev. Rul. 71-288,* 1971-2 CB 319)

Planning Pointer. Instead of guaranteeing corporate borrowings from third parties, the shareholders should consider borrowing the money themselves from the third parties and then either lending their borrowed money to the S corporation or contributing it to the corporation's capital. (For a discussion of which of these courses to follow, see Questions 11:23–11:25.)

Q. 11:16 If a shareholder substitutes his or her own obligation for corporate obligations to a third party, will this create basis for purposes of the limitation on losses and deductions?

Yes, it will. IRS has held that a shareholder would obtain basis when he substituted his own notes for a corporate note that he had guaranteed. Under the facts of the ruling, the creditor relieved the corporation from its liability on the old notes and substituted the shareholder as the primary obligor. Holding that the state law subrogated the shareholder into the position of the third-party lender (so that the corporation now owed the loan to the shareholder), IRS said he had basis in a loan made by him to the corporation. (*Rev. Rul. 75-144,* 1975-1 CB 277)

> **Planning Pointer.** A better procedure would be for the shareholder to avoid making the guarantee if he or she is requested to do so. Instead, the shareholder should personally borrow the money from the lender and give the lender a note. The borrowed funds should then be lent to the corporation in exchange for the corporation's note to the shareholder. Alternatively, the shareholder may contribute the capital to the corporation in exchange for stock or as additional paid-in capital. In any event, the shareholder will get credit for basis that may be used to offset corporate operating losses and deductions on his or her own income tax return.

Q. 11:17 Do loans from a related third party give the shareholder basis for deducting passed-through deductions and losses?

No, the shareholder himself or herself must have sufficient basis in the stock of the S corporation and in loans made to the S corporation. The courts have uniformly held that loans by related entities do not provide any basis for purposes of the pass-through limitation.

In *Prashker,* 59 TC 172 (1972), Mrs. Prashker was a shareholder in an S corporation and also the sole beneficiary and executrix of her husband's

Q. 11:17   The S Corporation Answer Book

estate. She caused the estate to lend the corporation $150,000, but was unable to use this as basis in loans made by her to the corporation. Had she made the estate checks payable to herself and then lent them to the corporation, she would have been able to deduct the losses. (See also *Rev. Rul. 69-125,* 1969-1 CB 207.)

There are about half a dozen other cases, all with the same result. (See *Robertson* (D. Nev. 1973), loan from a trust of which he was remainderman beneficiary; *Frankel,* 61 TC 343 (1973), *aff'd,* 506 F.2d 1051 (3d Cir. 1974), loan from a partnership in which all partners were also shareholders; *Lee et al.,* TC Memo 1976-265, loan from another corporation with the same shareholders; *Burnstein,* TC Memo 1984-74, *Shebester,* TC Memo 1987-246, and *Gurda,* TC Memo 1987-394, all involving loans from related corporations.)

Q. 11:18   Will co-making or cosigning a corporate loan give a shareholder basis for purposes of the limitation on deductions and losses?

Shareholders may be denied basis for purposes of the loss limitations when they are co-makers on loans to S corporations from third parties. The courts have generally looked upon the shareholder/co-maker as a mere guarantor or accommodation co-maker when the proceeds of the loan are used by the corporation. If the proceeds of the loan are not used by the corporation, then there is no indebtedness from the corporation to the shareholder for the debt, and so no basis in shareholder loans.

> **Planning Pointer.** A better procedure is for the shareholder to borrow the money directly and then either lend it to the corporation or contribute it to the corporation as additional capital. (See Question 11:20.)

Contributions to Capital—A Planning Tool

Q. 11:19   Is a loan the only way, other than a stock purchase, to increase the shareholder's basis?

No, a loan to the corporation is not the only way—other than a stock purchase—to increase the shareholder's basis for losses and deductions. The shareholder may also make a contribution to capital.

Q. 11:20 What is a contribution to capital?

Basically, a contribution to capital is a contribution of cash or other property to the corporation that increases the corporation's paid-in capital. A stock purchase also increases a corporation's paid-in capital, but with a contribution of capital, the shareholder does not receive stock.

Repayment of a loan may create income to the shareholder (from interest on the loan principal and payments deemed to be made on reduced basis, as described at Questions 11:11–11:12). Contributions to capital increase the shareholder's basis in his or her stock. Basis is used to measure the gain or loss upon sale (see Question 11:2), to characterize corporate distributions to shareholders (see Chapter 12), and to establish the limitation on losses and deductions.

Q. 11:21 What types of payments can be contributions to capital?

Contributions to capital can be direct payments of money or other property designated as such. However, as with shareholder loans (see Question 11:13), it is important to be able to establish a business purpose for the contributions to capital. Contributions designed merely to increase basis will not be permitted to do so.

For example, the Tax Court has held that basis did not exist when claimed contributions to the capital of an S corporation were found to be sham transactions made solely to obtain basis for deducting passed-through losses. (*Hodge,* TC Memo 1970-280) Admittedly, this case was a poor one. The taxpayers had contributed real estate, which they dealt with as their own after the so-called transfers to the corporation. They personally reported the income and expense from the property on their own tax returns, and one of them executed a notarized agreement in which he stated that he, individually, owned the property. Furthermore, they failed to prove a basis they could use even if the transfers were bona fide.

> **Planning Pointer.** It is advisable to document the business reasons for the contribution to capital—that is, why the corporation needs the money or property—in the corporate minutes authorizing the capital contribution. (The same is true even if the corporation authorizes issuance of additional stock.)

Q. 11:22 How do contributions to capital increase basis?

Contributions to capital increase the shareholder's basis in his or her

S corporation *stock*. The amount of the increase is the amount of money contributed or the fair market value of other property contributed. (Unless the contribution qualifies as a tax-free transaction under Section 351, the shareholder must recognize income to the extent that fair market value exceeds his or her basis in the contributed property.)

Subsequently, this basis is adjusted yearly as part of the shareholder's basis in his or her stock. (See Question 11:5.)

Q. 11:23 What are the advantages of a contribution to capital, as compared to a loan?

A contribution to capital (even using funds the shareholder has borrowed) offers the following advantages:

- It eliminates the need for the corporation to pay or impute interest and for the shareholder to recognize interest income;
- It eliminates the necessity of repayment;
- It eliminates the creation of income to the shareholder if principal is repaid after basis is reduced (see Questions 11:11–11:12 and 11:24);
- It may eliminate the problem of creating dividend income to the shareholder upon partial repayment (see Question 11:24 and Chapter 12);
- It will increase the shareholder's basis in his or her stock and therefore (1) decrease gain (or increase loss) upon sale or exchange of the stock (see Question 11:2) and (2) possibly increase the amount that the S corporation can distribute to the shareholder tax-free (see Chapter 12); and
- It eliminates the risk of creating debt that may be viewed as a second class of stock, thereby disqualifying the S corporation (see Questions 1:30–1:35).

Additionally, tax considerations aside, the contribution to capital will make the corporation's balance sheet look stronger. A loan will make the balance sheet look weaker.

Q. 11:24 How does a contribution to capital solve the problem of repayment of a reduced-basis loan?

As previously noted, a shareholder may use basis in loans to deduct corporate losses, but when a reduced-basis loan is repaid, IRS will treat part of the principal repaid as income. (See Questions 11:11–11:12.) Assuming for the moment that the S corporation has no accumulated earnings and profits (see Questions 12:4–12:6), all payments to a shareholder will be tax-free to the extent of basis. (This concept is discussed further at Question 12:7.) The impact is best illustrated by two examples.

■ **Example 1.** Assume that a corporation had losses that reduced shareholder A's basis in her stock to zero. Shareholder A lent the corporation $10,000, and additional losses reduced A's basis in these loans to $6,000. Upon a partial repayment of $1,000, $600 will be a repayment of loan basis (principal) and $400 will be gain because of the reduced basis.

■ **Example 2.** Assume the same facts as in Example 1, except that instead of making a $10,000 loan, A contributes $10,000 to the corporation's capital. Even though A's basis in her stock will be reduced to $6,000 by the subsequent losses, a payment of $1,000 (which is equivalent to repayment of the loan) will be completely tax-free. (It will, however, further reduce A's basis; see Question 11:7.)

Q. 11:25   What might make a contribution to capital inadvisable?

If the corporation has accumulated earnings and profits (E&P), it will not be able to make a tax-free return of the capital contributed until it has distributed all E&P. E&P distributions result in dividend income fully taxable to the shareholder. These concepts are discussed fully in Chapter 12.

Additionally, there can be at least one nontax reason for using loans, rather than contributions to capital: protection from creditors. If the S corporation becomes insolvent, contributions to capital will be lost; the creditors will receive everything. On the other hand, a shareholder who is also a creditor may be able to salvage some of the money he or she has put into the corporation.

Chapter 12

S Corporation Distributions to Shareholders

Fundamental Concepts

Q. 12:1 How, generally speaking, are S corporation distributions treated?

In an S corporation, profits, losses, and other items are passed through to the shareholders in the taxable year in which the corporation recognizes the items. The shareholders recognize these items, and pay tax on them when they pass through. (See Chapter 9.) This pass-through also affects the shareholders' bases in their S corporation stock. (See Questions 11:4–11:8.) What, then, happens when the S corporation actually distributes income to its shareholders? The general rules are as follows (Section 1368(b); see Question 12:3):

- Distributions to the shareholders are generally not taxable to them to the extent that they are recoveries of shareholders' bases; and
- Distributions in excess of basis are generally treated as capital gains, eligible for whatever tax-favored rates may be available.

However, when the corporation has earnings and profits, some distributions to shareholders may be taxable as dividends (at ordinary income rates when there is a distinction between ordinary income and long-term capital gain rates). (Section 1368(c)) (See Questions 12:9–12:20.)

Special rules apply to distributions after the election is terminated. (Section 1371(e)) (see Question 12:23.)

Q. 12:2 What concepts are important in characterizing distributions from an S corporation?

In characterizing distributions from an S corporation, it is necessary to determine several different items, including:

- The shareholder's basis in his or her S corporation stock (see Questions 11:4–11:8); and
- Whether the corporation has any accumulated earnings and profits (see Questions 12:4–12:6).

The following may also be relevant:

- The amount in the corporation's accumulated adjustments account (see Questions 12:10–12:17); and
- Whether the corporation has any previously taxed income (see Questions 12:21–12:22).

Q. 12:3 What are earnings and profits (E&P)?

Earnings and profits (E&P) consist of all recognized income (both taxable and nontaxable), reduced by all losses and payments (both deductible and nondeductible), from the date of incorporation (or from 1913 if that is after the date of incorporation). The concept is an economic concept and applies primarily to C corporations. (See Section 312 and the regulations thereunder.)

Q. 12:4 When will an S corporation have E&P?

Under present law, it is impossible for an S corporation to build up any current or accumulated E&P. This is because all of the items of income and deductions of an S corporation are treated as though received or paid by the shareholders. The no E&P rule applies to taxable as well as nontaxable items of income and expense. Since everything passes through to the shareholders (in a manner similar to that in which partnership items pass through to the partners), there can be no addition to an S corporation's E&P. (Section 1371(c)(1)) However, an S corporation may have E&P from any or all of the following:

1. E&P it accumulated while it was a C corporation;
2. E&P it accumulated in Subchapter S taxable years prior to 1983; and
3. E&P it acquired from another corporation.

Planning Pointer. When it is necessary to determine the amount of E&P, worksheets similar to those described in *Rev. Proc. 75-17,* 1975-1 CB 677, should be prepared. Reference should also be made to IRS Form 5452, "Corporate Report of Non-Taxable Dividends," and the worksheet illustration on the back of that form.

Q. 12:5 How can an S corporation acquire E&P from another corporation?

E&P will be acquired in the event of redemptions, liquidations, reorganizations, and the like (basically the types of transactions discussed in Chapter 5). (Section 1371(c)(2)) For example, if a C corporation that has E&P is merged into an S corporation, the surviving S corporation will inherit the C corporation's E&P.

It might also acquire E&P from another S corporation that either has its own E&P or has previously acquired it from a C corporation. If the S corporation acquiring the E&P also has E&P of its own, it must adjust its E&P to reflect the acquired E&P.

Q. 12:6 When is an S corporation's E&P reduced?

The E&P of an S corporation may be reduced by dividend distributions. (see Questions 12:9–12:18.) (Section 1371(c)(3)) These distributions of the S corporation's E&P will be taxable to the shareholders as ordinary income.

An S corporation's E&P may also be reduced by investment credit recapture for which the corporation is liable. If a C corporation reduced its taxes through use of the investment credit and later elected S corporation status, the early disposition of that property while the S corporation election is in effect will cause recapture income tax to the S corporation. (See Question 8:34.) This investment credit recapture tax will reduce the accumulated E&P of the S corporation. (Section 1371(d)(3))

Corporations Without E&P

Q. 12:7 How are distributions from an S corporation taxed if the corporation has no E&P?

Distributions to each shareholder from an S corporation that has no E&P are taxed as follows (Section 1368(b)):

- They are tax-free to the shareholder to the extent of that shareholder's basis in his or her stock (Section 1368(b)(1)); and
- They are treated as having been received from the sale or exchange of stock to the extent that they exceed the shareholder's basis in the stock. (Section 1368(b)(2)) (This rule generally leads to capital gain treatment unless the corporation is a collapsible corporation as defined in Section 341; even if favorable capital gain rates are not important, the characterization can be important—for example, in applying limitations on capital losses under Section 1211.)

Basis adjustments resulting from corporate income or loss from the current year are made before applying these rules. (see Question 11:5 for a discussion of basis adjustments.)

Property distributions are considered made at fair market value for purposes of these computations. (see Question 8:4 for a discussion of the impact of property distributions on the corporation.)

The table below illustrates the distribution rule discussed above:

Deemed Order of Distribution	Tax Treatment
Tax basis in stock (after current year's adjustments)	Tax-free
Excess over tax basis in stock	Treated as sale or exchange of S corporation stock

Effect of Tax-Exempt Income: An S corporation may derive tax-exempt income from such sources as municipal bond interest or proceeds from a life insurance policy on an officer-shareholder. When the S corporation receives this tax-exempt income, no taxable income is created at the corporate level, and therefore no taxable income passes through to the shareholders. However, the receipt of tax-exempt income by the corporation does serve to increase the shareholder's tax basis in his or her stock. (See Question 11:6.) Therefore, the distribution of an amount for which the basis was increased will be tax-free.

Q. 12:8 Is it important for an S corporation without E&P to make distributions to its shareholders each year?

Corporations with no E&P have a simple set of distribution rules. (See

Question 12:7.) Distributions are tax-free to the extent of the shareholder's tax basis in his or her stock (after the current-year adjustments of tax basis). Any excess is treated as gain from the shareholder's sale or exchange of the S corporation's stock. (Section 1368(b))

Since the income that is not distributed will increase the shareholder's tax basis in his or her stock (see Question 11:6)—and thus the amount of tax-free distributions that can be made in subsequent years, so long as the election is in effect—current distributions are not generally important.

Even if the election terminates, the S corporation will still have the post-termination transition period, during which it can make a tax-free distribution of its S corporation income. (See Question 12:23.)

Corporations With E&P

Q. 12:9 How are distributions from an S corporation generally taxed if the corporation does have accumulated E&P?

If the corporation does have E&P, distributions are generally treated as being made in this order (Section 1368(c)):

1. From the accumulated adjustments account (see Questions 12:10–12:15);
2. From accumulated E&P as a dividend; and
3. Then (as E&P has been exhausted), according to the rules for an S corporation with no E&P (see Question 12:7).

As with other S corporation distributions, there is no distinction between cash and property distributions, and the tax impact on each shareholder is determined by his or her basis in the S corporation stock he or she holds.

The following table summarizes these distribution rules:

Deemed Order of Distribution	Tax Treatment
Accumulated adjustments account, up to tax basis in stock	Tax-free (reduces basis in stock)
Accumulated adjustments account in excess of the tax basis in the stock	Treated as a sale or exchange of S corporation stock

Accumulated E&P	Ordinary dividend income (file Form 1099 DIV)
Basis in stock, if any remaining	Tax-free (reduces basis in stock)
Excess over tax basis in stock	Treated as sale or exchange of S corporation stock

Q. 12:10 What is the accumulated adjustments account that an S corporation with E&P generally distributes first?

The accumulated adjustments account is a memorandum account for corporations that have accumulated E&P. (See Questions 12:4–12:5.) It is used to account for income and expenses of S corporation years beginning after 1982 (Section 1368(e)(2)), and it basically represents the total of the S corporation's taxable income (see Questions 8:1–8:7), reduced by deductible expenses and by nondeductible expenses that are unrelated to tax-exempt income. (Section 1368(e)(1))

Q. 12:11 How are adjustments to the accumulated adjustments account made?

Adjustments to the accumulated adjustments account to reflect income and expenses are made in a manner similar to that in which adjustments to the shareholder's basis in stock are made under Section 1367. (See Questions 11:6–11:8.)

The adjustments are made at the end of the taxable year, before the distributions are characterized. (The example contained at Question 12:16 demonstrates the impact of this rule.)

Interaction With Four-Year Spread: It is possible that the S corporation had to change to a calendar or other "permitted" year in 1987 to comply with the calendar-year rules of the Tax Reform Act of 1986 (TRA '86). In that case, shareholder income from the short year resulting from the change may be spread over four years. (See Question 3:2.)

TRA '86, as amended by the Technical and Miscellaneous Revenue Act of 1988, and temporary regulations on the four-year spread specifically provide that basis is increased in the beginning of the spread period. However, the temporary regulations make no mention of the accumulated adjustments account. Failure to increase the accumulated adjustments account when basis is increased may create a trap. If accumulated adjustments are amortized, distributions of more than the amortized amount for the year may result in an inadvertent distribution of E&P.

Q. 12:12 How is the accumulated adjustments account reduced, and what is the impact?

The accumulated adjustments account is reduced by (Section 1368(e)(1)):

- Deductible expenses and losses;
- Nondeductible expenses unrelated to tax-exempt income;
- Distributions to shareholders of either cash or property (to the extent that the account is positive); and
- Certain redemptions (see Question 12:13).

When the accumulated adjustments account is reduced to zero, it is no longer available for tax-free distributions, and generally the corporation will next distribute E&P. (See Question 12:9 for this general rule, and Question 12:18 for an exception.)

The accumulated adjustments account can be reduced below zero. When that happens, the negative amount must be restored before the corporation can make further tax-free distributions. (See Question 12:15.)

Q. 12:13 How does a redemption reduce the accumulated adjustments account?

A redemption will affect the accumulated adjustments account if it is treated as an exchange for stock that (Section 1368(e)(1)(B)):

- Qualifies for capital gain treatment under Section 302(a); or
- Qualifies as a distribution to pay death taxes under Section 303(a).

In such cases, the accumulated adjustments account is reduced by the portion of the account that is allocable to the redeemed shares. The portion of the account that is allocable to the redeemed shares is the amount that bears the same ratio to the balance of the accumulated adjustments account that the number of shares redeemed bears to the total number of shares of stock immediately before the redemption. (Section 1368(e)(1)(B)) This can be expressed:

$$\frac{\text{Allocable portion}}{\text{Accumulated adjustments account}} = \frac{\text{Shares redeemed}}{\text{Total shares immediately before redemption}}$$

Q. 12:14 If distributions in a taxable year exceed the amount in the accumulated adjustments account, how are distributions allocated to that account?

Amounts in the accumulated adjustments account are allocated pro rata among all distributions made during the year. (Section 1368(c)(3)) Regulations may be promulgated that could vary this rule.

Even if shares change hands during the year, the accumulated adjustments account is a corporate account and thus is transferable when the shares to which it applies are transferred during the year.

Q. 12:15 Can the accumulated adjustments account become negative?

Yes, S corporation losses reduce the accumulated adjustments account and can cause it to become negative. Distributions to shareholders do not reduce the accumulated adjustments account when it is negative. (These distributions are not made out of the accumulated adjustments account.)

Q. 12:16 Can S corporation distributions be timed to prevent problems that arise from a zero or negative accumulated adjustments account?

As previously noted, losses can cause the accumulated adjustments account to become negative. (See Question 12:15.) If there is a negative—or zero-value—accumulated adjustments account, distributions will be deemed to come out of E&P, and thus will be taxable. (See Question 12:9.) This can become a tax trap, and thus—in contrast to the S corporation that has no E&P (see Question 12:5)—the S corporation that does have current E&P should consider current distributions, particularly if it is a marginal operation or has reason to anticipate losses.

■ **Example.** A former C corporation has accumulated E&P of $50,000. For its calendar year 1990 it elects S corporation status, and during 1990 it earns $10,000, which is passed through to its sole shareholder as 1990 taxable income. On February 15, 1991, the corporation distributes $10,000 to its sole shareholder. Subsequently, the corporation incurs a $15,000 loss for 1991. The entire loss is incurred after the distribution is made. Nonetheless, the distribution is fully taxable. This is because the accumulated adjustments account, which was a positive $10,000 for 1990, is completely eliminated and becomes a negative $5,000 because of the 1991 loss of $15,000. As there is no positive accumulated adjustments account, the entire $10,000 is deemed to be a fully taxable distribution of accumulated E&P.

These adverse tax consequences could have been avoided if the corporation had made the $10,000 distribution to the shareholder in December 1990 instead of February 1991. If the distribution had been made in 1990, the accumulated adjustments account would have had a positive amount ($10,000), and the entire distribution would have been tax-free. (The shareholder would have had to pay tax on the pass-through of the income, but not on the distribution—which would have been deemed to be the same $10,000 in current earnings instead of a different $10,000 out of accumulated E&P.)

Q. 12:17 Do tax-exempt earnings affect the accumulated adjustments account?

Nontaxable income and related expenses have no effect on the accumulated adjustments account. (Section 1368(e)(1)(A)) In effect, this means that receipt of tax-exempt income by the S corporation can create a problem—the tax-exempt income (although it is not taxed to the shareholders in the year of receipt by the S corporation) cannot be paid out tax-free to shareholders until all accumulated E&P has been paid out, as fully taxable dividend income.

This is true because, although the tax-exempt income does increase each shareholder's tax basis in his or her stock (see Question 11:6), only the accumulated adjustments account can be distributed before accumulated E&P. Thus, accumulated E&P must be distributed before any tax-exempt income can be distributed.

■ **Example.** An S corporation has a single shareholder. On January 1, 1990, the corporation has an accumulated adjustments account of

$10,000 and accumulated E&P of $50,000. The shareholder's basis in her stock is $75,000. During calendar 1990, the corporation has $20,000 of tax-exempt interest and no other income. It has broken even on its operations for the year. In November 1990, the corporation makes a distribution of $30,000. The shareholder intends to distribute the $10,000 in the accumulated adjustments account, plus the $20,000 of tax-exempt income that the corporation has just earned. However, the tax results for this will not be as expected. The first $10,000 is considered a distribution of the accumulated adjustments account. This distribution is tax-free because the tax on the accumulated adjustments had previously been paid by the shareholder via the pass-through of corporate taxable income. The next $20,000 comes from accumulated E&P and is fully taxable as ordinary dividend income. Tax-exempt income cannot be distributed until the entire $50,000 of accumulated E&P has been distributed.

Q. 12:18 Can a corporation with accumulated E&P distribute E&P before distributing the accumulated adjustments account?

Yes, the corporation may elect to avoid applying the accumulated adjustments account to any part of distributions made during a taxable year. (Section 1368(e)(3))

Q. 12:19 Why would a corporation want to distribute E&P before distributing the accumulated adjustments account?

Generally, an S corporation wants to distribute the accumulated adjustments account before it distributes E&P for the simple reason that the first represents tax-free income to the shareholders, while the second does not. (See Question 12:9.) However, an S corporation that has both accumulated E&P and passive investment income faces two severe consequences:

1. A tax on excess passive investment income (see Questions 8:10–8:12); and
2. Termination of the S corporation election if passive investment income exceeds 25% of gross receipts for three years. (See Chapter 7 for a discussion of this rule.)

By making this election to distribute E&P first, an S corporation with accumulated E&P could clear out its accumulated E&P account and thereby no longer be subject to limitations on passive investment income. Without the ability to make this election, the corporation would have to distribute the combined total of its accumulated adjustments account and its E&P account in order to pay out all of its E&P. With this election, it can eliminate its accumulated E&P by distributing an amount equal to that E&P.

■ **Example.** An S corporation has $100,000 in its accumulated adjustments account and $50,000 of accumulated E&P. Under the normal rules for distributions (see Question 12:9), the corporation would have to distribute the accumulated adjustments account first, and it would have to make a $150,000 distribution to cleanse itself of E&P. But the corporation can afford to distribute only $100,000. By electing under Section 1368(e)(3), the corporation will be able to treat the first $50,000 distributed as a distribution of accumulated E&P, and thus cleanse itself of E&P. The remaining $50,000 will be a distribution from the accumulated adjustments account.

The election will also permit a corporation to obtain a dividends-paid deduction for purposes of any accumulated earnings tax and personal holding company tax that might otherwise arise for its last C corporation year.

It can also enable a corporation to receive tax-exempt income and distribute it to shareholders tax-free to the extent of their bases in their stock. (See Question 12:17.)

Q. 12:20 How does the corporation elect to distribute accumulated E&P first?

To make the election, the corporation must attach a statement to its income tax return (Form 1120S) stating that it elects under Section 1368(e)(3) not to have Section 1368(c)(1) apply to distributions made during the taxable year. Pursuant to that election, the accumulated E&P of the corporation will be distributed prior to any distribution of the accumulated adjustments account.

All of the affected shareholders (that is, those who have received distributions from the S corporation during the corporation's taxable year) must consent to the corporation making this election. The consent should be attached to, or made a part of, the election attached to the tax return.

Q. 12:21   **The S Corporation Answer Book**

Q. 12:21 Are these distribution rules modified if an S corporation has undistributed pre-1983 S corporation income that has previously been taxed?

Yes, they are. Cash distributions of previously taxed income from years beginning before January 1, 1983, are tax-free and deemed made before any taxable distributions are made from E&P. (Section 1379(c), continuing the effectiveness of Former Sections 1375(d) and 1375(f) for current distributions of previously taxed undistributed taxable income from any taxable year beginning before January 1, 1983.)

This means that distributions of previously taxed income are deemed to occur after any payments from the accumulated adjustments account but before any payments from accumulated E&P. When combined with the general distribution rules (see Question 12:9), the order of distribution of taxable income, and the tax consequences thereof, are deemed to be as follows:

Deemed Order of Distribution	*Tax Treatment*
Accumulated adjustments account, up to tax basis in stock	Tax-free (reduces basis in stock)
Accumulated adjustments account in excess of the tax basis in the stock	Treated as a sale or exchange of S corporation stock
Previously taxed income for years prior to January 1, 1983 (personal to each shareholder and may be distributed using money only)	Tax-free (reduces basis in stock)
Accumulated E&P	Ordinary dividend income
Basis in stock, if any remaining	Tax-free (reduces basis in stock)
Excess over tax basis in S corporation stock	Treated as sale or exchange of S corporation stock

Q. 12:22 What is previously taxed income?

Previously taxed income is taxable income from any Subchapter S taxable years beginning before January 1, 1983, that has not been distributed to shareholders. It is personal to each shareholder and cannot be transferred—even by gift or by death. It can no longer be increased, but can be reduced and/or eliminated by distributions to shareholders. It can be distributed in the form of money only. Previously taxed income cannot be distributed in the form of property. (See Question 12:21.)

Post-Termination Distributions

Q. 12:23 Can a corporation make tax-free distributions of S corporation income after the election has been terminated or revoked?

Yes, during a "post-termination transition period," the S corporation may make tax-free distributions *of money only,* to the extent of the accumulated adjustments account. These distributions reduce each shareholder's basis in his or her stock. Note that, for this purpose, the corporation must use the accumulated adjustments account measure (see Questions 12:10–12:15), even if it has no accumulated E&P. (Section 1371(e)(1))

Also note that, as the accumulated adjustments account is the measure of the tax-free distribution, tax-exempt income cannot be distributed tax-free after termination or revocation under the Subchapter S rules. (See Question 12:17.) However, the tax-exempt income may be distributed tax-free under the Subchapter C rules if the corporation has no current or accumulated E&P.

Q. 12:24 What is the post-termination transition period?

The post-termination transition period may be either (Section 1377(b)(1)):

1. The period beginning on the day after the final day of the S corporation's last S corporation taxable year and ending on the later of (a) the date one year after the final day of the last S corporation year or (b) the due date, including extensions, for filing the S corporation's return for the last S corporation year (see Questions 14:2–14:3 for a discussion of due dates and extensions); or

2. A 120-day period that begins on the date of a determination that the corporation's S election has terminated for a previous year.

The latter provision permits the S corporation to take advantage of the post-termination distribution rule (see Question 12:23) if it has filed a return, more than a year has passed, and IRS decides that the election has been terminated. Such a determination would usually occur upon audit. A final determination, for purposes of beginning the 120-day period, is defined as (Section 1377(b)(2)):

1. A final court decision;
2. A closing agreement; or
3. An agreement between the corporation and IRS that the election has been terminated.

Q. 12:25 Can—and should—the corporation opt out of this post-termination transition-period rule?

The general rule is that during the post-termination transition period (see Question 12:24), money distributions reduce the basis in stock (and are tax-free) to the extent of the accumulated adjustments account. (See Question 12:23.) But the corporation—with the consent of all shareholders to whom distributions are made during the post-termination transition period—may instead elect to treat the distributions as ordinary dividends out of E&P. (Section 1371(e)(2))

This election will permit the corporation to avoid accumulated earnings tax or personal holding company tax, which are of no concern to the S corporation, but which can be a significant concern to a small, closely held C corporation.

Chapter 13

Compensation; Fringe and Retirement Benefits

Compensation

Q. 13:1 Can a shareholder who works fulltime for his or her S corporation take zero compensation and have the profits distributed as dividends to avoid unemployment tax, Social Security, and withholding requirements?

IRS takes the position that S corporation dividends paid to employee-shareholders in lieu of reasonable compensation should be treated as wages subject to federal payroll taxes. Thus, the payments would be subject to federal unemployment (FUTA) taxes, Social Security (FICA) taxes, and federal withholding tax requirements. (See *Rev. Rul. 74-44*, 1974-1 CB 287; *Rev. Rul. 73-361*, 1973-2 CB 331; *Letter Ruling 7949022*.)

In 1989, a federal district court upheld IRS when the Service imposed deficiencies, interest, and penalties for failure to file Forms 940 and 941 and pay Social Security and federal unemployment taxes. The shareholder was the corporation's only fulltime employee. Whenever he needed money and whenever the corporation showed a profit, he would have the corporation declare a dividend to him. No payroll tax returns were filed. The court stated: "An employer should not be permitted to evade FICA and FUTA by characterizing all of an employee's remuneration as something other than wages." (*Radtke* (E.D. Wis. 4/11/89))

Planning Pointer. If a corporation pays at least $7,000 in wages to its shareholder-employees, it will eliminate any assessment for failure to file and pay federal unemployment taxes. It will also avoid a penalty

Q. 13:1   **The S Corporation Answer Book**

for failure to file payroll tax returns. Ideally, however, the corporation should pay a figure that could be justified as "reasonable compensation"—even if such figure is at the low end of the reasonable spectrum.

Fringe Benefits

Q. 13:2   Can the S corporation deduct the cost of providing fringe benefits to a shareholder who is also an employee?

Fringe benefits are employee benefits (other than retirement plan benefits, as discussed at Question 13:7 et seq.). To the extent that a corporation can provide deductible fringe benefits to shareholder-employees, all shareholders benefit because the corporation can use the deduction to reduce the taxable income that passes through to them. (See Question 8:2.) The individual shareholder-employee (or his or her beneficiary) benefits because the corporation's payments are not included in his or her taxable income.

However, *no* S corporation may deduct the cost of fringe benefits to shareholder-employees who own more than 2% of the corporation's stock. Such a person is treated as a partner. (Section 1372) A partner is not considered an employee of the partnership and, therefore, is deprived of most tax-free fringe benefit opportunities. (This rule became fully effective in taxable years beginning in 1988.)

Fringe benefit payments on behalf of shareholders owning 2% or less of the S corporation's stock are, however, treated as deductible business expenses and, unlike payments on behalf of other shareholders, are excluded from the shareholder-employee's income. In other words, these 2%-or-less shareholders are treated like other employees.

Q. 13:3   How is ownership calculated for purposes of the rule treating more-than-2% shareholders as partners?

For purposes of the rule treating more-than-2% shareholders as partners for fringe benefit purposes, any person owning more than 2% of the stock, directly or indirectly, on *any day* during the year, is considered a 2%-or-more shareholder. The ownership may consist of more than

2% of the outstanding stock or ownership of voting stock that has more than 2% of the total combined voting power of all of the stock in the corporation. (Section 1372(b))

Indirect Ownership: The attribution rules of Section 318 are used to determine indirect ownership. Generally speaking, under these rules, an individual is deemed to own (Section 318(a)):

- Stock held by his or her spouse, children, grandchildren, and parents; and
- Stock held by a grantor trust of which the person is considered the grantor or other trust of which the person is considered the substantial owner.

Q. 13:4 How might the S corporation handle benefits for more-than-2% shareholders?

The Code does *not* bar the S corporation from paying the costs of fringe benefits for 2% shareholders (as defined at Question 13:4). What it does is prevent the corporation from deducting payments as a business expense and deprive the shareholders of the ability to exclude these payments from income. Because no deduction is available, the payment of the expense does not reduce the income that passes through to the shareholder—and generally unless holders of equal amounts of stock are all receiving fringe benefits of equal value, some shareholders are at least arguably bearing the expense of payments without correlative benefits.

This inequitable result comes about because Congress, in enacting the Subchapter S Revision Act of 1982, attempted to make an S corporation more like a partnership. However, Congress apparently overlooked the fact that partnerships have more flexibility than S corporations. In particular, they can either (1) make special allocations of tax items, as long as the allocations have substantial economic effect (see Section 704(b)), or (2) treat guaranteed service-related payments to partners as compensation in certain circumstances (see Section 707(c)). Thus, a partnership is able to reach an equitable result.

■ **Example.** Assume a 50% partner's distributive share of partnership income is $100, and the partnership pays $5 for health insurance for a partner. The net income taxed to the partner would be $100 (the distributive share with no offset for the health insurance). However,

Q. 13:4

the partnership could instead treat the health insurance premium as a guaranteed payment under Section 707(c), in which case the partner would recognize the $5 cost as compensation income and receive a pro rata share of the compensation deduction for the guaranteed payment.

Some published reports have argued that Section 1372 in effect incorporates Section 707(c) by reference, which would mean that an S corporation could reach the same result as in the example above, reducing pass-through income to $95. (The shareholder's Form K-1 would reflect $5 of nonexcludable health insurance.) However, this type of approach, is, to say the least, *extremely aggressive and risky in the absence of any specific endorsement from Treasury or IRS.*

In the absence of additional regulatory or legislative guidance, at least two other, *less aggressive approaches* are available:

1. Have the shareholder reimburse the S corporation for the benefits (which, particularly in the context of medical insurance and group term life insurance, gives the shareholder the advantage of whatever favorable rates the corporation is able to obtain); or
2. Treat the payment of fringe benefits to shareholders as compensation to them.

Q. 13:5 What deductible fringe benefits are available to 2%-or-less shareholders and other employees?

Deductible fringe benefit plans for 2%-or-less shareholders who are employees and nonshareholder-employees may include the following:

- Medical expense reimbursement;
- Health and accident insurance plans;
- Group-term life insurance;
- Employee death benefits; and
- Meals and lodging.

Under some circumstances, death benefits can also be provided to more-than-2% shareholders. (See Question 13:6.)

However, many of these benefits—particularly medical reimbursement and insurance plans and life insurance plans—may be subject to strict qualification and antidiscrimination rules that are beyond the scope of this book.

Q. 13:6 What tax-favored death benefits may S corporations pay on behalf of employees—including more-than-2% shareholders?

The Code generally permits an employer to pay a tax-free death benefit of up to $5,000 to an employee's spouse or other dependent. The employer can deduct this payment. (Section 101(b))

This exclusion is available for payments with respect to a more-than-2% shareholder (see Questions 13:2–13:3), but only if the payments are made as a distribution under a qualified pension or profit-sharing plan.

The S corporation can still provide these benefits separately, however, with respect to a nonshareholder-employee or an employee who is a 2%-or-less shareholder. If the payment is not a lump-sum distribution from a qualified plan, the employee must not have had a nonforfeitable right to the payment before he or she died.

This type of arrangement may be discriminatory. The corporation may select covered employees as it sees fit. If the corporation does not give a separate death benefit on behalf of an employee, the beneficiary of the employee's pension or profit-sharing death benefits may use the exclusion.

Retirement Plans

Q. 13:7 Can all shareholders participate in the S corporation's qualified retirement plan(s)?

The situation with regard to retirement plans is completely different from that with regard to fringe benefit plans. *No shareholder is excluded from participation on the basis of shareholdings. All shareholders can participate as long as they are employees who meet the eligibility and participation requirements.*

Q. 13:8 What are the tax advantages of qualified retirement plans?

The basic tax advantages of corporate pension and profit-sharing plans that apply to S corporations are:
- The corporation gets a current tax deduction for its contributions

Q. 13:8   The S Corporation Answer Book

to the plan, while covered employees are not taxed when the contributions are made;

- Earnings accumulate tax-free in the plan;
- Lump-sum plan distributions may qualify for special treatment (income averaging or tax-free rollover); and
- Death benefits payable under the plan may qualify for a $5,000 income tax exclusion (see Question 13:6).

Fundamentally, the rules for S corporation plans—including contribution and benefit limits, limits on includible compensation, and the like—are the same as for any qualified retirement plan. Similarly, the S corporation—like other companies—must be concerned with the top-heavy plan rules, which apply if more than 60% of the present value of accrued benefits or account balances is for key employees.

Although the rest of this chapter focuses on some situations and problems unique to S corporations these generic plan qualification issues should not be ignored. Where necessary, the assistance of a qualified specialist should be sought.

Q. 13:9   Can an S corporation take shareholder-employees' shares of undistributed net profits into account in setting a retirement plan benefit or contribution formula?

A plan is considered discriminatory if contributions or benefits do not bear a uniform relationship to total compensation. (Section 401(a)(5)) The result of such a finding is plan disqualification (with retroactive loss of deductions and other severe adverse consequences). Basing compensation on shareholders' shares of undistributed net profits means risking such a result.

In *Robertson*, 61 TC 727 (1974), shares of an S corporation's undistributed net profits were found not to be compensation and thus caused the plan to be disqualified. Employment contracts between the S corporation and its shareholders provided for a fixed annual salary plus a bonus equal to a percentage of the corporation's net profits for the year. These percentages in each employment contract were almost identical to the percentage of stock ownership.

The Tax Court pointed out that "it is obvious that this corporation could not enter into such an employment contract with non-shareholders because 100 percent of the net profits were already siphoned off to the shareholder-employees by use of the employment contract." The actual allocation of contributions to the S corporation's plan was based on regular salary plus a share of undistributed net profits in the case of shareholders, but on regular salary only in the case of nonshareholders. Thus, the corporation's plan discriminated in operation. Contributions did not bear a uniform relationship to compensation, and the entire plan was disqualified.

Q. 13:10 Are there any types of qualified plans that an S corporation may not adopt?

An S corporation *may* adopt a pension plan or a profit-sharing plan. However, an S corporation may *not* adopt an employee stock ownership plan (ESOP). An ESOP is a special form of stock bonus plan under which the plan must invest primarily in employer stock. (Section 409A(a)) S corporation rules prohibit the ownership of stock by any type of trust (other than by a qualified trust; see Question 1:19). (Section 1361)

And although an S corporation may technically adopt a stock bonus plan, as a practical matter it should not. A stock bonus plan is a profit-sharing plan that makes benefit payments in the stock of the corporation. Once stock is transferred to the plan for the payment of benefits, the corporation will lose the benefit of its S corporation election.

Q. 13:11 Can a shareholder borrow from the S corporation's qualified retirement plan?

A more-than-5% shareholder is not permitted to borrow from an S corporation's qualified plan. (Section 4975(b)) This is the one significant difference between treatment of S corporation plans and treatment of C corporation plans.

Such a loan by a qualified plan is considered a prohibited transaction, which may result in a penalty equal to 5% of the amount involved in the transaction for each year the loan remains outstanding. An additional 100% penalty is imposed if the loan is not repaid within 90 days after IRS mails a notice of deficiency for the 5% tax. (Section 4975) The loan is also a taxable distribution to the owner, subject to income and possibly penalty taxes. (Section 72(m)(5))

Newly Electing S Corporations: When a corporation elects S corporation status, previously permissible loans to shareholders will become prohibited transactions if they run afoul of the more-than-5%-shareholder rule discussed above. Therefore, outstanding loans should be checked *before* an election is made. The loans should be repaid prior to the effective date of the election, or, if this is not feasible or desirable, the advisability of the election should be reconsidered.

Chapter 14

Tax Administration of S Corporations

Returns

Q. 14:1 Must an S corporation file an income tax return?

Although items of income and deduction generated by an S corporation generally pass through to its shareholders, who include their pro rata shares on their individual returns (see Chapters 8 and 9), every S corporation must file a return, using Form 1120S and its related schedules, for each taxable year. (Section 6037(a)) That return must state:

- The items of the S corporation's gross income and deductions;
- The names and addresses of all persons owning stock in the corporation at any time during the taxable year;
- The number of shares of stock owned by each shareholder at all times during the taxable year;
- The amount of money and other property distributed by the corporation during the taxable year to each shareholder;
- The date of each such distribution;
- Each shareholder's pro rata share of each item of the corporation for the taxable year; and
- Such other information as the Secretary may by forms and regulations prescribe.

Q. 14:2 When must an S corporation file its income tax return?

The normal due date for a C corporation and for an S corporation using Form 1120S and its related schedules is the fifteenth day of the third month following the close of the corporation's taxable year. For a calendar-year S corporation, the date is March 15. (Section 6072(b))

Q. 14:3 How does an S corporation obtain an extension of time for filing its return?

The Form 1120S is normally due on the fifteenth day of the third month after the close of the taxable year, which is March 15 for a calendar-year corporation. Since a Form 1120S for an S corporation is due at the same time as a Form 1120 for a C corporation, the rules governing extensions of time for filing returns apply to S and C corporations with equal force. Form 7004, "Application for Automatic Extension of Time to File Corporation Income Tax Return," is available for an automatic extension of time for filing the S corporation return.

> **Planning Pointer.** If a shareholder of an S corporation needs an extension of time for filing his or her own return in situations in which the time for filing the corporate return has been extended, he or she might also request an automatic extension. An individual shareholder's request is made on Form 4868, which grants an automatic four-month extension.

Q. 14:4 Must an S corporation furnish its shareholders with copies of the Form 1120S?

An S corporation must furnish each person who was a shareholder at any time during the taxable year with a copy of all information shown on the Form 1120S that is required by regulations. (Section 6037(b))

The corporation is required to furnish this information on or before the date on which the Form 1120S is filed, so that the information is available to the shareholder in reporting pass-through items of income and deduction on his or her individual Form 1040.

As yet, regulations have not been issued. At a minimum, a copy of the Schedule K-1 must be furnished to shareholders. To be safe, a copy of the Form 1120S, including the Schedule K-1, should be furnished.

Q. 14:5 What happens if an S corporation fails to supply a shareholder with the information necessary to include the pro rata share of each S corporation item on his or her tax return for the taxable year?

The corporation may be subject to a penalty of $50 for failure to provide copies of the necessary information to those persons who are shareholders at any time during the taxable year. (Section 6670(a)(3)) The Conference Committee Report on the 1984 Tax Reform Act indicates that the $50 penalty relates to S corporations' failures to provide copies of their returns to shareholders. The penalty is $50 for each statement that is not furnished, but the total amount imposed for all such failures may not exceed $50,000.

S Corporation Audits Generally

Q. 14:6 How are audits of the S corporation and its shareholders handled?

Code Sections 6241–6245 contain the S corporation audit provisions. The purpose of these provisions is to avoid the situation in which each S corporation shareholder's individual tax liability is determined in a separate proceeding between IRS and the shareholder of the corporation. Otherwise, issues involving the income or deductions of a particular S corporation might be decided inconsistently among shareholders of the same corporation, because they are handled in separate administrative or judicial proceedings. The S corporation audit provisions attempt to determine the tax treatment of items from an S corporation at the corporate level in a single unified proceeding rather than in separate proceedings for each of the shareholders.

Q. 14:7 How do the S corporation audit provisions operate?

The statutory scheme is as follows:

Under the unified procedures for S corporations, all "Subchapter S items" will be determined in a single audit, rather than in separate audits. (Section 6241) A "Subchapter S item" is any item that the regulations provide is more appropriately determined at the corporate level than at the shareholder level. (Section 6245) (See Questions 14:9–14:10.)

Treatment as a Subchapter S item means that (Sections 6241 and 6242; Temp. Reg. §301.6241-1T):

1. IRS cannot adjust the treatment of a Subchapter S item on the corporate return except through a corporate proceeding; and
2. A shareholder cannot put Subchapter S items at issue in a proceeding relating to other items.

■ **Example.** A taxpayer may not offset a potential increase in taxable income based on changes in non-Subchapter S items by a potential decrease based on Subchapter S items.

Each shareholder must either (1) report his or her Subchapter S items in a manner that is consistent with the treatment on the corporate return, or (2) notify IRS that he or she is not doing so. (Section 6242; see Questions 14:9–14:13)

When the corporation is audited, IRS will usually deal with one shareholder, the tax matters person (TMP) (see Questions 14:20–14:22), although other shareholders will be permitted to participate in audit and Appeals Office conferences. (Section 6243) The manner and time for giving notice of proceedings is to be prescribed in regulations. Since the regulations on this portion of the statutory scheme have not yet been issued, it is not known exactly how this will happen.

Assessments, Claims, Judicial Proceedings: The partnership provisions in Sections 6221–6232, which relate to assessing deficiencies, filing claims for credit or refund, and judicial determination, apply to Subchapter S items. (Section 6244)

Under the unified audit rules for partnerships, IRS is authorized to settle with one or more partners. However, IRS must allow a partner to enter into a settlement on the same terms as those offered to another partner. If tax deficiencies proposed by IRS are not resolved at the District or Appeals Office level, a notice of final partnership administrative adjustment will be issued. Thereafter, the TMP can contest the proposed deficiencies in the Tax Court, a U.S. district court, or the Claims Court. As S corporation audits are supposed to follow the partnership rules, presumably these procedures apply to S corporation shareholders as well.

Q. 14:8 Are any S corporations exempt from these audit rules?

Certain S corporations (like certain partnerships) are exempt from the unified audit rules unless they elect to be covered by them. This exemption, and the election out of it, are discussed at Questions 14:14–14:19.

"Subchapter S Items"

Q. 14:9 What is a "Subchapter S item" for income tax purposes?

A Subchapter S item is any item of an S corporation that is more appropriately determined at the corporate level than at the shareholder level. (Section 6245)

The term "Subchapter S item" includes not only the corporation's particular items of income, gain, loss, deduction, or credit, but also its accounting practices and the legal and factual determinations underlying the determination of the existence, amount, timing, and characterization of these items. The temporary regulations include such items as (Temp. Reg. §302.6245-1T):

- The corporation's method of accounting, taxable year, and inventory method;
- Whether certain elections were made by the corporation;
- Whether the corporate property is a capital asset, Section 1231 property, or inventory;
- Whether an item is currently deductible or must be capitalized; and
- Whether the corporation engaged in activities with the intent to make a profit for purposes of Section 183. (See Question 1:4.)

The temporary regulations provide specifically that both the corporation's aggregate amount and each shareholder's share of all the following amounts are Subchapter S items:

- Items of income, gain, loss, deduction, or credit of the corporation;
- Expenditures by the corporation that are not deductible, such as charitable contributions;
- Corporate items that may be tax preference items under Section 57(a) for any shareholder;
- Tax-exempt income items; and
- Corporate liabilities.

In addition, the following, although one might not usually think of them as "items," are Subchapter S items:

- Information necessary to determine (1) shareholder amounts at risk for Section 465 purposes (see Questions 10:3–10:9), and (2) corporate-level alternative minimum tax, capital gains tax, built-in gains tax, and tax on excess passive investment income (see Chapter 8);
- Factors necessary to determine whether an entity (1) qualifies as an S corporation (see Chapter 1), (2) has properly made an S corporation election (see Chapter 2), or (3) has had its election revoked or terminated (see Chapter 4); and
- Certain information regarding shareholder contributions to the corporation and corporate distributions to shareholders (see Question 14:10).

Q. 14:10 Which factors affecting contributions and distributions are Subchapter S items?

The regulations provide some nonexhaustive illustrations of which factors concerning distributions and contributions are Subchapter S items and specifically provide that failure by the corporation to actually make a determination of these items does not prevent them from being Subchapter S items.

Contributions: With regard to contributions it receives, the S corporation must determine:

1. Character of the amount it received (contribution, loan, or repayment of a loan);
2. Amount of money received; and
3. Basis to the corporation of contributed property.

To the extent that a determination of an item relating to contributions can be made from determining these factors, the item is a Subchapter S item. However, to the extent that the determination of these factors requires other information, the item is not a Subchapter S item. An example of other information that would render an item not a Subchapter S item is the factors used in determining whether Section 47 requires a shareholder contributing property to recapture a general business credit in circumstances in which the determination has no relevance to the corporation.

Distributions: With respect to distributions, the S corporation must

determine, for purposes of its books and records or for purposes of furnishing information to a shareholder:
1. Character of the amount transferred to a shareholder (dividend, compensation, loan, or repayment of a loan);
2. Amount of money distributed to a shareholder;
3. Fair market value of property distributed to a shareholder;
4. Adjusted basis to the corporation of distributed property; and
5. Character of corporate property (e.g., whether the item is inventory or capital asset).

To the extent that the corporation can determine these matters, the item is a Subchapter S item. To the extent that a determination requires other information outside the control of the corporation, the item is not a Subchapter S item. Such other information might include the determination of a shareholder's basis in his or her S corporation stock or in indebtedness of the S corporation to the shareholder.

Q. 14:11 What does "corporate-level determination" mean?

The tax treatment of any Subchapter S item is to be determined at the corporate level unless regulations provide otherwise. (Section 6241) Temporary regulations contain a general rule that a shareholder's treatment of a Subchapter S item on the shareholder's return may not be changed except as provided in Sections 6241–6245 and the regulations thereunder. Temp. Reg. §301.6241-1T contains the following:

> Thus, for example, if a shareholder treats an item on the shareholder's return consistently with the treatment of that item on the S corporation return, the Internal Revenue Service generally cannot adjust the treatment of that item on the shareholder's return except through a corporate-level proceeding. Similarly, the shareholder may not put a subchapter S item in issue in a proceeding relating to nonsubchapter S items. For example, the shareholder may not offset a potential increase in taxable income based on changes in non-subchapter S items by a potential decrease based on subchapter S items.

These restrictions become inapplicable when such items cease to be Subchapter S items with respect to a shareholder. This can happen if (1) IRS notifies the shareholder that the items will be treated as non-Subchapter S items, (2) the shareholder sues after IRS fails to allow an administrative adjustment, (3) IRS and the shareholder settle with regard to the items, (4) IRS fails to notify the shareholder of administrative proceedings, or (5) certain other denominated circumstances occur. (Section 6231(b)(1), as made applicable to Subchapter S items under Section 6244.)

Q. 14:12 Must all shareholders follow the corporation's treatment in reporting Subchapter S items on their tax returns?

All S corporation shareholders must treat their Subchapter S items consistently with the manner in which these items are treated on the corporation's Form 1120S, unless the shareholder notifies IRS of the inconsistency. (Section 6242) The notice is given by filing a Form 8082, "Notice of Inconsistent Treatment or Amended Return (Request for Administrative Adjustment)." (See Question 14:13.)

Q. 14:13 When and how may a shareholder ask that Subchapter S items be treated differently from the way in which the S corporation treated them?

Shareholders of S corporations may notify IRS that they wish to treat one or more Subchapter S items in a manner different from the way the S corporation has treated the item(s) on its return by filing Form 8082, "Notice of Inconsistent Treatment or Amended Return (Request for Administrative Adjustment)."

When Request Is Permitted: The form is to be used by S corporation shareholders in any one of the following four situations:

1. The shareholder believes that *an item was not properly reported* on the Schedule K-1 or similar statement he or she received from the S corporation. This is true regardless of whether the item is required to be reported on the shareholder's tax return. For example, if the amount shown as the shareholder's percentage of stock ownership is incorrect, or if the amount of loan repayments when the loan basis has not been reduced is incorrect, a Form 8082 should be filed even though these items are not required to be reported on the individual shareholder's income tax return.

2. *The S corporation has not filed a tax return or has not given the shareholder a Schedule K-1 or similar statement* by the time the shareholder is required to file his or her tax return and there are Sub-

chapter S items that must be included on the shareholder's personal income tax return.
3. The shareholder is filing an *amended income tax return on which he or she is changing the amount or the treatment of any Subchapter S item* from the way said amount or item was reported on the original or previously filed income tax return.
4. After the shareholder has filed his or her individual income tax return, he or she finds that a *Subchapter S item* that was not otherwise required to be reported on the individual income tax return *was not properly reported on the Schedule K-1 or similar statement.* In this situation, the instructions call for the filing of an amended return to identify the inconsistency. Only the name, address, and identifying number need be entered on the amended return. Instead of entering any of the amounts that are not otherwise required to be reported on the amended return, enter the words "See Attached Form 8082" on the amended return.

Other Rules: If the shareholder does not notify IRS that he or she is reporting any Subchapter S item in a manner inconsistent with the way it was reported on the corporation's Form 1120S and related schedules, any deficiency resulting from a computation or adjustment to make the treatment of the item consistent with the amount or treatment of the S corporation return may be assessed immediately.

A separate Form 8082 must be filed for each S corporation for which a shareholder is reporting an inconsistent or amended item. If more than four inconsistent or amended items are being reported from any one S corporation, additional Forms 8082 will be needed, because the form has room for only four inconsistent or amended items.

The Form 8082 should be filed together with the shareholder's tax return to which it applies. An additional copy is to be filed at the Internal Revenue Service Center with which the S corporation filed its return.

"Small Corporation" Audit Exception

Q. 14:14 Are there any exceptions to this general rule that Subchapter S items must be determined at the corporate level?

Generally speaking, the answer to this question is no. The tax treatment of any Subchapter S item is to be determined at the corporate level unless regulations provide otherwise. (Section 6241) Temp. Reg. §301.6241-1T contains the general rule that a shareholder's treatment of a Subchapter S item on the shareholder's return may be adjusted only through a corporate-level proceeding. However, there is a special exception for small-corporation returns due (without extensions) on or after January 30, 1987. (Temp. Reg. §301.6241-1T(c)(2))

Q. 14:15 What is a "small corporation" to which the Subchapter S item rules do not apply?

For purposes of the small-corporation exception, a small corporation is an S corporation with five or fewer shareholders, each of whom is a natural person or an estate. Spouses (and their estates) are treated as one shareholder. Stock owned jointly as tenants in common or as joint tenants by persons other than a husband and wife is treated as owned by more than one shareholder—each tenant in common or joint tenant is considered a separate shareholder of the corporation. (Temp. Reg. §301.6241-1T(c)(2)(ii))

Planning Pointer. The five-or-fewer-shareholders limitation is applied to those who are shareholders at any one time during the taxable year of the corporation, not to the aggregate number of shareholders during the year. Thus, an S corporation could have six or more shareholders during the year so long as no more than five of them (counted as above) were shareholders at any one time. The corporation might have six or more shareholders and still qualify if shares were transferred from one person to another during the course of a taxable year.

Q. 14:16 Is every S corporation that meets the small-corporation ownership requirements eligible for this special rule?

This special exception for small S corporations does not apply to an S corporation for any taxable year in which it had a "pass-through" shareholder, which the temporary regulations define as a trust, a nominee, or other similar pass-through person through whom other persons have ownership in the S corporation's stock. However, a shareholder's estate is not treated as a pass-through shareholder for this purpose. (Temp. Reg. §301.6241-1T(c)(2)(iii))

Q. 14:17 When is eligibility for small-corporation treatment determined?

The determination of whether an S corporation meets the requirements for the exception for small S corporations is made annually, for each taxable year of the corporation. An S corporation can qualify in one taxable year but not in another, depending on whether the requirements are met with respect to the particular taxable year. (Temp. Reg. §301.6241-1T(c)(2)(iv))

Q. 14:18 When can the tax treatment of a small corporation's Subchapter S items be determined at the corporate level?

A small S corporation can elect to have the tax treatment of its Subchapter S items determined at the corporate level according to the general rule. A special election must be made in a statement attached to the corporation's return for the first taxable year for which the election is to be effective. The election must be:

1. Identified as an election under Temp. Reg. §301.6241-1T(c)(2)(v)(A);
2. Signed by all persons who were shareholders of the corporation at any time during the taxable year to which the return relates; and
3. Filed at the time and place prescribed for filing the Form 1120S.

Q. 14:19 When is an election to determine a small corporation's Subchapter S items at the corporate level effective?

The election is effective for the taxable year of the corporation to which it relates and to *all subsequent taxable years of the corporation unless it is revoked with the consent of IRS.* (Temp. Reg. §301.6241-1T(c)(2)(iv)(C))

Notice; Tax Matters Person

Q. 14:20 Must a shareholder be given notice of an administrative or judicial proceeding involving the S corporation?

Yes, each shareholder of an S corporation must be given notice of, and the right to participate in, any administrative or judicial proceeding for the determination of a Subchapter S item at the corporate level. (Section 6243)

Q. 14:21 Why and how might an S corporation designate one of its shareholders as a tax matters person (TMP) for a specific corporate year?

The instructions for the Form 1120S specify that an S corporation may designate one of its shareholders as a tax matters person (TMP) for a specific corporate tax year by attaching a statement to Form 1120S for that year. The statement must contain the following items:

1. Name, address, and taxpayer identification number of the corporation and of the individual shareholder designated as the TMP;
2. Declaration that the attached statement is a designation of the individual as TMP for the tax year to which the Form 1120S tax return relates; and
3. Signature of a corporate officer authorized to sign the corporation's income tax return.

These instructions also indicate that an S corporation may not designate a TMP through the use of this attached statement for any tax year other than the year for which the return is being filed. As indicated above (see Question 14:7), no regulations have been issued with respect to the procedural rules.

The following considerations with regard to a TMP in the partnership context give some indication as to the desirability of naming a TMP for any given taxable year.

To expedite the unified audit procedures, the partnership selects a TMP to function as the liaison between the partnership and IRS. If there is no such designation, the general partner with the largest profits interest at the end of the year is the TMP; if there are general partners with equal interests, the designation is made alphabetically. (Section 6231(a)(7))

> **Planning Pointer.** Because the TMP has significant powers and responsibilities, it is best to select one rather than letting the choice be made by default. Procedures are spelled out in Reg. §301.6231(a)(7)-1.

Q. 14:22 What are the powers and responsibilities of the TMP?

IRS and the Code provide guidance in the partnership context.

Presumably, although specific regulations have yet to be promulgated, the same is true in the S corporation context.

In a partnership, the TMP is authorized to extend the statute of limitations on assessment on behalf of the partnership. In addition, the TMP can control the choice of forum should litigation become necessary.

It is the responsibility of the TMP to keep the other partners informed of the progress of the partnership audit. (Section 6623(g)) However, the fact that the TMP is derelict in his or her duty is not a defense for the other partners to an action by IRS. (Section 6230(f))

Statute of Limitations and Other Matters

Q. 14:23 How long does IRS have to challenge items reported on returns of the S corporation and its shareholders?

In most instances, IRS must make an assessment within *three years* from the date on which the return is (1) due or (2) actually filed, whichever is later. In other words, if the return is filed before the due date, the time for making an assessment runs from the due date. (Section 6501(b)(1))

■ **Example.** RST Corporation files its Form 1120S for 1989 on March 1, 1990. IRS has until March 15, 1993, to make an assessment. March 15, 1993, is three years from the due date of the return, which was March 15, 1989.

As the tax treatment of Subchapter S items is determined at the corporate level, the return to which Section 6501 refers would seem to be the Form 1120S, not the shareholder's return. This conclusion is clear in the case of a partnership. (See Section 6501(o)(2), cross-referencing to Section 6229). Section 6244 provides that the partnership provisions of Section 6221 through 6232 apply to Subchapter S items. Under the law before the Subchapter S Revision Act of 1982 (Revision Act), the Tax Court had held that a shareholder was not protected with respect to adjustments on a Form 1120S for a year that was closed with regard to the S corporation's form 1120S if the year with regard to the shareholder's Form 1040 was still open. (*W. H. Leonhart,* TC Memo 1968-98, *affirmed per curiam,* 414 F.2d 749 (4th Cir. 1969); *Daniel M. Kelley,* TC Memo 1986-405) But the Ninth Circuit reversed *Kelley* on June 7, 1989, holding that IRS may not adjust a shareholder's Form 1040 based on an adjustment to a Form 1120S after the statute of limitations has run on Form 1120S.

A return for this purpose must give enough information to calculate tax, purport to be a return, be an honest and reasonable attempt to comply with the law, and be sworn to under penalty of perjury. Failure to include a W-2 form, for example, does not invalidate the return and extend the statute of limitations. (See *Blount,* 86 TC 383 (1986), *acq. in result, action on decision,* 1986-041.)

Q. 14:24 When does IRS have an extended time to challenge items of income and deduction on the returns of the S corporation and its shareholders?

The general three-year statute of limitations does not apply when no return is filed, the return is fraudulent, or there are substantial omissions of gross income.

No Return Is Filed: If a taxpayer fails to file a tax return, IRS can assess the tax *at any time.* There is no statute of limitations or definite date after which IRS cannot make a valid assessment. (Section 6501(c)(3)) However, the three-year statute of limitations will begin to run once the taxpayer files a late, nonfraudulent return. (See *Bennett,* 30 TC 114 (1958), *acq.,* 1958-2 CB 3; and *Rev. Rul. 79-178,* 1979-1 CB 435.) This is true even if the initial failure to file a return was fraudulent. (*Badaracco,* 104 S. Ct. 756 (1984))

Fraudulent Return: IRS may also make an assessment at any time if the taxpayer has filed a false or fraudulent return with the intent to evade taxes. (Section 6501(c)(1)) The subsequent filing of a nonfraudulent amended return does *not* start the three-year statute of limitations running on the original, fraudulent return. In other words, the filing of a nonfraudulent amended return has no effect on IRS's right to assess the tax attributable to a false or fraudulent return at any time. The taxpayer cannot escape penalties or "eradicate the fraud" merely by filing a nonfraudulent amended return. (*Badaracco, supra*)

Substantial Omission: Rather than failing to file or willfully attempting to evade taxes, a taxpayer might file a return that omits a substantial amount from gross income. (A substantial amount is one that (1) should have been reported and (2) is in excess of 25% of the gross income actually reported.) In such a case, IRS has *six years* to make an assessment. The filing of an amended return has no effect on the six-year period of limitations. (Section 6501(e)(1)(A); *Houston,* 38 TC 486 (1962); *Goldring,* 20 TC 79 (1953))

Planning Pointer. When computing the gross income of a trade or business, gross revenues are not reduced by the costs of goods or services sold. (Section 6501(e)(1)(A)(i)) If an item is omitted from gross income because the taxpayer believes that the item does not constitute gross income, a statement attached to the return, apprising IRS of the taxpayer's position, will prevent the six-year statute of limitations from applying. IRS will be required to make an assessment within three years. (Section 6501(e)(1)(A)(ii))

Q. 14:25 What is the "innocent spouse" rule?

There is a provision—the innocent spouse rule—that sets out standards that, if satisfied, relieve the "innocent" spouse of a portion of his or her liability on a joint return. (Section 6013(e)) The basis for relief under the innocent spouse rule depends to some extent on whether the liability for tax, penalties, interest, or other amounts is attributable to an item (or items) of:

1. Omitted income; or
2. Unjustified deductions, credits, or basis amounts.

To the extent that a liability for tax, penalties, interest, or other amounts is attributable to an unjustified deduction, credit, or basis amount, a taxpayer is relieved of liability under the innocent spouse rule if:

1. A joint tax return was filed;
2. A deduction, credit, or amount of basis for which there was no factual or legal justification was claimed by the other spouse;
3. The resulting understatement of tax is more than $500;
4. The resulting understatement is more than 10% of the taxpayer's adjusted gross income for the most recent taxable year ending before the date that IRS mailed its deficiency notice, if that adjusted gross income is $20,000 or less;
5. The resulting understatement is more than 25% of the taxpayer's adjusted gross income for the most recent taxable year ending before the date that IRS mailed its deficiency notice, if that adjusted gross income is more than $20,000;
6. The taxpayer establishes that he or she did not know of, and had no reason to know of, the understatement; and
7. It would be inequitable to hold the taxpayer liable for the deficiency stemming from the omitted income. (Sections 6013(e)(1)–6013(e)(4))

In determining the innocent spouse's adjusted gross income for the most recent taxable year ending before the deficiency letter was mailed, the income of a new spouse is taken into account, whether or not the couple filed a joint return. (Section 6013(e)(4)(D))

The Sixth Circuit has held that when liability must be more than 10% or 25% of adjusted gross income, interest accrued up to (but not after) the date of the deficiency notice is included in calculating the liability percentage. (*Farmer*, 794 F.2d 1163 (6th Cir. 1986))

Q. 14:26 How is gross income of an S corporation shareholder calculated for purposes of extending the statute of limitations under the substantial omission rule and for applying the innocent spouse rule?

As noted above (see Questions 14:24–14:25), in some instances it is necessary to determine whether there has been an omission of gross income from an individual's tax return and whether that omission is greater than 25% of gross income. This is necessary for the computation under Section 6501 concerning the six-year statute of limitations, and also for Section 6013(e), governing the innocent spouse rule. Thus, when the taxpayer is an S corporation shareholder, the question arises of how the items shown on the Form 1120S affect the individual's Form 1040.

The Code specifically provides that when it is necessary to determine the gross income of a shareholder of an S corporation, his or her gross income will include the pro rata share of the gross income of the S corporation. (Section 1366(c)) Thus, this provision adopts the approach that courts had taken before it was adopted as part of the Subchapter S Revision Act of 1982, which is that the facts on the Form 1120S are incorporated by reference into the individual's tax return. Thus, the three-year statute of limitations generally applies. The courts have used the same logic in applying the 25%-omission-of-gross-income test for purposes of the innocent spouse rule. (See, on the statute of limitations, *Roschuni*, 44 TC 80 (1965), and *Benderoff*, 398 F.2d 132 (8th Cir. 1968), *rev'g* 270 F. Supp. 87 (S.D. Iowa 1967); see, on the innocent spouse rule, *Ketchum*, 77 TC 1204 (1981), and *Tuchman*, TC Memo 1981-731.) Note, however, that these cases involve instances in which reference to the S corporation is made on the Form 1040.

No Reference to S Corporation on Individual's Return: The *Roschuni* and *Benderoff* cases were distinguished in *Reuter,* TC Memo 1985-607. In *Reuter,* the Tax Court found that petitioners' individual income tax returns for the taxable year did not contain a reference to the fact that the taxpayers owned stock in an S corporation. As a result, it held that the six-year statute of limitations under Section 6501(e)(1)(A)(ii), instead of the three-year statute of limitations, applied. The court found that the facts of *Reuter* closely mirror the facts in *Taylor,* 417 F.2d 991 (5th Cir. 1969). In *Taylor,* the taxpayers failed to report their share of S corporation income and there was no reference to the S corporation in the taxpayers' individual tax returns or on any attached schedules. Also, the court in *Taylor* refused to look to the S corporation information return. Since the information on the Form 1120S was not taken into account by the court, the omission of gross income was greater than 25%, and the six-year statute of limitations applied.

Q. 14:27 Can an S corporation be used to shield a person's business from his or her creditors?

The Tax Court in *Scott,* 70 TC 71 (1978), answered this question in the negative. The husband had his wife form a new S corporation with a total capitalization of $500. He managed the business of the corporation and took only a small salary. The first two jobs the corporation handled were shifted from the husband's old corporation, which he then liquidated.

The Tax Court looked to state law to determine whether the wife was liable as a transferee to the extent of the dividends she received from her S corporation. Its opinion distinguished between two lines of cases. The two conflicting principles are as follows:

1. When the earnings of a business conducted in the wife's name are attributable solely to the judgment and business ability of the husband, without the investment of any capital by the wife, the profits of the business are liable for the insolvent husband's debts.
2. An insolvent husband may gratuitously provide his services in managing his wife's separate property or her separate business, without subjecting either the value of his services or the profits realized by his wife to the claims of his creditors.

The Tax Court held that the second principle applies only if the business actually is the wife's and is not a device to keep from the husband's creditors the income of a business that is really his own. The entire arrangement was held to be a device to defraud creditors by placing the profits of a business (which was really the husband's) beyond their reach. Therefore, the wife was held to be liable as a transferee for her husband's tax liabilities to the extent of the S corporation's distributions to her.

Glossary

Following is a list of terms (arranged in alphabetical order) designed to provide the reader with an additional guide to understanding the complex concepts that apply to S corporations and the terminology employed in this book. Basic definitions are provided here, with cross-references to the more complete discussions in the text. If a term used in a definition appears in italics, it is also defined in this glossary.

Accumulated adjustments account: S corporations with accumulated *earnings and profits* use this account to measure taxable income and expenses for years beginning after 1982. Amounts in this account are deemed to be distributed to taxpayers first (as a tax-free return of capital to the extent of basis and then as payments for the sale or exchange of stock), ahead of distributions from earnings and profits (which are taxed as dividends), unless an election to reverse this order is made. See Questions 12:9–12:20. The account is also used to measure cash amounts an S corporation can distribute tax-free during the *post-termination transition period.* See Questions 12:23–12:24.

Affirmative refusal to consent: See *qualified Subchapter S trust successor beneficiary's affirmative refusal to consent.*

Alternative allocation method: See *two-taxable-years allocation method.*

Amount at risk: The measure of a shareholder's currently deductible losses under the *at-risk rules.* It consists of cash and property contributed to an S corporation activity (or permitted aggregation thereof) plus funds borrowed with recourse to the shareholder and noncorporate assets the shareholder has pledged as security for debt. It is decreased by loss deductions claimed. See Questions 10:6–10:8.

At-risk rules: The rules that limit the losses S corporation shareholders (along with certain other taxpayers) may deduct currently to the *amount at risk.* Their application is similar to that of the *basis limitation,* except that they generally apply on an activity-by-activity basis, rather than to the investment in the corporation as a whole, and thus can result in additional limitations on loss deductions. Aggregation of some or all activities is permitted in certain circumstances. See Questions 10:3–10:9.

Backup Section 444 election: See *Section 444 fiscal-year election.*

Basis: See *shareholder's basis.*

Basis limitation: A rule limiting the amount of S corporation losses that each shareholder may deduct currently to the sum of his or her individual *shareholder's basis in stock* plus *shareholder's basis in loans.* See Questions 10:1–10:2.

Built-in gain: For purposes of the *built-in gains tax,* the excess of fair market value of an asset on the day a former *C corporation's S corporation election* becomes effective over the corporation's adjusted basis in the asset on that date. See Question 8:21.

Built-in gains tax: A corporate-level tax imposed on certain former C corporations because of a taxable disposition within 10 years after the effective date of the *S corporation election.* The tax generally applies to former C corporations that elected S corporation status after December 31, 1986, to be effective in a taxable year beginning after that date (a transitional rule provides relief to some small companies until 1989). The tax also applies to certain assets acquired directly or indirectly from a C corporation in tax-free transactions, even if the S corporation making the disposition has never been a C corporation. The tax itself is equal to the highest corporate tax for the particular type of income times the *net recognized built-in gain* for the year. See Questions 8:21–8:33.

Buy-sell agreement: See *shareholders' agreement.*

C corporation: A corporation that pays tax on its own income under the general rules of Subchapter C of the Internal Revenue Code. See Question 1:1.

Calendar year: An accounting period that ends each December 31, which is the period most S corporations must adopt as a *permitted year.* See Questions 3:1 et seq.

Capital gains tax: See *tax on long-term capital gains.*

Closing of the books method: A method of allocating income, deductions, losses, and credits between the S corporation and C corporation portions of an *S corporation termination year.* The books are deemed closed as of the effective date of a *termination* or *revocation,* and all items recognized during the S corporation period pursuant to the corporation's normal accounting method are allocated to that period. This method must be used if more than 50% of the stock has been sold or exchanged during the S termination year. The corporation may elect to use it only if all persons who were shareholders at any time during the S corporation period of the year and all who were shareholders on the first day of the C corporation year consent. See Questions 4:21–4:22. It may also be used

Glossary

when there is a change in the identity of S corporation shareholders during the year, provided all persons who were shareholders during the year consent. See Questions 9:10–9:12.

Contribution to capital: A contribution of cash or other property that a shareholder makes to an S corporation (or any other corporation) that increases the corporation's paid-in capital but for which the shareholder does not receive stock. The contribution increases that *shareholder's basis in stock*. See Questions 11:19 et seq.

Disqualifying act: An act by the corporation or shareholder that causes the corporation to cease to be an *eligible corporation* and that generally results in *termination*. See Questions 4:3 et seq.

Earnings and profits (E&P): The measure of corporate earnings available for dividend distributions, consisting of all recognized taxable and nontaxable income less losses and payments made (1) in a C corporation year since the later of 1913 or the date of incorporation, and (2) in an S corporation year prior to one beginning in 1983. See Questions 12:3–12:6.

Eligible corporation: A corporation that is eligible to elect and maintain *S corporation* status because it meets statutory tests pertaining to the type of corporation, number and type of shareholders, and equity structure, and has made a valid *S corporation election*. See Question 1:2 and Chapter 1 generally.

Eligible shareholder: A shareholder that an S corporation is permitted to have—basically, an individual U.S. citizen or resident alien. Estates and certain trusts also qualify. See Questions 1:2, 1:17–1:20, and 1:28–1:29.

Excess net passive income: The amount on which the corporate-level *tax on excess passive income* is imposed if (1) the corporation has *earnings and profits* accumulated as a *C corporation* and (2) *passive investment income* exceeds 25% of gross receipts. It is determined by applying to net passive investment income—that is, passive investment income less directly related allowable deductions—the ratio of passive investment income less 25% of gross receipts to total passive investment income. See Questions 8:11.

Fifteenth day of third month: The date by which an *S corporation election* (or *revocation*) must be made if it is to be effective in the year in which it is made. See Questions 2:2–2:6.

Fiscal year: An accounting period that ends on a date other than December 31. See Question 3:1. An S corporation may generally use a fiscal year as a *permitted year* only if it is a *natural business year*. In some circumstances, an S corporation may also make a *Section 444 fiscal-year election*. See Questions 3:4 et seq.

Form 720: The IRS form on which a corporation that has made a *Section 444* *fiscal-year election* makes its yearly return concerning that election, showing what, if any, *required payment* is due. Any payment due is submitted with the form. See Question 3:19.

Form 1120S: The IRS form on which an S corporation computes its taxable income and reports it to IRS. See Questions 8:2 et seq. and Questions 14:1–14:3.

Form 1128: The IRS form that an existing S corporation uses to request a change in its taxable year. See Questions 3:13 and 3:15.

Form 2553: The IRS form on which the *S corporation election* is made. See Questions 2:1 and 3:11–3:12.

Form 8082: The IRS form that an S corporation shareholder uses to notify IRS that his or her tax return treats a *Subchapter S item* in a way that is inconsistent with the corporation's treatment of it. See Questions 14:12–14:13.

Form 8716: The IRS form on which an S corporation makes a *Section 444 fiscal-year election*. See Questions 3:15–3:16.

Fringe benefits: Employee benefits and perquisites, other than *qualified retirement plans*. An S corporation cannot deduct the cost of any fringe benefit provided to an employee who is a *more-than-2% shareholder*. See Questions 13:2–13:4.

Inadvertent termination: An accidental *termination*, via a *disqualifying act* or violation of the restrictions on *passive investment income*, that IRS may overlook if certain statutory conditions are met. See Questions 4:6–4:8.

Ineligible corporation: A corporation that is precluded by statute from electing S corporation status. See Question 1:8.

Ineligible shareholder: A shareholder that an S corporation is not permitted to have, including a corporation, partnership, or nonresident alien. Certain trusts are also ineligible. See Questions 1:10, 1:17–1:19, and 1:28–1:29.

Invalid election: Generally, an *S corporation election* that has never been effective because (1) the corporation was not, in fact, an *eligible corporation* or (2) the election itself was in some way deficient. The term can also be used to describe an election that was not effective for the first year in which it purported to be effective because the corporation did not meet the filing deadline for that year. See Questions 6:14 et seq.

LIFO recapture amount: The amount on which the *LIFO recapture tax* is based. See Question 8:37.

LIFO recapture tax: A tax imposed on a former *C corporation* converting to S corporation status on or after December 17, 1987 (with transitional exceptions). The tax is imposed on the excess of FIFO inventory value over LIFO inventory value as of the close of the last C corporation year. It is paid in four equal, interest-free installments. See Questions 8:36–8:39.

Glossary

Long-term capital gains tax: See *tax on long-term capital gains*.

More-than-2% shareholder: A shareholder for whom an S corporation cannot provide deductible *fringe benefits* if he or she is an employee. Deductions are disallowed if a person meets this test on any day of the taxable year, and family attribution rules are used. See Question 13:3.

Natural business year: A *fiscal year* that is a *permitted year* because the corporation can show that 25% of gross receipts have been realized in the last two months of such a year for each of the last three years. See Question 3:4.

Net recognized built-in gain: The measure used for the *built-in gains tax* (as that tax was amended by the Technical and Miscellaneous Revenue Act of 1988). Net built-in gain consists of the lesser of (1) the S corporation's taxable income for the year, calculated as if taxable income consisted only of *recognized built-in gain* and *recognized built-in loss*, reduced by any net operating loss carryforwards from *C corporation* years; or (2) taxable income, generally determined as if the corporation were a *C corporation*. See Question 8:26.

Net unrealized built-in gain: The amount (if any), for purposes of the *built-in gains tax*, by which the fair market value of all assets on the first day of the first S corporation year exceeds the bases of those assets. It takes into account built-in losses (that is, assets for which adjusted bases exceed fair market values) as well as gains and limits tax to total built-in gain in the aggregate. See Question 8:27.

One class of stock: An S corporation may have only one class of stock, which must be equal in all respects except voting rights. See Questions 1:30–1:35.

Passive activity loss (PAL) rules: Rules, enacted in the Tax Reform Act of 1986, that restrict deductions, losses, and credits from business activities in which certain taxpayers do not materially participate. These items may be used only to offset *passive income*. The rules apply to the *pass-through items* of S corporation shareholders, among others, unless they can show material participation. See Questions 10:10 et seq.

Passive income: Income to certain taxpayers (including S corporation shareholders) that is subject to the *passive activity loss rules* because the taxpayer does not materially participate in the business activity producing the income. See Questions 10:10 et seq.

Passive investment income: Corporate receipts from royalties, rents, dividends, interest, annuities, and sales and exchanges of stock and securities. An S corporation that has C corporation *earnings and profits* faces two problems if passive investment income exceeds 25% of gross receipts: (1) a corporate-level tax and (2) *termination* if the situation continues for three consecutive years. See Questions 7:1 et seq. See also Questions 8:10–8:14 and 6:7.

Pass-through items: S corporation items of income, loss, deduction, and credit that are reported by the shareholders on their individual tax returns (the term is used because the S corporation is a conduit through which the items pass to the shareholders). Shareholders generally report these items on their tax returns for the year in which the S corporation year ends. See Questions 9:1 et seq.

Permitted year: A year an S corporation may use for tax accounting purposes—generally a *calendar year* (one ending December 31) or one for which the S corporation can establish, to IRS's satisfaction, a business purpose. For purposes of a *Section 444 fiscal-year election,* a permitted year is known as a "required year." See Questions 3:2–3:6.

Post-termination transition period: A statutory period following *termination* or *revocation,* during which an S corporation may make distributions of money out of the *accumulated adjustments account* that will be tax-free to the extent of each shareholder's basis in his or her stock. See Questions 12:23–12:25.

Previously taxed income: Undistributed taxable income from any Subchapter S taxable year beginning before 1983. Tax-free cash distributions of this income can be made to shareholders who actually included the income in their gross income. The distributions are deemed made after distributions from the *accumulated adjustments account* but before distributions from *earnings and profits.* See Questions 12:21–12:22.

Pro rata daily allocation method (pro rata method of allocation): A method of allocating income, deductions, losses, and credits between the S and C corporation portions of an *S corporation termination year.* Actual dollar amounts are divided by the number of days in the year and multiplied by the number of S corporation days and the number of C corporation days. This method is not used insofar as income items result from a Section 338 step-up election. Otherwise, it is used unless more than 50% of the stock has been sold or exchanged in the termination year or the corporation elects to make allocations using the *closing of the books method.* See Questions 4:6–4:21. It is also used for determining each shareholder's *pro rata share* of *pass-through items* for a taxable year that is not an *S corporation termination year* when a stock transfer during the year has resulted in a change in the identity of shareholder(s). Items are allocated equally to each day of the year on a per-share basis, and a shareholder's actual share is determined by applying this daily per-share amount to the number of shares he or she held on each day of the year. (If a shareholder dies during the year, that shareholder and his or her estate are considered separate shareholders.) See Questions 9:8 and 9:13. This method is used unless a shareholder terminates his or her interest in the corporation and an election is made to use the *two-taxable-years allocation method.*

Pro rata share: An individual shareholder's share of S corporation *pass-through items.* See Questions 9:8–9:9.

Glossary

Qualified retirement plan: A pension or profit-sharing plan that qualifies under the Internal Revenue Code for deductible contributions by an employer that are not included in employee income until plan distributions are made. An S corporation may adopt any type of qualified plan a *C corporation* can, except an employee stock ownership plan (ESOP), and *more-than-2% shareholders* who are employees may be covered by the plan like other employees. However, most S corporations, like other small businesses, must take into account the "top-heavy plan" rules, which impose special requirements to protect the rank-and-file when too high a proportion of plan benefits is earmarked for owners and certain other key employees. See Questions 13:7–13:11.

Qualified Subchapter S trust (QSST): A trust that meets the requirements of Section 1361(d) to be an S corporation shareholder. Generally, this is a trust that must distribute all of its income currently to one beneficiary who is an individual. The beneficiary must elect to have the trust treated as a QSST. See Questions 1:20–1:27.

Qualified Subchapter S trust election: The special election to have a trust treated as a *qualified Subchapter S trust* that the beneficiary must make with respect to each S corporation in which the trust owns stock (1) when the corporation makes an *S corporation election* or (2) within a statutory period after the trust becomes a shareholder, whichever is earlier. See Questions 1:24–1:27.

Qualified Subchapter S trust successor beneficiary's affirmative refusal to consent: The document a successor beneficiary must file with IRS if he or she wants to end the trust's status as a *qualified Subchapter S trust*. See Question 1:27.

QSST: See *qualified Subchapter S trust*.

QSST election: See *qualified Subchapter S trust election*.

Recognized built-in gain: For purposes of the *built-in gains tax*, gain that a former *C corporation* recognizes if (1) it disposes of an asset it held on the first day of the first taxable year in which its *S corporation election* was effective and (2) the disposition occurs within the 10-year period beginning on that date. The amount is the entire amount recognized under normal accounting principles unless the corporation can show that the asset appreciated during this period by establishing fair market value and adjusted basis at the time the election became effective; if it can, the difference between these amounts is the recognized built-in gain. This amount may be used in calculating *net recognized built-in gain*. See Question 8:26.

Recognized built-in loss: For purposes of the *built-in gains tax*, a loss that a former *C corporation* recognizes if (1) it disposes of an asset it held on the first day of the first taxable year in which its *S corporation election* was effective, and (2) the disposition occurs within the 10-year period beginning on that date. This amount may be used in calculating *net recognized built-in gain*. As built-in loss decreases built-in gain tax liability, the burden is on the S corporation to prove what assets it owned, and their value, on the effective date of the election. See Question 8:26.

Required payment: A payment in the nature of a deposit on deferred shareholder taxes that an eligible S corporation must make if it elects a fiscal year using a *Section 444 fiscal-year election*. The payment is refunded, without interest, if the corporation terminates the election. See Questions 3:18–3:21 and 3:23.

Required year: See *permitted year*.

Revocation: Voluntary cessation of S corporation status by action of holders of more than 50% of the outstanding stock. See Questions 4:10–4:13.

S corporation: A corporation that is eligible to and does, in fact, elect to be taxed under Subchapter S of the Internal Revenue Code. Basically, shareholders pay tax on the corporation's income by reporting their *pro rata shares* of *pass-through items* on their own returns. For more on the definition, see Questions 1:1 et seq.

S corporation audit: A uniform audit procedure, enacted as part of the Subchapter S Revision Act of 1982, that generally requires all *Subchapter S items* to be determined at the S corporation level. This restriction that Subchapter S items be determined at the corporate level applies to IRS and to shareholders, although a shareholder may dispute the corporation's treatment of an item by taking a different position on his or her return and notifying IRS of this. However, certain *small corporations* are exempt from these requirements for returns originally due after January 30, 1987, unless they elect to be covered. See Questions 14:6–14:22.

S corporation election: The corporate election of S corporation status, made on *Form 2553*. See Questions 2:1 et seq.

S corporation termination year: A taxable year (either a *calendar year* or another *permitted year*) during which S corporation status is ended by *termination* or *revocation*. Both S corporation and C corporation returns must be filed for this year, with the tax burden split between the shareholders and the C corporation according to a *pro rata daily allocation method* or a *closing of the books method*. See Questions 4:17 et seq.

Section 444 fiscal-year election: An election qualifying S corporations can make to use a fiscal year with a three-month-or-less deferral of income to shareholders, even though the year is not a *required year*. In return for this election, the S corporation must make *required payments* in the nature of a deposit on shareholder taxes due. If the corporation is eligible, it may make an election either alone or as a backup to a request for a *natural business year*. See Questions 3:7–3:10 and 3:15–3:16.

Glossary

Shareholder consent to election: The document that each shareholder, and in some cases certain former shareholders, must file in order for the *S corporation election* to be effective. See Questions 2:8–2:13.

Shareholders' agreement: An agreement, sometimes called a "buy-sell" agreement, that all of the shareholders of a privately held corporation, and the corporation itself, often make to govern operations of the corporation and define how shares of stock will be transferred. In all small corporations, such an agreement can be used to set estate tax value of stock, define what happens if a shareholder is disabled, restrict the transfer of stock to outsiders, and the like. In the S corporation context, it can also serve the function of protecting the corporation against a *disqualifying act* and provide other mechanisms for maintaining, and ending, S corporation status. See Questions 6:9–6:10.

Shareholder's basis: The measure of a shareholder's investment in an S corporation. See Questions 11:1 et seq.

Shareholder's basis in loans: The measure of loans made directly by a shareholder to an S corporation, which can be used to provide additional basis for the deduction of losses after the *shareholder's basis in stock* is exhausted. It is calculated using the initial amount of the loan, adjusted to reflect S corporation *pass-through items*. See Questions 11:8 et seq.; see also Questions 10:1–10:2 regarding the limitations on losses.

Shareholder's basis in stock: The measure of a shareholder's equity investment in an S corporation, which is used to measure gain or loss when the stock is sold, characterize certain distributions, and (along with *shareholder's basis in loans*) determine whether passed-through losses are currently deductible. It is calculated using the initial investment in stock, plus any contributions to capital, with annual adjustments to reflect S corporation *pass-through items* and certain distributions. See Questions 11:3 et seq. See also Questions 10:1–10:2 regarding the limitations on losses.

Small corporation: For purposes of the *S corporation audit* rules, a corporation that—for returns originally due after January 30, 1987—will be exempt from the rules unless it elects to have them apply. Basically, it is an S corporation that at no time during the taxable year had more than five shareholders and had no shareholders that were "pass-through" or conduit entities such as trusts. See Questions 14:14–14:19.

Straight debt: A debt obligation an S corporation can issue, to shareholders or nonshareholders, under a statutory safe harbor without running afoul of the *one class of stock* requirement and jeopardizing its election. See Question 1:35.

Subchapter S items: Items that, for purposes of the *S corporation audit* rules, IRS has deemed to be more appropriately determined at the corporate level than at the shareholder level. They include determination of the amount of each shareholder's *pro rata share* of *pass-through items*, most basic accounting questions, and matters pertaining to the validity of the *S corporation election*, the *at-risk rules*, and distributions and contributions. See Questions 14:9–14:11.

Tax matters person (TMP): A shareholder that the S corporation may designate each year as the person authorized to act on its behalf (and on behalf of the other shareholders) in conjunction with an *S corporation audit*. See Questions 14:21–14:22.

Tax on excess passive income: A tax that, subject to certain exceptions, is imposed directly on an S corporation if (1) the corporation has *earnings and profits* accumulated as a *C corporation* and (2) *passive investment income* exceeds 25% of gross receipts. The tax is imposed at the corporate rate, which is applied to *excess net passive income*. See Questions 8:10–8:14.

Tax on long-term capital gains: A tax that is imposed directly on an S corporation if (1) net long-term capital gains for a taxable year exceed $25,000 and is more than 50% of taxable income, (2) taxable income exceeds $25,000, and (3) the corporation neither (a) is subject to the *built-in gains tax*, nor (b) has had an *S corporation election* in effect for three taxable years preceding the year in question (or been an S corporation for its entire existence, if less than three years). The tax is the lower of (1) the current capital gains rate applied to net long-term capital gains in excess of $25,000 or (2) regular corporate income tax on the corporation's entire taxable income (with certain special adjustments). See Questions 8:15–8:20.

Termination: A cessation of S corporation status by operation of statute because the corporation either (1) fails to continue to meet the requirements for S corporation status or (2) has *earnings and profits* accumulated as a *C corporation* plus excess *passive investment income* for three consecutive years. See Questions 4:3 et seq.

Two-taxable-years allocation method: An alternative method of allocating shareholders' *pro rata shares* of *pass-through items* in a year that is not an *S corporation termination year* but in which a shareholder has terminated his or her interest in the corporation. Under this method, the corporation's books are used to allocate all items to the portion of the year in which they occurred. Everyone who held stock at any time during the year must consent to this election. See Questions 9:10–9:12.

Voting trust: A trust formed to vote shares of stock and that can, under certain circumstances, be an *eligible shareholder* of an S corporation. See Question 1:19.

Code Sections

Code Section	Text Section	Code Section	Text Section
6(c)(2)(A)	1:13	101(b)	13:6
6(c)(2)(B)	1:13	108	9:15
6(c)(3)(A)	1:14	108(a)	8:7;
6(c)(3)(B)	1:14		9:15
6(c)(4)	1:13;	108(b)	8:7;
	1:14		9:15
11	8:25	108(c)	8:7;
11(b)	8:11		9:15
26(a)	10:37	162(a)	1:6
26(b)	10:37	163(d)	10:34
28(d)(2)	10:37	165(g)	10:1;
29(b)(5)	10:37		11:5
38(c)	10:37	166(d)	10:1;
39	10:37		11:9
47	8:34;	167	10:23
	14:10	170	9:4
47(a)(1)	10:38	172	8:18
47(a)(2)	10:38	174	10:11
47(a)(3)	10:38	179(b)(1)	9:15
47(a)(4)	10:38	179(d)(8)	8:7;
47(a)(5)	10:38		9:15
48(q)(6)	11:6	183	1:5;
57(a)	14:9		1:6;
58(b)	10:10		9:4;
58(b)(3)	10:10		14:9
58(c)(1)	10:10	183(e)	1:5
67	9:4	183(e)(4)	1:5
72(m)(5)	13:11	194(b)(2)(B)	8:7;

The S Corporation Answer Book

Code Section	Text Section	Code Section	Text Section
	9:15	368(a)(1)(B)	5:1
212	9:4	368(a)(1)(C)	5:1
243	8:18	368(a)(1)(D)	5:1
248	8:2	368(a)(1)(E)	5:1
267(a)(1)	8:5	368(a)(1)(F)	5:1;
267(a)(2)	8:6		5:16
267(b)	10:6	368(a)(1)(G)	5:1
267(b)(2)	8:5	368(c)	5:3
267(b)(10)	8:5	381	5:18
267(b)(11)	8:5	385	1:34
267(b)(12)	8:5	401(a)(5)	13:9
274(n)	9:4	409A(a)	13:10
280A	10:23	441(d)	3:1
291	8:2	441(e)	3:1
302(a)	12:13	441(f)	3:1
303(a)	12:13	444	3:2;
311(a)	8:4		3:3;
312	12:3		3:7;
318	13:3		3:8;
318(a)	8:33;		3:9;
	13:3		3:10;
331	5:13		3:11;
337 (former)	7:6		3:12;
338	4:19;		3:13;
	4:21;		3:15;
	5:13		3:16;
341	12:7		3:18;
351	1:17;		3:20;
	11:4;		3:21;
	11:22		3:22;
354	5:1;		3:23
	8:4	444(d)(3)	3:8
355	5:1;	465	10:3;
	5:10;		10:36;
	8:4		14:9
356	5:1;	465(a)(2)	10:7
	8:4	465(b)(3)	10:6
358	11:4	465(b)(4)	10:6
361	5:3;	465(b)(5)	10:8
	8:30	465(c)(1)	10:5;
368(a)(1)	5:1;		10:6
	5:3	465(c)(2)(A)	10:5
368(a)(1)(A)	5:1	465(c)(2)(B)(ii)	10:5

Code Sections

Code Section	Text Section	Code Section	Text Section
465(c)(3)	10:5	469(m)(1)	10:50
465(c)(3)(A)	10:3	469(m)(2)	10:50
465(c)(3)(B)	10:4;	469(m)(3)	10:10
	10:5	469(m)(3)(A)	10:50
465(c)(3)(C)	10:5	469(m)(3)(B)	10:50
465(c)(3)(D) (former)	10:3	469(m)(3)(B)(ii)	10:50
465(e)	10:9	481	10:28;
469	7:1;		10:33
	10:24;	542(c)(6)	7:26
	10:33;	542(d)(1)	7:26
	10:36;	585	1:8
	10:37	593	1:8
469(a)	10:10	611	8:2;
469(a)(1)(B)	10:37		11:7
469(b)	10:38	613A	10:33
469(c)(1)	10:11	613A(d)	10:33;
469(c)(1)(B)	10:24		10:36
469(c)(2)	10:39	613A(c)(13)(B)	11:7
469(c)(6)	10:11	617	8:8;
469(d)(1)	10:38		9:5
469(d)(2)	10:37;	632(b)	8:23
	10:38	633(d)(2)	8:32
469(e)(1)	10:29	633(d)(5)	8:33
469(e)(1)(B)	10:29	633(d)(6)	8:33
469(f)(1)	10:49	633(d)(8)	8:32
469(f)(2)	10:49	663(c)	1:23
469(g)(1)	10:38;	671	1:19
	10:48	672	1:19
469(g)(1)(A)	10:48	673	1:19
469(g)(1)(B)	10:48	674	1:19
469(g)(2)	10:48	675	1:19
469(g)(3)	10:48	676	1:19
469(h)	10:24	677	1:19
469(i)(4)	10:42	678	1:19
469(i)(5)	10:41	702(b)	7:10
469(i)(6)	10:42	704(b)	13:3
469(i)(6)(B)	10:42	704(e)(3)	9:14
469(j)(3)	10:37	707(b)	10:6
469(j)(6)	10:48	707(c)	10:17;
469(j)(8)	10:39		13:4
469(j)(9)	10:48	806(e)(2)(C)	3:2
469(k)	10:38	901	8:8;

Code Section	Text Section	Code Section	Text Section
	9:5	1361(d)(1)(A)	1:20
936	1:8;	1361(d)(1)(B)	1:20
	1:9	1361(d)(2)	1:24;
1006(g)(1)	8:19		1:25;
1014	11:4		1:26;
1031	7:7;		1:27
	8:30	1361(d)(2)(A)	1:25
1033	8:30	1361(d)(2)(B)(ii)	1:27
1201(a)	8:25	1361(d)(2)(C)	1:26
1211	10:33;	1361(d)(3)	1:20;
	10:36;		1:23
	10:38;	1361(d)(3)(A)(i)	1:21
	12:7	1361(d)(3)(A)(ii)	1:21
1222(9)	7:11	1361(d)(3)(A)(iii)	1:21
1231	8:3;	1361(d)(3)(A)(iv)	1:21
	9:4;	1361(d)(3)(B)	1:21
	9:8;	1362(a)	4:12
	10:38;	1362(a)(2)	2:8
	14:9	1362(b)	2:2
1232 (former)	11:11	1362(b)(2)	2:2
1245	10:5	1362(d)(1)	4:10;
1256	8:19		4:15;
1256(g)(8)	8:19		6:10
1271	11:11	1362(d)(1)(B)	4:11
1271(a)(1)	11:11	1362(d)(1)(C)	4:13
1272	11:11	1362(d)(3)	4:3;
1273	11:11		6:1;
1274	11:11		6:7;
1275	11:11		7:3;
1361	13:10		7:5
1361(b)	1:2	1362(d)(3)(C)	7:6;
1361(b)(1)(D)	1:30		7:7;
1361(b)(2)	1:8		7:11
1361(c)(1)	1:15	1362(d)(3)(D)	7:1
1361(c)(2)	1:19	1362(d)(3)(D)(i)	7:6;
1361(c)(2)(A)(i)	1:19		7:12
1361(c)(2)(A)(ii)	1:19	1362(d)(3)(D)(ii)	7:26
1361(c)(2)(A)(iii)	1:19	1362(d)(3)(D)(iii)	7:26
1361(c)(2)(A)(iv)	1:19	1362(e)(1)	4:17
1361(c)(4)	1:30	1362(e)(2)	4:19;
1361(c)(5)	1:35;		4:20;
	6:6		4:22
1361(c)(6)	1:9	1362(e)(3)	4:19;

Code Sections

Code Section	Text Section	Code Section	Text Section
	4:22	1367(a)(1)(B)	11:6
1362(e)(5)(A)	4:23	1367(a)(1)(C)	11:6
1362(e)(6)(C)	4:21	1367(a)(2)	11:8
1362(e)(6)(D)	4:21	1367(a)(2)(A)	11:7
1362(f)	4:6	1367(a)(2)(B)	11:7
1362(g)	2:17;	1367(a)(2)(C)	11:7
	6:13	1367(a)(2)(D)	11:7
1363(b)	8:2;	1367(a)(2)(E)	11:7
	8:3	1367(b)(1)	11:6
1363(c)(1)	8:8	1367(b)(2)	11:9
1363(c)(2)	8:8;	1367(b)(2)(A)	11:8
	9:5	1367(b)(2)(B)	11:6;
1363(d)	8:4;		11:8
	8:36;	1367(b)(3)	10:1;
	8:39		11:5;
1363(e)	8:4		11:9
1366(a)	3:8;	1368(b)	12:1;
	3:18;		12:7;
	9:1;		12:8
	9:2	1368(b)(1)	12:7
1366(a)(1)	9:13	1368(b)(2)	12:7
1366(a)(1)(A)	9:4;	1368(c)	12:1;
	10:38		12:9
1366(b)	8:3;	1368(c)(1)	12:20
	9:1;	1368(c)(2)	10:30
	9:3	1368(c)(3)	12:14
1366(c)	14:26	1368(e)(1)	12:10;
1366(d)	10:1;		12:12
	10:3;	1368(e)(1)(A)	12:17
	10:6;	1368(e)(1)(B)	12:13
	10:33;	1368(e)(2)	12:10
	10:36	1368(e)(3)	12:18;
1366(d)(2)	10:2;		12:19;
	10:33		12:20
1366(d)(3)	10:2	1371(a)(2)	5:13
1366(e)	9:14	1371(c)(1)	12:4
1366(f)(2)	8:25	1371(c)(2)	12:5
1366(f)(2) (former)	8:19	1371(c)(3)	12:6
1366(f)(3)	8:11	1371(d)(1)	8:35;
1367	10:1;		9:6
	12:11	1371(d)(2)	8:34;
	9:4;		9:6
1367(a)(1)(A)	11:6	1371(d)(3)	12:6

Code Section	Text Section	Code Section	Text Section
1371(e)	12:1		7:5;
1371(e)(1)	12:23		8:10;
1371(e)(2)	12:25		8:11
1372	8:2;	1375(b)	7:4;
	13:2;		8:11
	13:4	1375(b)(1)(B)	8:12
1372(b)	13:3	1375(b)(2)	8:11
1372(e) (former)	7:6	1375(b)(3)	8:11
1372(e)(4) (former)	7:6	1375(b)(4)	8:10
1372(e)(5)	7:13;	1375(c)(2)	8:20
	7:17	1375(c)(2) (former)	8:31
1372(e)(5) (former)	7:6;	1375(d)	8:13
	7:7	1375(d) (former)	12:21
1372(e)(5)(B)	7:8	1375(f) (former)	12:21
1374	5:18;	1377(a)(1)	9:8;
	8:15;		9:12
	8:21	1377(a)(2)	9:9;
1374 (former)	8:15		9:10;
1374(a) (former)	8:18		9:12
1374(b)	8:25	1377(b)(1)	12:24
1374(b) (former)	8:19	1377(b)(2)	12:24
1374(c) (former)	8:16	1378(a)	3:2
1374(c)(2)	8:28	1378(b)	3:3
1374(c)(3) (former)	8:17	1379(c)	12:21
1374(c)(4) (former)	8:19	1504	1:8;
1374(c)(4)(B)(ii) (former)	8:19		1:9
1374(d) (former)	8:19	1504(b)	1:8;
1374(d)(1)	8:28		1:9
1374(d)(2)(A)	8:26	2036(c)	1:31
1374(d)(2)(B)	8:27	4975	13:11
1374(d)(3)	8:26	4975(b)	13:11
1374(d)(4)	8:26	6013(e)	14:25;
1374(d)(5)	8:24;		14:26
	8:26	6013(e)(1)	14:25
1374(d)(5)(B)	8:26	6013(e)(2)	14:25
1374(d)(5)(C)	8:28	6013(e)(3)	14:25
1374(d)(6)	8:30	6013(e)(4)	14:25
1374(d)(8)	8:30	6013(e)(4)(D)	14:25
1374(e)	8:29	6037(a)	14:1
1375	7:3;	6037(b)	14:4
	8:9	6072(b)	14:2
1375(a)	7:4;	6144(e)	4:26

Code Sections

Code Section	Text Section	Code Section	Text Section
6166	1:28	6243	14:6;
6221	14:7;		14:7;
	14:23		14:11;
6222	14:7;		14:20
	14:23	6244	14:6;
6223	14:7;		14:7;
	14:23		14:11;
6224	14:7;		14:23
	14:23	6245	14:6;
6225	14:7;		14:7;
	14:23		14:9;
6226	14:7;		14:11
	14:23	6501	6:17;
6227	14:7;		14:23;
	14:23		14:26
6228	14:7;	6501(b)(1)	14:23
	14:23	6501(c)(1)	14:24
6229	14:7;	6501(c)(3)	14:24
	14:23	6501(e)(1)(A)	14:24
6230	14:7;	6501(e)(1)(A)(i)	14:24
	14:23	6501(e)(1)(A)(ii)	14:24;
6230(f)	14:22		14:26
6231	14:7;	6501(o)(2)	14:23
	14:23	6623(g)	14:22
6231(a)(7)	14:21	6653	3:20
6231(b)(1)	14:11	6670(a)(3)	14:5
6232	14:7;	7503	2:6
	14:23	7519	3:2;
6241	14:6;		3:3;
	14:7;		3:9;
	14:11;		3:18;
	14:14		3:19
6242	14:6;	7519(b)	3:18
	14:7;	7519(d)(3)	3:8
	14:11;	7519(f)(3)	3:24
	14:12	7519(f)(4)	3:20

Regulation Sections

* denotes proposed regulations
** denotes temporary regulation

Regulation	Text Section	Regulation	Text Section
§1.47-4(a)	9:6	§1.469-1T(e)(3)(ii)(A)**	10:39
§1.47-4(a)(2)	9:7	§1.469-1T(e)(3)(ii)(B)**	10:39
§1.47-4(d)	8:35; 9:6	§1.469-1T(e)(3)(ii)(C)**	10:39
		§1.469-1T(e)(3)(ii)(D)**	10:39
§1.67-1T(a)**	9:4	§1.469-1T(e)(3)(ii)(E)**	10:39
§1.67-1T(c)**	9:4	§1.469-1T(e)(3)(ii)(F)**	10:40
§1.67-2T(b)(1)**	9:4	§1.469-1T(e)(3)(vii)**	10:40
§1.163-8T**	10:35	§1.469-1T(f)(2)(i)(B)**	10:38
§1.165-3(a)(1)	7:18	§1.469-1T(f)(2)(i)(C)**	10:38
§1.442-1(b)(1)	3:5; 3:13	§1.469-1T(f)(3)(ii)**	10:38
		§1.469-1T(f)(4)**	10:38
§1.444-1T(b)(5)(iii)**	3:9	§1.469-1T(f)(4)(i)**	10:38
§1.444-1T(c)(2)**	3:21	§1.469-1T(h)(2)(ii)**	10:13
§1.444-2T**	3:8	§1.469-1T(k)**	10:49
§1.444-2T(b)(3)**	3:9	§1.469-2T(b)**	10:28; 10:33; 10:38
§1.444-3T**	3:15		
§1.444-3T(b)(3)**	3:15		
§1.444-3T(b)(4)(ii)**	3:16	§1.469-2T(c)**	10:28; 10:38
§1.444-3T(b)(4)(iii)**	3:16		
§1.465-1T**	10:5	§1.469-2T(c)(2)**	10:29
§1.465-3*	10:9	§1.469-2T(c)(2)(i)(A), Ex. 2**	10:43
§1.465-10*	10:3		
§1.465-10(c)*	10:6	§1.469-2T(c)(2)(i)(A)(*1*)**	10:43
§1.469-1T(e)**	10:11	§1.469-2T(c)(2)(i)(A)(2)**	10:43
§1.469-1T(e)(1)(i)**	10:11	§1.469-2T(c)(2)(i)(A)(3)**	10:43
§1.469-1T(e)(2)**	10:11	§1.469-2T(c)(2)(i)(C)(*1*)**	10:43
§1.469-1T(e)(3)(i)**	10:39	§1.469-2T(c)(2)(ii)**	10:43

Regulation	Text Section	Regulation	Text Section
§1.469-2T(c)(2)(iii)**	10:43; 10:47	§1.469-2T(e)(3)(ii)(B)**	10:46
		§1.469-2T(e)(3)(ii)(C)**	10:46
§1.469-2T(c)(2)(iii)(B)**	10:43	§1.469-2T(e)(3)(ii)(D)(*1*)(*i*)**	10:45
§1.469-2T(c)(2)(iii)(D)**	10:43	§1.469-2T(e)(3)(ii)(D)(*1*)(*ii*)**	10:45
§1.469-2T(c)(2)(iv)**	10:43	§1.469-2T(e)(3)(ii)(D)(*3*)**	10:44
§1.469-2T(c)(2)(v)**	10:43	§1.469-2T(e)(3)(iii)**	10:47
§1.469-2T(c)(3)**	10:29	§1.469-2T(e)(3)(iv)**	10:46
§1.469-2T(c)(3)(i)(B)**	10:30	§1.469-2T(e)(3)(v)**	10:44
§1.469-2T(c)(3)(ii)**	10:29	§1.469-2T(e)(3)(vi)(B)**	10:46
§1.469-2T(c)(3)(iii)(B)**	10:29	§1.469-2T(e)(3)(viii), Ex. 1**	10:46
§1.469-2T(c)(4)**	10:31		
§1.469-2T(c)(4)(i)**	10:31	§1.469-2T(f)(2)**	10:32
§1.469-2T(c)(4)(ii)**	10:31	§1.469-2T(f)(2)(iii)**	10:38
§1.469-2T(c)(5)**	10:28	§1.469-2T(f)(3)**	10:32
§1.469-2T(d)(1)**	10:33	§1.469-2T(f)(4)**	10:32
§1.469-2T(d)(2)**	10:33	§1.469-2T(f)(5)**	10:32
§1.469-2T(d)(2)(i)**	10:33; 10:34	§1.469-2T(f)(6)**	10:32; 10:40
§1.469-2T(d)(2)(iii)**	10:34; 10:35	§1.469-2T(f)(7)**	10:29; 10:32
§1.469-2T(d)(2)(iv)**	10:34	§1.469-3T(a)**	10:37
§1.469-2T(d)(2)(vii)**	10:33	§1.469-3T(b)(1)**	10:37
§1.469-2T(d)(5)(i)**	10:29	§1.469-3T(b)(1)(B)**	10:37
§1.469-2T(d)(5)(i)(A)**	10:43	§1.469-3T(b)(2)**	10:37
§1.469-2T(d)(5)(i)(B)**	10:43	§1.469-3T(b)(4)**	10:37
§1.469-2T(d)(5)(ii)**	10:43	§1.469-3T(d)(1)**	10:37
§1.469-2T(d)(5)(iii)(A)**	10:43	§1.469-3T(d)(2)(i)**	10:37
§1.469-2T(d)(6)**	10:3	§1.469-3T(e)**	10:37
§1.469-2T(d)(6)(i)**	10:36	§1.469-3T(f)**	10:38
§1.469-2T(d)(6)(ii)(B)**	10:36	§1.469-4T(a)(2)**	10:13
§1.469-2T(d)(6)(iii)**	10:36	§1.469-4T(a)(3)**	10:13
§1.469-2T(d)(6)(iv)**	10:36	§1.469-4T(a)(3)(ii)**	10:14
§1.469-2T(d)(6)(v)**	10:36	§1.469-4T(a)(3)(iii)**	10:14
§1.469-2T(d)(7)**	10:33	§1.469-4T(a)(4)(i)**	10:13; 10:15
§1.469-2T(d)(8)**	10:33; 10:36		
		§1.469-4T(a)(4)(ii)(B)**	10:16; 10:17
§1.469-2T(e)(1)**	10:26; 10:33; 10:42		
		§1.469-4T(a)(4)(ii)(C)**	10:16
		§1.469-4T(a)(4)(iii)**	10:22
§1.469-2T(e)(3)(i)**	10:44	§1.469-4T(a)(4)(iv)(A)**	10:23
§1.469-2T(e)(3)(i)(E)**	10:46	§1.469-4T(a)(4)(iv)(B)**	10:23
§1.469-2T(e)(3)(ii)(A)**	10:44	§1.469-4T(a)(4)(v)**	10:20;

Regulation Sections

Regulation	Text Section	Regulation	Text Section
	10:21	§1.469-4T(o)(7)(ii)**	10:20
§1.469-4T(a)(5)(i)**	10:13	§1.469-4T(p)**	10:13
§1.469-4T(b)(2)(i)**	10:16	§1.469-5T(a)**	10:25
§1.469-4T(c)(2)**	10:14	§1.469-5T(a)(7)**	10:25
§1.469-4T(c)(2)(ii)(A)(1)**	10:14	§1.469-5T(b)(2)**	10:25
§1.469-4T(c)(2)(ii)(A)(2)**	10:14	§1.469-5T(f)(1)**	10:24
§1.469-4T(c)(2)(iv)**	10:14	§1.469-5T(f)(2)(i)**	10:24
§1.469-4T(d)(1)**	10:14	§1.469-5T(f)(2)(ii)**	10:24
§1.469-4T(d)(2)**	10:14	§1.469-5T(f)(3)**	10:24
§1.469-4T(e)(1)(ii)**	10:14	§1.469-5T(f)(4)**	10:27
§1.469-4T(f)(1)**	10:18	§1.469-5T(g)**	10:25
§1.469-4T(f)(1)(ii)**	10:16	§1.469-5T(h)(3)**	10:25
§1.469-4T(f)(2)(i)**	10:16	§1.469-5T(j)(1)**	10:25
§1.469-4T(f)(2)(ii)**	10:16	§1.469-6T**	10:48
§1.469-4T(f)(2)(iii)**	10:16	§1.469-7T**	10:34
§1.469-4T(f)(3)(i)**	10:16	§1.469-9T**	10:38;
§1.469-4T(f)(4)(i)**	10:18		10:41
§1.469-4T(f)(4)(ii)**	10:18	§1.469-10T**	10:38
§1.469-4T(f)(5)**	10:18	§1.469-11T(a)**	10:50
§1.469-4T(g)(3)**	10:19	§1.469-11T(a)(2)**	10:32
§1.469-4T(h)(1)(ii)**	10:22	§1.469-11T(a)(4)**	10:50
§1.469-4T(h)(2)**	10:22	§1.469-11T(a)(5), Ex. 1**	10:50
§1.469-4T(j)**	10:17	§1.469-11T(b)(2)**	10:50
§1.469-4T(j)(3)**	10:17	§1.469-11T(b)(3)**	10:50
§1.469-4T(j)(3)(iii)(A)**	10:17	§1.469-11T(b)(4)**	10:50
§1.469-4T(k)(1)(ii)**	10:23	§1.469-11T(c)(2)(ii)**	10:50
§1.469-4T(k)(2)(iii)(A)**	10:23	§1.469-11T(c)(3)(i)**	10:50
§1.469-4T(k)(2)(iii)(B)**	10:23	§1.469-11T(c)(3)(ii)**	10:50
§1.469-4T(k)(3)**	10:23	§1.469-11T(c)(5)**	10:51
§1.469-4T(k)(4)**	10:23	§1.469-11T(c)(5)(iii),	
§1.469-4T(k)(6)**	10:23	Ex. 7**	10:51
§1.469-4T(k)(7)**	10:23	§1.469-11T(c)(7)(i)**	10:50
§1.469-4T(m)(1)**	10:13	§1.469-11T(c)(7)(ii)**	10:50
§1.469-4T(n)**	10:13	§1.1361-1A(f)*	1:29
§1.469-4T(o)**	10:20	§1.1361-1A(h)(3)(ii)*	1:19
§1.469-4T(o)(1)**	10:20	§1.1361-1A(i)(2)*	1:21
§1.469-4T(o)(3)**	10:20	§1.1361-1A(i)(3)*	1:25
§1.469-4T(o)(4)**	10:20	§1.1361-1T(a)**	1:25
§1.469-4T(o)(5)**	10:20	§1.1361-1T(b)**	1:27
§1.469-4T(o)(6)(i)**	10:21	§1.1361-1T(c)**	1:26
§1.469-4T(o)(6)(ii)**	10:21	§1.1362-1*	2:3
§1.469-4T(o)(7)(i)**	10:20	§1.1362-1(c)(4)*	2:6

Regulation	Text Section	Regulation	Text Section
§1.1362-1(e)*	2:3	(former)	7:6;
§1.1362-3(b)(1)*	4:12		7:7;
§1.1362-3(b)(2)*	4:13		7:13;
§1.1362-3(b)(3)*	4:13		7:17
§1.1362-3(b)(5)*	4:15	§1.1372-4(b)(5)(iv)(b)	
§1.1362-3(c)*	4:3	(Example 3) (former)	7:9
§1.1362-3(c)(1)*	4:16	§1.1372-4(b)(5)(x) (former)	7:12
§1.1362-3(d)*	4:3	§1.1372-5(a) (former)	2:18
§1.1362-3(d)(4)*	7:6;	§1.1372-5(b) (former)	2:17
	7:7	§1.1375-1A(b)(1)(i)	8:11
§1.1362-3(d)(4)(ii)(A)*	7:7	§1.1375-1A(c)(2)	8:20
§1.1362-3(d)(4)(ii)(B)*	7:12	§1.1375-1A(d)(1)	8:13
§1.1362-3(d)(4)(iv)*	7:9	§1.1375-1A(d)(2)	8:14
§1.1362-3(d)(5)(iv)*	7:13;	§1.1375-1A(f)	7:1
	7:15;	§1.6037-1(c)	6:17
	7:17;	§1.7519-2T(a)(2)**	3:19
	7:19;	§1.7519-2T(a)(6)(ii)**	3:23
	7:20	§18.1362-1T(b)**	2:3
§1.1362-3(d)(5)(vi)*	7:1;	§18.1362-2T(a)**	2:9
	7:26	§18.1362-2T(b)(1)**	2:8
§1.1362-3(d)(5)(ix)*	7:26	§18.1362-2T(b)(2)**	2:8
§1.1362-4(a)*	4:21	§18.1362-2T(c)**	2:12
§1.1362-4(b)*	4:20	§18.1362-3T**	4:12
§1.1362-4(c)(2)*	4:22	§18.1362-4T**	4:22
§1.1362-4(c)(3)*	4:21	§18.1366-5**	3:2
§1.1362-4(c)(4)*	4:21	§18.1366-5(d)**	3:2
§1.1362-4(d)*	4:23	§18.1366-5(f)**	3:2
§1.1362-5(b)*	4:7	§18.1377-1T**	9:12
§1.1362-5(c)*	4:8	§301.6231(a)(7)-1	14:21
§1.1362-6(a)*	2:18	§301.6241-1T**	14:7;
§1.1362-6(b)*	2:17		14:11;
§1.1362-6(c)*	2:18		14:14
§1.1363-1(c)*	8:8;	§301.6241-1T(c)(2)**	14:14
	9:5	§301.6241-1T(c)(2)(ii)**	14:15
§1.1366-2	9:4	§301.6241-1T(c)(2)(iii)**	14:16
§1.1371-1(g) (former)	1:34	§301.6241-1T(c)(2)(iv)**	14:17
§1.1372-2(b)(1) (former)	2:3	§301.6241-1T(c)(2)(iv)(C)**	14:19
§1.1372-2(b)(3) (former)	2:16	§301.6241-1T(c)(2)(v)(A)**	14:18
§1.1372-4(b)(3) (former)	4:16	§301.7503-1(a)	2:6
§1.1372-4(b)(5)(iv)		§302.6245-1T**	14:9

Revenue Rulings

Rev. Rul.	Text Section	Rev. Rul.	Text Section
61-112, 1961-1 CB 399	7:22	71-549, 1971-2 CB 319	6:16
64-162, 1964-1 (Part 1)		72-320, 1972-1 CB 270	5:10
CB 304	11:11	73-361, 1973-2 CB 331	13:1
64-232, 1964-2 CB 334	7:23	73-496, 1973-2 CB 312	5:11
64-249, 1964-2 CB 332	1:29	74-44, 1974-1 CB 287	13:1
64-250, 1964-2 CB 333	5:16	75-144, 1975-1 CB 277	11:6
65-40, 1965-1 CB 429	7:23	75-261, 1975-2 CB 350	2:8
65-83, 1965-1 CB 430	7:23	75-349, 1975-2 CB 349	7:23
65-91, 1965-1 CB 431	7:19;	76-23, 1976-1 CB 264	1:28
	7:20	76-48, 1976-1 CB 265	7:21
65-292, 1965-2 CB 319	8:18	76-469, 1976-2 CB 252	7:23
66-116, 1966-1 CB 198	2:8	78-274, 1978-2 CB 220	2:18
67-269, 1967-2 CB 298	1:33	78-332, 1978-2 CB 223	2:18
68-227, 1968-1 CB 381	2:8	78-333, 1978-2 CB 224	2:18
68-364, 1968-2 CB 371	7:7	78-364, 1978-2 CB 225	2:18
68-537, 1968-2 CB 372	11:11	79-52, 1979-1 CB 283	5:8
69-125, 1969-1 CB 207	11:17	79-178, 1979-1 CB 435	14:24
69-192, 1969-1 CB 207	7:7	80-236, 1980-2 CB 240	11:13
69-566, 1969-2 CB 165	5:7	81-197, 1981-2 CB 166	7:24
70-50, 1970-1 CB 178	11:15	83-116, 1983-2 CB 264	2:6
70-206, 1970-1 CB 177	7:23	85-86, 1985-1 CB 291	11:6
70-232, 1970-1 CB 177	5:9	85-161, 1985-2 CB 191	1:32
70-615, 1970-2 CB 169	2:8	86-110, 1986-2 CB 150	4:7
71-266, 1971-1 CB 262	5:11	87-57, 1987-2 CB 117	3:6
71-288, 1971-2 CB 319	11:15	89-45, 1989-14 IRB 15	1:22
71-455, 1971-2 CB 318	7:10	89-55, 1989-15 IRB 14	1:22

Revenue Procedures

Rev. Proc.	Text Section	Rev. Proc.	Text Section
75-17, 1975-1 CB 677	12:4		3:14;
87-32, 1987-2 CB 396	3:3;		3:17
	3:4;	*88-13*, 1988-1 CB 639	3:17
	3:5;	*89-12*, 1989-1 IRB 22	1:18
	3:6;	*89-38*, 1989-24 IRB 75	10:18
	3:11;		

Revenue Procedures

Letter Rulings

Letter Ruling	Text Section	Letter Ruling	Text Section
7718003	7:24	7949022	13:1
7718007	7:16	8007089	5:6
7730071	2:18	8010028	6:12
7731004	7:23	8114094	7:24
7732053	7:25	8116081	7:25
7741019	2:18	8221053	7:23
7743011	2:18	8225141	7:23
7743074	7:10	8752017	10:30
7745041	5:12	8818049	5:13
7752040	7:19	8836031	2:15
7805036	2:18	8842007	2:18
7809078	2:18		

Cases

Appley, TC Memo 1979-433, **1:6**

Badaracco, 104 S. Ct. 756 (1984), **14:24**
Bader, TC Memo 1987-30, **11:14**
Benderoff, 398 F.2d 132 (8th Cir. 1968), rev'g 270 F. Supp. 87 (S.D. Iowa 1967), **6:17; 14:26**
Bennett, 30 TC 114 (1958), acq., 1958-2 CB 3, **14:24**
Blake, TC Memo 1981-579, **1:6**
Blount, 86 TC 383 (1986), acq. in result, action on decision, 1986-041, **14:23**
Blum, 59 TC 438 (1972), **11:14**
Bramlette Bldg. Corp., Inc., 52 TC 200 (1969), aff'd, 424 F.2d 751 (5th Cir. 1970), **7:17**
Branch, et al. (D. Ga. 1967), *vacating a prior adverse decision* (D. Ga. 1967), **7:7**
Brown, TC Memo 1977-15, **1:6**
Burnstein, TC Memo 1984-74, **11:17**

City Markets, Inc., TC Memo 1969-202, aff'd, 443 F.2d 1240 (6th Cir. 1970), **7:14**

Clemens, TC Memo 1969-235, aff'd, 453 F.2d 869 (9th Cir. 1971), **2:11**
Combs, Leslie, II, TC Memo 1989-206, **6:17**
Curran, TC Memo 1970-160, **1:4**

Demler, TC Memo 1966-117, **1:4**
DuPont, 234 F. Supp. 681 (D. Del. 1964), **1:4**

Eppler, 58 TC 691 (1972), aff'd in an unpublished opinion (7th Cir. 1973), **1:6**
Erwin, Edward R., III, TC Memo 1989-80, **11:14**

Farmer, 794 F.2d 1163 (6th Cir. 1986), **14:25**
Fear, Douglass, D., TC Memo 1989-211, **11:14**
Feingold, 49 TC 461 (1968), **7:14**
Feldman, 47 TC 329 (1966), **2:4**
Forrester, 49 TC 499 (1968), **2:11**
Frankel, 61 TC 343 (1973), aff'd, 506 F.2d 1051 (3d Cir. 1974), **11:17**

Frentz, 44 TC 485 (1965), *aff'd*, 375 F.2d 662 (6th Cir. 1967), **1:3; 2:4**

Fulk & Needham, Inc., 228 F. Supp. 39 (D. N.C. 1968), *aff'd*, 411 F.2d 1403 (4th Cir. 1969), **1:28**

Goldring, 20 TC 79 (1953), **14:24**

Greene, 70 TC 534 (1978), **7:18**

Gripentrog, TC Memo 1975-334, **2:5**

Gurda, TC Memo 1987-394, **11:17**

H. & L. Reid, Inc., 375 F. Supp. 1099 (E.D. Mich. 1973), **7:14; 7:17**

Helis v. Usry (D. La. 1971), *aff'd*, 464 F.2d 330 (5th Cir.1972), **7:7**

Helvering v. Southwest Consolidated Corp., 315 U.S. 194 (1942), **1:33**

Hicks Nurseries, Inc., 62 TC 138 (1974), *rev'd on other grounds*, 517 F.2d 437 (2d Cir. 1975), **2:12**

Hodge, TC Memo 1970-280, **11:21**

Hoffman, 47 TC 218 (1966), **6:12**

Houston, 38 TC 486 (1962), **14:24**

Johnston, TC Memo 1976-142, **6:7**

Jones, TC Memo 1973-238, **2:5**

Kean, 51 TC 337 (1968), *aff'd on this point*, 469 F.2d 1183 (9th Cir. 1972), **1:16; 2:11, 2:12**

Kelley, Daniel M., TC Memo 1986-405, **14:23**

Kennedy, et al., TC Memo 1974-147, **7:22**

Ketchum, 77 TC 1204 (1981), **14:26**

Lausmann, TC Memo 1979-420, **7:14**

Leavitt, Estate of Daniel, 90 TC 206 (1988), **11:14**

Lee, et al., TC Memo 1976-265, **11:17**

Lemler, TC Memo 1979-308, **1:6**

Lemler, TC Memo 1980-507, **1:6**

Leonhart, W.H., TC Memo 1968-98, *affirmed per curiam* 414 F.2d 749 (4th Cir. 1969), **14:23**

LeVant, 45 TC 185 (1965), *rev'd on other issue*, 376 F.2d 434 (7th Cir. 1967), **1:33**

Leve, TC Memo 1985-255, **2:5**

Lillis, TC Memo 1983-42, **7:14**

Llewellyn, 70 TC 370 (1978), **7:8**

McIlhenney, TC Memo 1979-43, **7:14**

Mitchell Offset Plate Service, Inc., 53 TC 235 (1969), *acq.*, 1970-2 CB xvi, **2:5**

Mora, TC Memo 1972-123, **2:5**

Neal, 313 F. Supp. 393 (D. Cal. 1970), **11:14**

Novell, TC Memo 1970-31, **11:12**

Ober, TC Memo 1980-513, **2:5**

Old Virginia Brick Co., Inc., 367 F.2d 276 (4th Cir. 1966), *aff'g* 44 TC 69 (1965), **1:28**

Packard, 85 TC 397 (1985), **1:7**

Papermaster (E.D. Wis. 1980), **10:1**

Parkin, TC Memo 1986-59, **2:5**

Perry, 47 TC 159 (1966), *aff'd*, 392 F.2d 458 (8th Cir. 1968), **11:14**

Pestcoe, 40 TC 195 (1963), **2:4**

Pike, 78 TC 58 (1982), **1:7**

Prashker, 59 TC 172 (1972), **11:17**

Cases

Radtke, E.D. Wis. 4/11/89, **13:1**
Ratcliff, TC Memo 1980-12, **1:3**
Raynor, 50 TC 762 (1968), **11:14**
Reuter, TC Memo 1985-607, **14:26**
Robertson (D. Nev. 1973), **11:17**
Robertson, 61 TC 727 (1974), **13:9**
Roschuni, 44 TC 80 (1965), **14:26**

Sanborn, TC Memo 1983-579, **7:8**
Scott, 70 TC 71 (1978), **14:27**
Seely, TC Memo 1986-216, **2:11**
Selfe v. U.S., 778 F.2d 769 (11th Cir. 1985), **11:14**
Shebester, TC Memo 1987-246, **11:17**
Sieh, 56 TC 1386 (1971), *aff'd* (8th Cir. 1973), **7:7**
Simons, 208 F. Supp. 744 (D. Conn. 1962), **2:4**

Taylor, 417 F.2d 991 (5th Cir. 1969), **14:26**

Taylor, George R., TC Memo 1987-399, **2:4**
Thompson, 66 TC 737 (1976), *acq. in result,* 1977-1 CB 1, **2:5; 2:15**
Thompson, 73 TC 878 (1980), **7:23**
Tuchman, TC Memo 1981-731, **14:26**

Uri, TC Memo 1989-58, **10:3**

Valley Loan Association, 258 F. Supp. 673 (D. Colo. 1966), **7:7**
Versitron (Ct. Cl. 1976), **2:18**

Wiebusch, 59 TC 777 (1973), **11:4**
Winn, 67 TC 499 (1976), *aff'd on this point,* 595 F.2d 1060 (5th Cir. 1979), **7:24**

Zalewski, Thaddeus J., TC Memo 1988-340, **2:4**
Zaretsky, TC Memo 1967-247, **2:5**

Index

(References in the index are to question numbers.)

- A -

Accumulated adjustments account. *See* Earnings and profits
Acquired corporation
  assets of, 5:13
  reorganization, status after, 5:14
Acquiring corporation
  and S corporation status, 5:11–5:12
    basis step-up, acquired corporation's assets, 5:13
Affiliated groups
  eligibility as S corporations, 1:8
Airfields
  passive investment income, 7:19
Allocation
  income, ownership change
    alternative, 9:10, 9:12
    death of shareholder, 9:13
    deductions, limitations, 9:15
    loans from shareholder's family, 9:14
    method, differences between, 9:11
    pass-through allocation, 9:12
    pro rata method, 9:8–9:9
At-risk rules, 10:3–10:9
  aggregation of activities, 10:4
  amount at risk, calculation of, 10:6
  defined, 10:3
  losses
    deductions, 10:8
    disallowed under rules, 10:7
  negative amount at risk, 10:9
  passive activity loss rules, effect on, 10:36
  trade or business, activities constituting, 10:5
Audit
  exempt organizations, 14:8
  small corporations, 14:14–14:19
  generally, 14:6–14:8

-B-

Bankruptcy reorganization. *See* Reorganizations
Basis for gain or loss
  capital contributions to increase, 11:19–11:25
  loans
    allocation of payments, more than one loan, 11:12
    capital contributions compared to, 11:23
    cosigning of, 11:18
    defined, 11:9
    increase of basis, structuring of loans, 11:13–11:18

losses, limitations, 11:14, 11:18
payments made by shareholder-
guarantor, 11:15
reduction of basis, 11:10–11:11
shareholder, to S corporation,
11:9–11:18
substitution of shareholder
obligation for corporate
obligation, 11:16
third parties, loans from, 11:17
worthless debt deduction, 11:9
stock, shareholder's basis,
11:1–11:25
decrease in basis, items causing,
11:7–11:8
determination of, 11:4–11:18
functions of, 11:1–11:3
increase in basis, items causing,
11:6
losses, limitations, 11:3
sale or exchange of stock, 11:2
worthless stock, 11:5
yearly adjustments, 11:5
Beneficiary
death of, termination of S corporation election, 6:4
"Boot," 5:1
Brother-sister corporations
election of status as S corporation,
1:9
Built-in gain tax. *See* Capital gains
and losses, long-term
**Buy-sell provisions, shareholders'
agreements,** 6:10

-C-

Capital assets
dispositions, 8:3
sale of
gross receipts, 7:11
Capital contributions
basis for gain or loss, increase,
11:19–11:25
advantages, 11:23
defined, 11:20
how basis is increased, 11:22
inadvisability, 11:25
loans, compared to, 11:23
payments, 11:21
and repayment of reduced basis
loan, 11:24
Capital gains and losses
distributions in excess of basis, 12:1
long-term
built-in gain tax, 8:15, 8:21–8:33
carryover basis transactions,
8:30
corporations subject to,
8:22–8:23
defined, 8:21
dispositions triggering, 8:24
limitations, 8:28
"loss" property, 8:29
losses, minimization by, 8:27,
8:29
minimization of, 8:27, 8:29
net recognized built-in gain
defined, 8:26
net unrealized built-in gain,
8:29
tax-free transactions, 8:30
transitional relief, 8:32–8:33
corporate-level capital gain tax,
8:15, 8:16–8:20
computation, 8:19
passive investment income,
gains taxed as, 8:20
pass-through of income, 9:4
**Capital structure of S corpora-
tions,** 1:30–1:35
Casualty insurance companies
eligibility as S corporation, 1:13
Charitable contributions
deduction of, 8:2
pass-through of income, 9:4
Charters
income, classification, 7:24
Commissions
gross receipts, 7:7
Compensation
shareholder's, tax treatment of, 13:1
Consolidations, 5:4–5:9

Index

election to become S corporation, effect on, 5:4
Convertible debentures
second class of stock, treatment as, 1:33
Corporate-level determination of Subchapter S items, 14:11, 14:18
Creditors
shielding of business from, 14:27

-D-

Death benefits, 13:6
Debt
worthless
basis limitations, 10:1
deduction, impact on basis adjustments, 11:9
Deductions
accrued expenses, 8:6
charitable contributions, 8:2
fringe benefits, 8:2
gross receipts, impact on, 7:8
limitations, 8:7
net operating losses, 8:2
Dispositions
property, passive activity loss rules, 10:43–10:49
Distributions to shareholders, 12:1–12:25
appreciated property, 8:4
characteristics of, 12:2
earnings and profits
defined, 12:3
reduction of, 12:6
taxation as dividends, 12:9–12:20
accumulated earnings and profits, 12:9, 12:18–12:20
in excess of basis
capital gain treatment, 12:1
exempt income, 12:7–12:8
fundamental concepts, 12:1–12:6
portfolio income, 10:30
S corporations without earnings and profits, 12:7–12:8
termination of status as S corporation, following, 12:23–12:25

Dividends
status as S corporation, effect on, 6:7
Domestic corporation, defined, 1:3
Domestic international sales corporation (DISC)
eligibility as S corporation, 1:8
Double taxation
avoidance, 1:1
termination or revocation of S corporation status, effect on, 4:2

-E-

Earnings and profits (E&P)
accumulated adjustments account, 12:10–12:19
accumulated earnings and profits distributed prior to, 12:18–12:20
allocation of distributions, 12:14
defined, 12:10
and exempt income, 12:17
four-year spread, interaction with, 12:11
negative status, losses causing, 12:15–12:16
previously taxed income, 12:21–12:22
reduction of, 12:12
redemption of stock, 12:3
zero accumulated adjustments account, 12:16
acquired from another corporation, 12:5
corporations without
distributions to shareholders, 12:7–12:8
defined, 12:3
distributions taxed as dividends, 12:9–12:20
passive investment income in excess of 25% limitation, 7:3–7:4, 8:10–8:14
previous years as C corporation, 4:3
reduction of, 12:6

reorganization, carryover, 5:18
Election of status as S corporation,
2:1–2:18. *See also* Status as
S corporation
  amendment of, 2:15
  consents, 2:8–2:18
    extension of time for filing,
      2:12–2:13
    failure to consent, 2:11
    how and when to make, 2:9–2:10
    new shareholders, 2:14
  effective date, 2:7
  form, 2:1
  invalid election, 6:14–6:17
    "cure" for, 6:15
    mistaken for valid, 6:17
    original, 6:14
    reelection after, 6:16
  and investment tax credit
    recapture, 8:35
  mergers, effect of, 5:4
  nominee shareholders, 6:5
  protection of, 6:8–6:13
    failure to protect, 6:13
  reelection of
    IRS consent, 2:18
    after termination, 2:17
  requirements for, 1:2
  time to elect, 2:2
    extension, 2:4
    mailing of, 2:5
    new corporation, 2:3
    nonbusiness due date, 2:6
  withdrawal of, 2:16
Employee stock ownership plans (ESOPs)
  adoption of, consequences, 13:10
Entertainment expenses
  80% limitation, 9:4
ESOPs. *See* Employee stock ownership plans
Estates. *See* Trusts and estates
Estimated tax
  termination of status as S corporation, 4:25
    underpayment, 4:26

Exempt income
  and accumulated adjustments
    account, 12:17
  distributions to shareholders,
    12:7–12:8

-F-

Farms
  passive investment income, 7:22
Financial institutions
  eligibility as S corporations, 1:8
Fiscal-year election
  backup election, 3:16
  business purpose, establishment to
    justify, 3:6
  deferral period, 3:7
  definition of fiscal year, 3:1
  denial of, 3:12
  distinguished from calendar year,
    3:1
  fee imposed by IRS, 3:17
  Form 8716, 3:15
  how to make, 3:15
  IRS expeditious approval of, 3:14
  limitations, avoidance of, 3:9
  maintenance, 3:18–3:24
  new corporation, denial of election,
    3:12
  number allowable, 3:10
  partnership interest held, 3:8
  required payments, 3:18–3:24
    failure to make, 3:20
    form, 3:19
    how to make, 3:19
    termination, following, 3:20,
      3:23–3:24
  termination, 3:18–3:24
  tiered-structure entities, 3:8
  transfer of assets, avoidance of
    limitations, 3:9
Foreign countries
  taxes paid to, 8:2
Foreign taxes
  pass-through of income, 9:4
Forms
  1120S, 14:1–14:4, 14:26

Index

2553, 2:1
8082, 14:12–14:13
8716, 3:15
Fringe benefits, 13:2–13:6
  cost of, deductibility, 13:2
  death benefits, 13:6
  deductions, 8:2
  more-than-2% shareholders, 13:3–13:4
  nondiscrimination rules, 13:5
  2%-or-less shareholders, 13:5

-G-

Gain or loss
  property disposition
    passive activity loss rules, 10:43–10:49
Grantor trust
  consents, election as S corporation 2:8
  termination of S corporation election, 6:3
Gross receipts. *See* Passive investment income

-H-

Hobby-loss rules, applicability, 1:5
Hotels
  passive investment income, 7:15
Husband and wife
  innocent spouse rule, 14:25–14:26
  as shareholders, 1:15

-I-

Income
  calculation of
    statute of limitations, extension of, 14:26
  passive investment. *See* Passive investment income
  pass-through, 9:1–9:6
  previously taxed
    distribution to shareholders, 12:21–12:22
  taxable. *See* Taxable income

types of, effect on status as S corporation, 6:7
Income tax returns. *See* Returns
Incorporation
  status as S corporation, effect on, 5:16
Indebtedness
  status as S corporation, effect on, 6:6
Ineligible corporations, 1:8, 1:11
Innocent spouse rule
  defined, 14:25
  statute of limitations, 14:26
Installment sales
  corporate-level capital gain tax, 8:18
  gains from, gross receipts, 7:9
Insurance companies
  eligibility as S corporations, 1:8, 1:12
    casualty insurance, 1:13
Interest
  debt incurred to purchase or carry shares
    passive activity loss rules, 10:35
  exempt, pass-through of income, 9:4
  income
    passive investment income, 7:26
Inventories
  LIFO method
    recapture, 8:36–8:39
      amount of, 8:37
      computation of tax, 8:38
      reporting of tax, 8:39
Investment income
  passive activity income, 10:29
Investment tax credit
  pass-through of income, 9:6
  recapture, 8:34–8:35
    earnings and profits reduced by, 12:6
    increase in basis of stock caused by, 11:6
    ownership change as cause of, 9:7

-L-

Lending and finance companies
  passive investment income
    exception, 7:26
Life insurance plans, 13:5
LIFO inventories. *See* Inventories
Like-kind exchanges
  gross receipts, 7:7
Loans
  second class of stock, treatment as, 1:34
  shareholder to S corporation
    basis for gain or loss, 11:9–11:18
  shareholder's family to corporation, 9:14
Long-term capital gains and losses.
See Capital gains and losses
Losses
  limitations on, 1:6, 10:1–10:51
    at-risk rules. *See* At-risk rules
    basis, 10:1–10:2
    hobby-loss rules, 1:5
    passive activity loss rules, 10:10–10:51
    pass-through, 9:1–9:6

-M-

Material participation. *See* Passive activity loss rules
Medical reimbursement plans, 13:5
Mergers, 5:4–5:9
  election of status as S corporation, effect on, 5:4, 5:7–5:9
  surviving C corporation, 5:6
  taxable year prior to, 5:5
Minor shareholders
  consents, election of status as S corporation, 2:8
Miscellaneous itemized deductions
  2% of adjusted gross income, 9:4
Mobile homes
  passive investment income, 7:16
Motels
  passive investment income, 7:15

-N-

Net operating losses
  deduction of, 8:2
New corporation
  election of status as S corporation, time for, 2:3
  fiscal-year election, denial of, 3:12
Nominees
  number-of-shareholders test, 1:16
  stock of S corporation held for partners, 1:17
Nondiscrimination rules
  fringe benefits, 13:5
Nonresident aliens
  as shareholders, 4:3–4:4
Notice, administrative proceeding, 14:20

-O-

Oil and gas wells
  depletion
    pass-through of income, 9:4
    percentage depletion, 8:2
Options
  second class of stock, treatment as, 1:33
Organizational expenses
  amortization of, 8:2
Ownership
  changes in, 9:7–9:15
    allocation of income items, 9:8–9:15
      alternative, 9:10, 9:12
      death of shareholder, 9:13
      methods, difference between, 9:11
      pass-through allocations, 9:12
      pro rata method, 9:8–9:9
    investment tax credit recapture, 9:7
  considerations of S corporations, 1:9–1:29

-P-

Parent-subsidiary corporations, 5:10

Index

Parking facilities
  passive investment income, 7:19
Partners and partnerships
  income
    gross receipts, 7:10
    interest in, fiscal-year election, 3:8
  S corporations
    as partner, 1:18
    distinguished from partnership, 1:3
    tax matters person, 14:21-14:22
    transfer of assets to S corporations, 1:17
Passive activity loss (PAL) rules, 10:10-10:51
  activities subject to, 10:11
  activity
    determination of scope, 10:12
    identification of, 10:15
    rules, 10:13, 10:15-10:22
    S corporation as, 10:13
  aggregation rules, 10:16-10:19, 10:22
  carryovers, 10:38
  deductions, limited by, 10:10
  disallowed credits, 10:28-10:38
    carryovers, 10:38
    passed through, 10:37
    reporting, 10:38
  disallowed losses, 10:28-10:38
    and at-risk rules, 10:36
    and basis limitation rules, 10:36
    carryovers, 10:38
    deductions, 10:33
    defined, 10:28
    reporting, 10:38
  effective dates, 10:50
  fragmentation election, 10:20-10:21
  interest, debt to purchase or carry shares, 10:35
  loans, shareholder to corporation, 10:34
  material participation, 10:24-10:27
    substantiation, 10:27
    taxable year, 10:26
    tests for, 10:25
  overview, 10:21-10:23

  pass-through of income, 9:4
  phase-in rules, 10:50-10:51
  portfolio income, 10:29
  preenactment interest, change of, 10:51
  pro rata share items, 10:31
  property dispositions, 10:43-10:49
    gain or loss, recognition of, 10:43
    interest, disposition of entire, 10:48
    revocation of S corporation election, impact of, 10:49
    shareholder, 10:44-10:47
    substantially appreciated property, 10:43
    suspended losses triggered by, 10:48
    termination of S corporation election, impact of, 10:49
  rental activities, 10:11, 10:39-10:42
    defined, 10:39
    real estate, 10:41-10:42
    shareholder, rented from, 10:40
  revocation of S corporation election, impact of, 10:49
  significant participation, 10:32
  special circumstances rules, 10:13
  termination of S corporation election, impact of, 10:49
  trade or business, 10:11, 10:32
  trade-or-business aggregation rules, 10:16, 10:18-10:19
  types of S corporation activities applicable to, 10:23
  undertakings
    aggregation of, 10:16
    control of, 10:17
    identification of, 10:14
    professional service, 10:22
    rental real estate, 10:23
    rules, 10:13-10:14
    similar, 10:18
    trade-or-business, 10:16-10:21
Passive investment income, 7:1-7:26
  airfields, 7:19

characterization of, 7:13–7:26
charters, 7:24
defined, 7:1
excess, taxation of, 8:10–8:14
  built-in gain tax and, 8:31
  limitation on, 8:12
  tax rate, 8:11
  waiver by IRS, 8:13–8:14
  when S corporation subject to, 8:10
excess net, 7:4
farming, 7:22
gross receipts, 7:5–7:12
  calculation of, 7:7, 7:11
  capital assets, sale of, 7:11
  deductions, impact of, 7:8
  defined, 7:6
  installment sale proceeds, 7:9
  partnership income, 7:10
  stock, sale of, 7:12
hotels, 7:15
interest income, 7:26
mobile homes, 7:16
motels, 7:15
parking lot facilities, 7:19
problems caused by, 7:2–7:3
recreational facilities, 7:21
reduction of, planning for, 7:27
rental income, 7:13–7:26
  office buildings, 7:17
    demolition, prior to, 7:18
  personal property, 7:23
  storage and warehousing activities, 7:20
reorganization, carryover from, 5:18
status as S corporation, effects on, 6:7
taxation of, 7:4
termination of status as S corporation, 4:3
trailer parks, 7:16
25% limitation, 7:3–7:4, 8:10–8:14

Penalties
information to shareholders, failure to furnish, 14:5

required payments, failure to make, 3:20
tax return preparers
  failure to take basis limitation into account, 10:1
termination of status as S corporation, underpayment of estimated tax, 4:26

Pension and profit-sharing plans, 13:7–13:11
contributions to, 13:9
discriminatory practices, 13:9
loans to shareholders, 13:11
newly electing S corporations, 13:11
participation standards, 13:7
stock bonus plans, 13:10
tax advantages, 13:8

Personal property
renting or leasing income, classification of, 7:23

Planning
stock classes, use of, 1:31

Portfolio income
defined, 10:29
distributions, 10:30
loans, shareholder to corporation, 10:34
pro rata share items, 10:31

Possessions corporations
eligibility as S corporations, 1:8

Profit motive requirement, S corporations, 1:4

Property
appreciated, distribution to shareholders, 8:4

Proprietorship
S corporation distinguished from, 1:3

Proxies
second class of stock, treatment as, 1:33

-Q-

Qualified oil corporation

Index

election to be treated as S corporation, 1:14
Qualified retirement plans. *See* Pension and profit-sharing plans
Qualified Subchapter S trusts
  beneficiaries
    consent to S corporation election, 1:24
    death of, 1:27
    how to make election, 1:25
    more than one, 1:23
    revocation of election, 1:26
  defined, 1:20
  eligible trusts, 1:21–1:23
    IRS rulings, 1:22
  stock ownership, 1:19

-R-

Real estate
  option to acquire payment for gross receipts, 7:7
  rental
    passive activity loss rules, 10:41–10:42
Recapitalization, 5:1
  status as S corporation, effect on, 5:15
Recreational facilities
  passive investment income, 7:21
Redemption of stock
  accumulated adjustments account, reduction of, 12:13
Related-party transactions
  losses, recognition of, 8:5
Rental income
  as passive investment income, 7:13–7:26
    office buildings, 7:17–7:18
    storage and warehousing activities, 7:20
  personal property, 7:23
  sale construed as rental, 7:25
Rental property
  passive activity loss rules, 10:39–10:42

Reorganizations
  acquisitions, 5:11–5:12
    basis step-up for acquired corporation's assets, 5:13
  bankruptcy, 5:17
  defined, 5:1
  divisions, 5:10
  mergers and consolidations, 5:4–5:9
  surviving corporation, carryovers, 5:18
  tax-free
    and built-in gain tax, 8:30
    S corporation as party to, 5:2
  types of, 5:1
Required payments. *See* Fiscal-year election
Requirements for S corporation status, 1:2
  profit motive, 1:4
Retirement plans. *See* Pension and profit-sharing plans
Returns
  extension for, 14:3
  failure to file, 14:24
  forms. *See* Forms
  fraudulent, 14:24
  information necessary, 14:1
  joint
    innocent spouse rule, 14:25–14:26
  pass-through of income, 9:4
  penalties, 14:5
  shareholders, copies to, 14:4–14:5
  Subchapter S items, 14:12. *See also* Subchapter S audits
  substantial omissions, 14:24
  termination or revocation of S corporation status, due date, 4:21
  time for filing, 14:2
Revocation of status as S corporation. *See also* Termination of status as S corporation
  accounting for, 4:16–4:24
  causes, 6:1
  defined, 4:10

distributions to shareholders
following, 12:23–12:25
double taxation provisions, effect
on, 4:2
effective date, 4:13
how to make, 4:12
notification to IRS, 4:16
passive activity loss rules, impact
on, 10:49
reasons for, 4:14
shareholders, number needed for,
4:11
taxable year, during, 4:17–4:24
allocation of income, losses, and
deductions, 4:19
pro rata allocation method,
4:19–4:21
returns, due date, 4:24
tax calculation, 4:23
withdrawal of, 4:15

-S-

Safe-harbor rules
"straight-debt," 1:35
Sale of property
gross receipts, 7:7
Second class of stock, 1:2,
1:32–1:34, 4:4
Section 444 election. *See* Fiscal-
year election
Section 1231 gains and losses
pass-through of income, 9:4
Shareholders
agreements between, 6:9–6:12
and IRS, 6:11
provisions, types of, 6:10
without creating second class of
stock, 1:32
basis in stock, 11:1–11:25
consents to election of status as
S corporation, 2:8
extension of time for filing,
2:12–2:13
failure to consent, 2:11
how to make consents, 2:9
new shareholders, 2:14

when to make consents, 2:10
death of, 1:28, 6:3
allocation of income items,
ownership change, 9:13
dispositions by
passive activity loss rules,
10:44–10:47
allocation methods, 10:46
contributions of property to
S corporation, 10:47
valuation date, 10:45
fringe benefits to, deductibility,
13:2–13:6
more-than-2% shareholders, 13:4
as partners, 13:3
death benefits, 13:6
2%-or-less shareholders, 13:5
husband and wife, 1:15
income, pass-through, 9:1–9:6
ineligible, 6:5
life estates, 1:29
loans to corporations
passive activity loss rules, 10:34
loans to shareholders
pension and profit-sharing plans,
13:11
losses
pass-through, 9:1–9:6
nominee for another, 6:5
nonresident aliens, 4:3–4:4
number-of-shareholders test, 1:16
revocation of status as S corporation, number needed for, 4:11
statements to, failure to furnish,
14:5
taxation of, 9:1–9:15
losses, limitations on, 10:1–10:51
at-risk rules. *See* At-risk rules
basis, 10:1–10:2
passive activity loss rules,
10:10–10:51. *See also* Passive
activity loss rules
termination of status as S corporation
death of shareholder, 6:3
intentional, 6:2

Index

transfer to disqualified shareholder, 4:5
Small corporation, audit exemption. *See* Subchapter S audits
Status as S corporation
dividend payments, effects of, 6:7
election. *See* Election of status as S corporation
income, types of, 6:7
indebtedness, effect of, 6:6
loss of. *See also* Revocation of status as S corporation; Termination of status as S corporation
   acquired corporation, 5:14
   acquisitions, 5:11–5:12
      basis step-up, acquired corporation's assets, 5:13
      causes, 6:1
      divisions, 5:10
      mergers, 5:7–5:9
      prevention, 6:8–6:12
         shareholders' agreements, 6:9–6:11
         voting trusts, 1:19, 6:12
      passive investment income, effect of, 6:7
      recapitalization, effect of, 5:15
Statute of limitations, 14:23–14:26
extension of, 14:24
innocent spouse rule, 14:26
Stock
basis. *See* Basis for gain or loss
classes of, 1:31
   second class, 1:32–1:34
      termination of status as S corporation, 4:4
differences in, use as planning tool, 1:31
equality of shares, 1:30
redemption. *See* Redemption of stock
sale of
   gross receipts, 7:12
trust as owner, 1:19
worthless, basis for gain or loss
   adjustments, 11:5
   limitations, 10:1

Stock bonus plans, consequences of adoption, 13:10
Stockholders. *See* Shareholders
Subchapter S audits, 14:7–14:23
"small corporation" exemption, 14:14–14:19
   corporate-level determination, 14:18
   defined, 14:15
   effective dates, 14:19
   eligibility for, 14:16–14:17
Subchapter S items, 14:9–14:13
   contributions, factors affecting, 14:10
   corporate-level determination, 14:11
   defined, 14:9
   distributions, factors affecting, 14:10
   inconsistent treatment, notice of, 14:13
   returns, 14:12–14:13
tax matters person
   designation of, 14:21
   responsibilities of, 14:22
Subchapter S trusts. *See* Qualified Subchapter S trusts
Subsidiaries
80% ownership rule, 1:9
inactive, exception for, 1:9
S corporations as, 1:10
Substantiation
passive activity loss rules, material participation, 10:27

-T-

Tax administration, 14:1–14:27
Tax shelter, appropriateness as, 1:7
Taxable income
capital assets, treatment of, 8:3
computation, 8:2
   elections, made by corporation or shareholder, 8:8
   related-party transactions, losses, 8:5

long-term capital gain
  built-in gain tax, 8:15, 8:21–8:33
  corporate-level capital gain tax, 8:16–8:20
  passive investment income, excess, 8:10–8:14
  principles, 8:1–8:9

Taxable year
  business-purpose fiscal year, approval by IRS, 3:14
  change of, 3:13
  choice of, restrictions, 3:2
  election of, 3:11–3:17
  fiscal year. *See* Fiscal-year election
  four-year spread, 3:2
  merger, prior to, 5:4
  natural business year
    determination, 3:4
    election, 3:11
  ownership tax year, 3:5, 3:11
  passive activity loss rules, material participation, 10:26
  permitted year, defined, 3:3
  revocation of status during, 4:17–4:24
  rules, 3:1–3:24
  termination of status during, 4:17–4:24

Tenants in common
  consents, election of status as S corporation, 2:8

Termination of status as S corporation, 4:1–4:26. *See also* Revocation of status as S corporation
  accidental, preservation of status in event of, 4:6
  accounting for, 4:16–4:24
  causes, 6:1
  death of beneficiary, 6:4
  death of shareholder, 6:3
  disqualification
    causes of, 4:3
    intentional, 4:4–4:5
  distributions to shareholders following, 12:23–12:25

double taxation, 4:2, 6:13
effective date, 4:9
estimated tax, 4:25
  underpayment, 4:26
inadvertent, 4:7–4:8
intentional, 6:2
and investment tax credit recapture, 8:35
losses, basis limitations, 10:2
notification to IRS, 4:16
passive activity loss rules, impact on, 10:49
reasons for, 4:14
reelection, 6:13
  after invalid election, 6:16
and reorganization, 5:3
second class of stock, 1:2, 4:4
taxable year, during, 4:17–4:24
  allocation of income, losses, and deductions, 4:19
    pro rata allocation method, 4:19–4:21
  returns, due date, 4:24
  tax calculation, 4:23

Tiered-structure entities
  fiscal-year election, 3:8

Trade-or-business purposes
  at-risk rules, 10:5
  passive activity loss rules, 10:32

Trailer parks
  passive investment income, 7:16

Travel expenses
  pass-through of income, 7:16

Trusts and estates
  consents, election of status as S corporation, 2:8
  stock of S corporation, ownership by, 1:19
  termination of status as S corporation, 6:3–6:4

-U-

U.S. possessions
  taxes paid to, 8:2

Index

-V-

Voting trust
    stock of S corporation, ownership by, 1:19

-W-

Warrants
    second class of stock, treatment as, 1:33